CHASING
SHADOWS

CHASING SHADOWS

THE LIFE & DEATH OF PETER ROEBUCK

TIM LANE AND ELLIOT CARTLEDGE

hardie grant books

Published in 2015 by Hardie Grant Books

Hardie Grant Books (Australia)
Ground Floor, Building 1
658 Church Street
Richmond, Victoria 3121
www.hardiegrant.com.au

Hardie Grant Books (UK)
5th & 6th Floors
52–54 Southwark Street
London SE1 1UN
www.hardiegrant.co.uk

A Cataloguing-in-Publication entry is available from the catalogue
of the National Library of Australia at www.nla.gov.au

Chasing Shadows: The life & death of Peter Roebuck

ISBN 978 1 74379 012 0

Cover design by Blue Cork
Typeset in Sabon by Kirby Jones
Printed in Germany by Arvato GGP

FSC
www.fsc.org
MIX
Paper from
responsible sources
FSC® C014496

The paper this book is printed on is certified
against the Forest Stewardship Council®
Standards. FSC promotes environmentally
responsible, socially beneficial and economically
viable management of the world's forests.

CONTENTS

INTRODUCTION

'Mind you, a lot can happen in a week. It just did.'

– Peter Roebuck's final column, 13 November 2011

Friday, 11 November 2011
Newlands, Cape Town

At one of the world's most picturesque sporting grounds a strange cricket match has been unfolding. Twenty-three wickets fell on day two, a Thursday. Fans back home in Australia, waking up to the score, thought they had missed a day. First South Africa crumbled for 96, to trail by 188 runs on first innings. Then Australia were reduced to a calamitous 9 for 21, on their way to an eventual 47, Vernon Philander on debut displaying a nerveless mastery of conditions to claim 5 cheap wickets. The turnaround was stunning. By 11.11 next morning, on the eleventh day of the eleventh month of 2011, South Africa required 111 to win. They got them by lunchtime, captain Graeme Smith bringing up his own hundred one over and the winning run, a clip through midwicket, an over later. Cock-a-hoop twenty-four hours earlier, the Australians were in a state of disbelief. 'No Test cricket on the weekend for the Capetonians,' tweeted former South African fast bowler Shaun Pollock, 'they will have to head for the beach!'

Tickets for Saturday and Sunday, the scheduled days four and five, had been selling well, making the premature end a disaster for vendors, caterers and the ground's custodian, the Western Province Cricket Association. For the travelling media, however, it was a rare opportunity for free time on a weekend. Members of the Australian Broadcasting Corporation commentary team were staying at the nearby Southern Sun Hotel. Somewhat unusually, Peter Roebuck was with them. Well known for his eccentrically private ways, Roebuck had been inclined over the years to stay at lesser establishments of his own choosing. As his Fairfax newspaper colleague Greg Baum puts it, 'Even in more lavish times for Fairfax, when we were nearly always staying in the team hotel, he would stay in a two-star hotel somewhere else and eat at a ten-dollar diner around the corner.'

Inside that cheap diner, Roebuck would most likely be found with his nose buried in a book. How he found time to refresh his knowledge stores with new material and to be abreast of so much was a constant source of mystery to his various friends and admirers in the media; the fact that he generally steered clear of the after-hours pockets of journalists as they dined – and wined – was no doubt part of his secret.

Years earlier, in Peshawar, where Mark Taylor was busy making a triple century, all but one of the ABC team were staying in and enjoying the relative opulence of the Pearl Continental. Roebuck joked daily that he was lodging at a place called Green's.

The establishment is still operating today, a decidedly no-frills option. That was more Roebuck's style.

Unusually for one whose spirits vacillated, he had appeared in fine fettle this whole Cape Town Test. Baum arrived at the ground early on Friday. He noticed Roebuck discussing player matters with Tony Irish, CEO of the South African Players Association. Allan Border was there and Roebuck talked to him too. 'It did strike me at the time,' says Baum, 'that he was particularly jovial. He could be excessively that, and then excessively morose too, but it did seem like he was in a good place.'

Much of the press pack was in a similar good place. It is an ongoing sore point for newspaper reporters, as opposed to those who inhabit the supposedly cushy TV and radio boxes, that when the match is over their work goes on, sometimes increasing in volume and intensity. Roebuck worked on both sides. A weekend of no cricket in one of the world's more scenic cities was a rare luxury. Some put their feet up and thought about the next match. Or golf. There were wineries, restaurants, beaches, trips to Robben Island and the top of Table Mountain to consider.

Friends were contacted, bookings made, plans set.

Saturday, 12 November 2011
Southern Sun Hotel

Given his penchant for less sophisticated digs, it was rare for this elusive pimpernel of a colleague to be just down the hallway, and equally unusual for him to be sharing breakfast with them. Roebuck was as happy as some had ever seen him. Part of the reason for his contentment at breakfast that Saturday was tangible, for he wasn't unaccompanied. Sitting at a table adjacent to fellow ABC commentator Drew Morphett, he introduced his companion with obvious pride. 'I'm really excited,' he told Morphett. 'I'd like to introduce you to my future daughter-in-law.'

The woman was to marry one of the young Zimbabwean men who lived at Roebuck's home in Pietermaritzburg, on the other side of the country, and studied at the University of KwaZulu-Natal. He regarded the members of this community as his adopted sons and they referred to him as 'Dad'.

Another ABC commentator, former fast bowler Geoff Lawson, also recalls Roebuck's demeanour that morning as unusually buoyant – 'as effusive and alive and aware as you've ever seen him. One of us said, "You're in a good mood today", and he said, "I'm going to see my boys. It's Saturday and I get to see them play cricket."' While the cricket he planned to watch would not be Test cricket, and the ground on which it was to be played was not a Test ground, it's likely the occasion meant more to Roebuck than the match he had sat witness to the previous three days. He told Morphett and Lawson he was heading to Basil D'Oliveira Oval and Basil's grandson would be playing.

The name Basil D'Oliveira is inextricably bound to the struggle of cricket and sport on its way to multiracial equality in South Africa. Born in Cape Town of Indian and Portuguese descent, and thus classed under South African law as 'coloured', D'Oliveira was an all-round cricketer of rich and obvious talent who had no hope of representing his country so long as apartheid flourished. In 1960, aged twenty-eight, he emigrated to England to further his career, and by scoring 158 in the Oval Test of 1968 he played what venerated sportswriter Ian Wooldridge described as probably the most significant modern Test innings.

4

His form commanded selection for England's forthcoming tour to South Africa. D'Oliveira was overlooked. It was patently obvious why. He was coloured, and his selection would have triggered the tour's cancellation; South Africa's prime minister, B.J. Vorster, had stated D'Oliveira's inclusion would not be acceptable to the ruling regime. But his omission caused uproar in England. When seam bowler Tom Cartwright was subsequently injured, D'Oliveira was his replacement – to no avail, as despite eleventh-hour negotiations, the tour was scrapped. Already barred from the Olympics and international soccer, South Africa's home series against Australia in 1969–70 would be their last exposure to sanctioned international cricket until the fall of apartheid.

Of all the issues on which Peter Roebuck would write over a thirty-year period, there was none he was more passionate about than race. He had staunchly opposed sporting links with South Africa during the boycott years, and when apartheid fell and South Africa's cricket team returned to the stage, he declared that he regarded the nation's previous history in the sport as null and void.

Roebuck's views on race and racial discrimination extended well beyond southern Africa. To the consternation of certain media peers, he argued vehemently that cricket's non-white nations were unjustly targeted in regard to suspect bowling actions. He was seen to back teams from the subcontinent on issues such as on-field behaviour. His dedication to the cause of racial equality obscured, in the opinion of some, his better judgement. Unquestionably, though, he put his money and his endeavour where his mouth was, his commitment to those disadvantaged by decades of disenfranchisement extending to the way he lived his life and where he lived it. Although a dual British and Australian citizen, he bought a house in Pietermaritzburg and there provided for the upkeep and education of a small community of young men, mostly plucked from St Joseph's orphanage in Harare.

So a visit to Basil D'Oliveira Oval was for Roebuck a special occurrence. 'He was that excited,' says Morphett. 'The world was good.'

By nightfall it would turn to disaster. A sexual assault claim against Roebuck was raised that day with local police, stemming from a meeting at the Southern Sun with a young Zimbabwean man the previous Monday evening. If the account of the complainant from that encounter is accepted, Roebuck must have been feeling sharp pangs of anxiety that he would be hearing more about it. And if so, his relaxed state during the days since Monday was a masterful disguise.

It may have seemed to Roebuck like history repeating itself. Just over ten years earlier, three young, white, South African men staying at his house in Somerset while receiving cricket tutelage accused him of hitting them painfully on their buttocks with a stick. Perhaps more incriminating, they said Roebuck insisted on inspecting whatever welts were left behind by the punishment. A court in Taunton found Roebuck guilty of common assault and delivered a three-month jail sentence, suspended for two years.

And yet even attentive listeners in Australia, tuning in to their car radios, couldn't help noticing how relaxed Roebuck sounded during the three days of that game in Cape Town, how serene. 'We'd done a Test match,' says Morphett, 'and there'd been no mention of it. It wasn't like we were broadcasting with a bloke on death row with a threat hanging over his head.'

When police first entered the Southern Sun on Saturday, Roebuck was absent. They returned in the evening. Two officers knocked on the door of room 623. It was answered promptly and the occupant did not appear surprised to see them; allegedly, he raised the matter that was of interest to police before they announced the purpose of their visit. From there things turned ugly. Jim Maxwell, the ABC's senior commentator, was summoned. He found his friend half-dressed and in considerable distress. He was then asked to leave. 'Jimmy had poked his nose in there and seen all this investigation going on,' says Morphett. 'The coppers got Jimmy's name and phone number, all that. And then eventually they said, "You'll have to leave now, Mr Maxwell, because we're investigating this matter ..."'

August 2015

So does this story warrant reconsideration?

The authors have found this to be a contentious question. Apprehension has been voiced and determined opposition expressed in certain quarters to the writing of this book. Some of it is born of collegial concern but elsewhere there is a distinct reluctance to help uncover the truth. The former response harks from the hurt felt by family and friends once the sexual assault allegations became public and partial histories were dressed up as defining commentary. The latter approach, however, much like the charade that passed for an investigation into Roebuck's death, invariably leads only to further speculation.

Roebuck's life was perplexing. The circumstances of his death are disconcerting, baffling. Many troubling questions still outnumber answers. Why did such deep-seated and interminable antipathy linger between Roebuck and certain influential figures?

He'd created the impression he was estranged from his family – why? The man who made the damning complaint of sexual assault disappeared without trace – how? What caused South African police to so quickly label the death as suicide? Why haven't results of forensic tests been released? Why was the inquiry into his death conducted furtively? Is there evidence of other forces at play, darker forces whose failings Roebuck in his life had exposed?

This is not a study undertaken lightly. A prominent man's legacy is at stake. It is an evocative tale of a spectacular and ultimately tragic life; and, as Roebuck himself reminded us, on the occasion of the death of young Ben Hollioake, 'Mere death does not bestow nobility, let alone sanctity'. When ignominy visits, a degree of shock is often followed by obfuscation. Those genuine in their concerns about Roebuck's legacy were strident in their belief that he was a singularly private man: and a man of such privacy, shyness, coyness – whatever it was – would strenuously resist having some part of his humanity held up for public examination. And the part necessarily requiring deepest exploration, given the circumstances of his death, is his most private part of all, his sexual existence. No one, to our knowledge, among those who worked with Roebuck through the years can articulate with any certainty the nature of his private life.

Perhaps we should have inquired earlier, when the chance was there to ask him. It is something long-serving cricket writer Mike Coward voiced at the time of Roebuck's passing, the idea that maybe his pressbox friends and colleagues should have 'taken the initiative' and delved more. Roebuck did not ask us many questions about our lives. But maybe that was partly because we didn't ask him enough about his. A lot of us were slightly intimidated, or slightly in awe; also, because we didn't know what was underneath the outer layer, we didn't know whether we should dig too deep.

'Cricketers,' Roebuck wrote, 'are fair game on the field and otherwise off limits ... There is no need to scour a man's private life in search of his character.'

Some would argue nothing could be further from the truth. Considering the strong positions Roebuck took publicly on matters of race, and the fact that his death occurred at the moment of realisation that he was being investigated over an alleged sexual assault of a relatively disempowered black Zimbabwean, the potential clearly exists for a conclusion of hypocrisy. Various reports and online discussions in the weeks after his death suggested his mentoring of young African men may have been organised with the ulterior motive of satisfying his own sexual desires. If this is true, the aforementioned hypocrisy could be seen to be on a grand scale.

In writing this book, a determining of the truth was the main spur. Right from the outset there were warning signs of how elusive truth can be. On stepping off a plane at Heathrow airport, one of the co-authors spotted the familiar face of a senior Australian sporting (not cricket) administrator. Pleasantries were exchanged. Then the administrator said: 'I reckon they threw him out the window.'

Even if one rules out assassination as a fanciful idea, is it possible Roebuck was honey-trapped? He had been a trenchant critic of both Zimbabwe's national administration and those who ran the country's cricket. Is it possible he was being set up to be publicly humiliated, and his death was an unplanned consequence? Roebuck's was the third mysterious death to befall a well-known cricket figure in the space of nine years. Like Roebuck, neither

Hansie Cronje nor Bob Woolmer was an old man. Roebuck had been an ongoing digger into cricket match-fixing. Is there a scintilla of a possibility that the three deaths are connected? All these questions warrant reconsideration as to what happened that night at the Southern Sun Hotel.

Then there is the central character himself. A brilliant student who, despite first-class honours in law at Cambridge, opted for cricket; a diligent and hard-working batsman; the eccentric, sometimes shambolic figure who stimulated, amused, irritated, delighted and infuriated those who knew and worked with him in press and commentary boxes around the world; an enigma, a tightly-wound riddle; a cerebral loner who celebrated a team game; a voice and a writer known to millions who preferred to spend his evenings alone.

'One has as many personalities as they have friends,' said Coward, quoting Ralph Waldo Emerson, at Roebuck's memorial service.

In the second half of his life he was a disenchanted Englishman, on the outer in his homeland, adopted as an exotic in Australia, South Africa, India. Reading his work back now – constant references to a yearning for brighter lights, wider spaces – it is entirely plausible to imagine such an outcome as a fait accompli. When Bob Woolmer died in the Caribbean during the 2007 World Cup, Roebuck wrote a column in which he referred to a hotel room's 'accusing walls'. It was a phrase picked up on, when Roebuck himself died in unusual and controversial circumstances, by the Booker prize–winning author Howard Jacobson:

> Those 'accusing walls' could only have been described by a man who has felt accused by them himself ... The

walls clearly accused Roebuck more than other men. What they accused him of is immaterial. If you're at all complex as a human being, you will feel yourself to be guilty of every crime and omission in the book. Look at photographs of the young Roebuck and you see a shy boy uncomfortable in his skin. Shyness leaves a legacy even when it's overcome. You know your soul to be an awkward thing and you can never forgive it for that. The reason you die in every hotel room you wind up in is that death is all you've ever thought you deserved ... Peter Roebuck was too lonely. I never met him but I know he was too lonely.

Who was that little boy in the photographs? What happened to him that brought about such a closed-off, masked persona? One mask for his family, another for teammates, one for his beneficiaries in Africa, another for steadfast friends in Sydney. Tormented might be too melodramatic a word, but complicated is not. Roebuck was not an easy person with whom to strike up an instant rapport. There was awkwardness, a sense of being removed from and at odds with others. Whatever happened along the way to that little boy, he became edgy, fretful, forever pursuing fulfilment.

That pursuit consisted of a constant flitting around the globe, as spontaneous as his sudden disappearances from social functions, without a backwards glance. Jacobson, who never met him, thought the restlessness mirrored a struggle for acceptance of his own self. Roebuck fought for acceptance in a number of aspects of his life, embracing the struggle, conquering it. He proclaimed the worthiness of striving to overcome obstacles. He testified time and again that it was never about reaching the pinnacle, only about how one's character got shaped on the way there. It is not inconceivable to contend, now, that he was only ever referring to himself. We are left mourning a man not just at war with his perceived enemies but at war inside.

'I think Roebuck was the most unusual character I've ever come across,' says Matthew Engel, for twelve years the editor of *Wisden*. Therein lies as good a reason as any for what follows on these pages. Yet it wasn't the ultimate motivation. That was, and is, a quest for clarity on the matter of what really happened to Peter Roebuck. In seeking it, the authors have also sought to establish a fuller answer to a question many of Roebuck's friends and colleagues asked often: just who was this man?

'You'll never know Peter,' urges his mother, Elizabeth, 'until you have looked back. You'll be chasing shadows.'

1

IN HIS OWN WORLD

'The idea that children inhabit some innocent reverie has been disproved a hundred thousand times. No one familiar with schoolboys or their own consciences could argue otherwise.'

- *IT TAKES ALL SORTS*, 2005

'You're like Don Quixote ... chasing windmills,' the English cricket writer Scyld Berry said to Roebuck, and he reckons he never saw him look so hurt. 'It was just for a few seconds. Then he closed up and moved on.' Before he did, though, Roebuck gave a hint as to the source of his pain. 'My dad,' he replied, 'said that to me once when I was young.'

That the reminder of a father's chiding words hit such a raw nerve says something poignant, for Roebuck generally gave the impression of having no nerves, raw or otherwise. Not only did he not exhibit any response to pain, he appeared not to feel it. He admitted, 'I did cry during my first hiding, but resolved never to repeat the mistake.' In a brief character assessment, discovered among his late father's papers and appended by Roebuck as an epilogue to his own autobiography, his father described his second son as being 'beyond the range of normal weaponry'. As such, wrote Jim Roebuck, he 'can strike as hard and often as he wants without fear'.

The father had experienced first-hand what later was so readily apparent to others: his son's tungsten-like exterior. It was a very real part of the person people came to know, reflected not only in his writing and broadcasting but in his outward being, and manifesting not in a huff-and-puff kind of way but in a manner that was credible, admirable. When Roebuck's considered professional view was that strong words were required, he appeared to have no squeamishness in expressing them. And once that was done, the possibility of recrimination was treated simply as not a matter to be considered. While it is true that journalists who deliver opinion and judgement must be resolute, few enjoy bumping into the subject of a damning assessment the following day. Roebuck was different. Asked about a stinging indictment of Brett Lee for bowling beamers, and the likelihood of backlash, he batted it away as an irrelevancy, something simply not worthy of consideration. It was the response of one pretty much as his father described, seemingly beyond the range of normal weaponry.

'He wanted to remain elusive, a puzzle, part of one circle or another yet somehow apart and outside of all circles.' That is the fondly expressed view of Toby Jones, a long-time friend and associate from Sydney's Cranbrook School, where Roebuck taught from 1978 to 1986. Another interpretation is that he was pathologically secretive – a 'house with fierce dogs outside', as Viv

Richards put it to his Somerset teammate when Roebuck plunged into one of his malaises. Roebuck did not shy away from the description. He included it within the pages of his 1983 diary of a county cricket season, *It Never Rains*.

Graham Greene's pessimistic assessment – 'The world is not black and white. More like black and grey' – amused and resonated with Roebuck, and might have been written to describe how many people viewed him. Or, indeed, how he saw himself. He told one friend who got closer than most: 'A lot of people know one-third of me, you know two-thirds. That's enough.'

Those who liked and admired him took the position that regardless of an almost total unapproachableness on personal matters, intangibly expressed but real nonetheless, he possessed an unimpeachable morality. Those who disliked him – some instinctively, others gradually – read his unusual nature as evidence of something amiss. The fact that he refused to lash out, in keeping with his father's assessment, at most of those detractors only served to strengthen the view of the believers.

Then there are the ones in between. David Frith, the Anglo-Australian cricket historian and writer, sums it up: 'Most other people in cricket you can say, "What a great bloke, wish he was still here", or "What a bastard". With Roebuck, it's neither. There has never been anyone like him in my experience, so you can say it was interesting knowing him and I'm sorry it ended that way.'

Roebuck's was a life lived in fragments, in a way reflective of his personality. Born English, he enjoyed stints in Greece, took out Australian citizenship, built a house in South Africa and, at the end, was thought to be contemplating a move to India. While he never married or formed a conventional settled relationship, he assembled what he regarded as his own family: young men from a Zimbabwean orphanage. He formed connections but had few enduring close friendships.

He appeared to all and sundry as a man who was uniquely alone.

He was born into a devoutly Catholic family. The adage of that religion's great order of educators, the Jesuits, is oft stated: 'Give me a child for the first seven years and I'll give you the man.' It speaks of imparting the beliefs, values and perceptions of one generation to the next.

He once told a close friend of having virtually no memory of life until around the age of ten. That he wrote of those years in his autobiography, *Sometimes I Forgot to Laugh*, suggests he was doing so on the basis of information conveyed to him, or his imagination was hard at work. A third alternative is his self-described childhood amnesia was a means – the like of which became familiar in later years – of deflecting attention from his family background.

Peter Michael Roebuck was born in Oddington, near Oxford, to a father who had left school at fourteen and a bright, vivacious mother determined to improve the family's lot. The Roebucks were of strictly modest means and education would be their saviour. Awarded a mature-age scholarship to Ruskin College in Oxford via his trade union, Jim Roebuck 'set about studying with the intensity often detected in the desperate', as his son recalled in print many years later. There Jim, a widower, met Elizabeth Morrison, a brilliant student and gifted sportswoman who would represent England at lacrosse and earn an Oxford blue for cricket. She was a wicketkeeper. Little wonder the son came to so fervently believe in the capacities of education to inspire and uplift.

A veteran of World War II who survived the D-Day landings, Jim had earlier married a Belgian woman named Rosa. That union produced a son and daughter, James and Rosalie, but Rosa died in late 1950 following complications from the second birth. Jim became a single father of two in straitened circumstances, forced to relinquish care of his children. James was sent to live with his father's parents and Rosalie with a nurse from the hospital. It was an episode never mentioned again.

The father's subsequent achievements at university were a triumph of tenacity. More than fifty years later his middle son described his efforts thus:

> He completed the course and passed the exams, not
> a bad effort for a lad from the bottom set of a run-
> down school located in the poorest parts of a northern
> industrial city who had left school at fourteen, had fought
> in war, had lost his first wife, had been left with two young
> children and had had no way of supporting them or
> himself except by taking a humdrum job in a warehouse.

It is a moving tribute, and relevant, given the acknowledged tension in the relationship between father and son. Roebuck went on to describe his father as a 'crumpled, emotional, bad-tempered figure who sat in the sitting-room watching *Match of the Day* and scribbling poetry with a pencil', but he admitted that in those troubled early years he did not know his father's story. He was far more attached to his mother.

Within a year of their chance meeting at a lacrosse match, Jim and Elizabeth were married. A daughter, Margaret, was born in 1954 and Peter arrived on 6 March 1956. It was the year of Suez, Elvis, and Jim Laker, and the newest addition to the Roebuck family would be remarkably quick to acquire curiosity about all such matters and more. The family unit eventually encompassed six offspring, Beatrice and Paul arriving after Peter, and Jim's firstborns coming back under the family roof. There was a philosophy of all within clan Roebuck being equal, something Elizabeth proudly emphasises when she says the prefix 'step' was never used to describe the relationship of James or Rosalie with the rest. The Roebucks were in it together.

For all the subsequent speculation about a lack of connection with his birth family, Roebuck wrote of them with pathos and cared deeply for Elizabeth, despite his clear ambivalence towards his father. Upon meeting five of the six surviving members of the family unit, we found no absence of togetherness or love. It was largely the opposite. They remain loyal, united.

This blended household of six children and two parents of quite different personalities headed north-east to Scarborough. In four years there Elizabeth suffered a miscarriage, losing a son six months into the pregnancy. The mental scars took a long time to heal. Only decades later, said Roebuck, did the children fully realise the extent of their mother's suffering. Whether he as a young child bore some guilt about it, as children inadvertently can, is not clear. The wound was sufficiently deep for the family to leave the north and find their way to the West Country, settling in Bath. It was here that seven-year-old Peter was drawn to cricket, enthralled by the coverage – on the family's first TV set – of the epic 1963 series between England and West Indies, including the stirring climax at Lord's where Colin Cowdrey came to the wicket with a broken arm to force a draw. From that day, Roebuck decided he would be a cricketer.

Rather than bringing the young boy out of his shell, cricket appears to have initially sparked an inner life. Rosalie, his sister, describes endless hours spent exercising his imagination with a game. 'Most normal children want to be with other people and play with other people. Peter,' she says, 'spent an awful lot of time in the attic, on his own, playing Owzthat. He lived for that game.' Owzthat was a table-cricket game of the time played with two dice-like, six-sided metal barrels, the engraved outcomes on which denoted runs and wickets.

While such games have long engaged the young, filling vast spaces of otherwise lonely time, Roebuck's imaginings went beyond those of most young dreamers. Not for him the simplicity of Trueman bowling to Lawry, or Cowdrey facing Davidson. He created and occupied a world of his own, taking charge as captain and selecting fantastic figures like JFK, John Lennon and Charles Dickens as teammates. He took on the name Davies for himself and, he wrote, 'batted at first wicket down and led many courageous fightbacks'.

Imagining oneself merely as Ted Dexter putting Australia to the sword at Lord's was apparently not enough. Roebuck's fantasy was much more elaborate, in line with his vision. Davies was a figure whose qualities were a montage of great leaders, not just of Roebuck's time but through all time, going right back to God, who family members recall taking part in these imaginary contests. Whoever played under him, though, Davies was the leader. He was famous, a philanthropist, reformist, writer, creator and cricketer. Davies was brave and led his men fearlessly into battle against the odds. And Davies was Roebuck.

* * *

Though he claimed to not have stood out academically, his mother recalls him recording an IQ of 148, a figure bettered by Beatrice, who was younger, with 152. Beatrice says all the siblings were highly intelligent and all were sporty. Peter, despite his range of talents, was not seen within the family as anything special.

By necessity the Roebucks were isolated from their local community. There was a tribe of children to house and feed, and none of the homes they lived in through the years had room for visitors. 'We simply weren't in that world,' says Beatrice. 'There were six children, it was very structured, and our parents did not have money. Everything was on the breadline all the time. Looking back, we weren't able to reciprocate things like sleepovers or birthday parties, so we simply didn't have them. It was a close, but closed, family unit.'

Roebuck, in his own words, refused to invite school friends around 'for it was too tense and exposing'. Still, he was relatively popular, excelled at ball games, and worshipped Bath's rugby team. Paul Roebuck remembers his older brother's fierce competitiveness and angry reactions to rare defeats. He was emotionally responsive in the way of so many competitive boys. Cards, tennis, golf and darts were among their pursuits, Peter usually holding sway but storming off and banging doors if he didn't. Paul also recalls moments of levity and kindness, and a passion for rock and folk music. 'He was totally nuts about Bob Dylan. For a time, he wore Dylan hats in the house the entire day.' Hours listening to records in the attic doubled as tutelage for the youngest sibling; Peter would play Paul a song and invite him to cast his opinion on the meaning of the lyrics.

The other siblings remember with considerable amusement plays that the young Roebuck wrote and performed, and a seemingly ingrained impracticality. Later came impassioned debates on politics and religion and the 'testing out' of suitors for the Roebuck girls. He was an eager reader, and entertaining company within select peer groups, indulging in the odd juvenile lark and delighting in the surrealism of Monty Python. In sport he embraced leadership roles. The two oldest siblings, though, acknowledge a vulnerable side.

'Peter needed protecting, but I'm not sure he got a lot of protection,' says Rosalie, adding 'he lived in his own world and sometimes his world coincided with ours'. James describes someone who was 'slightly different', who stammered, not because he didn't know what to say but because he couldn't get the words out quickly enough. Speaking for himself, Roebuck was unsentimental about how he may have contributed to such perceptions. 'I preferred to lead a double life, gregarious among school chums, withdrawn at home. It is a common enough resolution to the embarrassment of family.'

As the middle boy – eight years younger than James, seven and a half years older than Paul – he was considerably apart from both. It was only as he reached his mid-teens that Paul became a regular companion, up in the attic. Peter was generous with his time. In theory, though, the key male presence in his life as a growing boy was Jim, the father with whom he found it difficult to connect. Rosalie describes Jim as a well-intentioned perfectionist who expected certain standards. James says, 'Our dad was quite demanding ... and quite difficult. To a certain extent he was a bit remote. He worked, he wrote his poetry, he oversaw Peter's cricket practice and it had to be done right.'

Initially Roebuck rejected his father's cricket coaching. He felt a burden, a weight of expectation, on him. In adolescence, he wrote, he 'kept away from his sometimes tortured assistance'. It does not sound so far removed from the perfectionism of Roebuck's own approach to coaching in later years. Perhaps it was this that prompted him to retrospectively observe of his father's efforts: 'If someone is to blame, might not they also deserve some credit?'

Credit was thin on the ground early and the strains between father and son extended beyond cricket practice. Roebuck wrote of a football game in which he ran around aimlessly without touching the ball as a 'protest against paternal influence'. Not that he was unfavourably disposed to football; it was his winter game and while ensconced in Bath he enthusiastically followed the local team. He described its star players as the only sporting heroes he ever knew.

But there was no contest when it came to Roebuck's practical sporting commitment. Cricket was more his style. He was an individual drawn to a team sport but a team sport notable for the individuality of its contributors. As he wrote in his mid-twenties, by this time a professional cricketer: 'I was <u>always</u> going to be a cricketer. Nothing else that I do, do I much value. Oh yes, I can write, I am clever, maybe I can teach but if I fail in cricket, I'll regard myself as a failure.'

It is hard to imagine a more eloquent statement of Roebuck's paradoxical way. A man whose vision extended far beyond the field of play would commit totally to a game. His self-image would be inextricably bound to success or failure at cricket. Roebuck was known to say that he regarded enjoyment in life as irrelevant. Only the struggle interested him. Here was a young man whose pursuit of personal fulfilment derived from playing a game he refused to enjoy. It sounds perverse. One who specialises in human behaviour describes it as a 'damaged way' of viewing life.

* * *

If Roebuck was searching for a more accommodating, more charismatic male figure such a person emerged at Somerset's unconventional Millfield School. There he encountered a man who evidence suggests became his greatest influence. R.J.O. 'Boss' Meyer founded the school in 1935 after returning from India with seven Indian boys, six of whom were princes. Millfield was one of the first co-educational English independent schools. Meyer was unpredictable, unorthodox and occasionally exasperating, described as a genius by fellow Cambridge cricketer and headmaster Dennis Silk, who wrote of Meyer after his death in 1991: 'He was much more a man of the world than any other headmaster I have known, and he was unencumbered with undue reverence for scholarship. The boys and girls at Millfield were led by a man who wanted them to know excellence in whatever field they could achieve it, and he did not much mind whether it came about in music or cricket, classics or the long jump.'

Reference to long jump wasn't random: the women's gold medallist at the 1964 Olympics in Tokyo was Millfield alumna Mary Rand (nee Bignal). Silk might also have mentioned men's breaststroke, for Duncan Goodhew, a year younger than Roebuck, became another Millfield Olympic champion at Moscow in 1980. According to Elizabeth Roebuck, the philosophies of R.J.O. Meyer were simple ones: everybody has some talent, some capacity, and everybody is equally important, and our job in life is to encourage that.

Meyer had been a Somerset cricketer of note who brought to the game some of the idiosyncratic flair that marked his approach to education. Once, playing for the Gentlemen at Lord's under the captaincy of Freddie Brown, he was at the bowling crease when Don Bradman arrived in the middle. Meyer was a man of theories and he had one about the Australian run-machine. As Roebuck liked to relate, he asked Brown for a field with eight men spread around the leg-side boundary. When Brown obliged, Meyer delivered a high, dipping full toss that Bradman dispatched between the outfielders. 'Orthodox field, please!' Meyer immediately called out to Brown.

Boss ran Millfield in accordance with how he believed education should be made available. School fees were adjustable depending on parental means. The wealthy might pay three or four times the standard rate, while the financially needy paid little or nothing. 'In that sense he might have been mistaken for a socialist,' said Silk, 'and how he would have chuckled at such an imputation.'

On a needs basis the Roebucks were closer to the second category than the first and the school came to their rescue. Meyer was conscious of Peter's growing reputation as a young cricketer because, according to Beatrice, 'Peter, as a twelve-year-old, bowled out Millfield's first team with these funny little leg-spinner things.' Nevertheless, there was the mandatory interview. Meyer tested the skills of the young cricketer opposite him by unexpectedly producing an orange from his desk, throwing it approximately in young Roebuck's direction, and noting that it was well caught.

'They wanted Peter,' says Beatrice, and Elizabeth and Jim said, 'You can't have Peter unless we all come. And – give us a house and two jobs.' 'Oh,' adds Beatrice, 'and they wanted scholarships as well.'

Boss Meyer agreed to the bold proposition. Clan Roebuck entered Millfield as a package, with the hard-bargaining parents joining the school as teachers. Meyer's determination to have

Peter, the talented cricketer and gifted student, opened the door. Given that his father's cricket coaching had already caused him to feel he had 'to carry the weight of the family', it can be imagined this new circumstance may have represented a disconcerting dynamic for a boy scarcely in his teens, particularly one uneasy about the 'embarrassment of family'. Eldest brother James concedes that having two parents on the staff may not have been especially beneficial.

'Boss was a very charismatic figure,' says Elizabeth, 'and he made you do things you didn't think you could. But he was bit of a gambler and he had a reputation. He once said to me, "Oh, you've got all these children but you look just sweet seventeen!" Jim said afterwards, "Well … he's won you over." The children were drawn to him like moths to a flame. It was a hopeless school at the time, except that it was wonderful for individuals. I think by the time Boss went it was bankrupt.'

References to Meyer, including his flaws, were not uncommon in Roebuck's writing. 'Blessed with principles rather than scruples,' Roebuck observed – and 'did not always distinguish between the school funds and his own.' Inevitably a showdown loomed with the school's board of governors. A groundswell formed. Financial issues and reputations were at stake. Roebuck, despite identifying improper behaviour on the headmaster's part, remained critical of those who challenged him.

Upon leaving the school he founded, Meyer moved to Campion, a private English-language school in Athens. Presumably it was no coincidence when Roebuck arrived there in 1977 for a brief teaching engagement. During this interlude he glimpsed, tantalisingly, another example of his erstwhile headmaster's mercurial methods:

Boss suggested that I help an especially bright girl
with aspirations to go to Oxford, an achievement the
old rogue felt might give the school a push along.
Her English was polite, immaculate and detailed but
somewhat stilted. His recommended method of instilling
a more carefree outlook was unorthodox.

Ultimately Roebuck concluded men of Meyer's calibre and nature cannot be 'subdivided'. Rather, they should be taken as a whole. The interpretation that he saw himself, in some way, walking in Meyer's shoes is hard to resist.

'I'm sure he was inspired by Meyer,' says Vic Marks, 'and he would have wondered at Meyer's eccentricities and his confidence to do it his way come what may.' Marks, a Somerset teammate, was regarded by many as Roebuck's closest friend through their playing years. 'He spoke of Boss with great affection and admiration and I bet in some way Pete wanted to emulate him. That experience would have encouraged any eccentricity about how you went about things, to not be constrained by the normal boundaries.'

'Boss,' confirms Rosalie, 'was incredibly bright, charismatic and incredibly perceptive. He and Peter were on the same wavelength.'

Meyer's encouragement to his students to know excellence in whatever field they could achieve it carried significance for Roebuck all his life. As for his choice to direct his energies to the field of cricket, rather than a more cerebral profession, Roebuck would write: 'A man must follow his spirit for otherwise something dies within.'

Not that he didn't shine academically. His parents, as school staff members, had a close-up view. 'Teachers were always calling us in or coming to see us to tell us stories,' says Elizabeth. 'In the upper sixth, Peter had a wonderful English teacher, Len Smith. He saw us in the staffroom one day and said: "Your son has just given the most inspiring comparison between T.S. Eliot and D.H. Lawrence ... They [his classmates] just sat there and didn't even notice the bell." That's when we began to realise that perhaps Peter might get to Cambridge.'

* * *

As for his cricketing ambitions, Roebuck's father had much earlier opted to apply the blowtorch. Peter Wight, an ex-Somerset player who hailed from Guyana, had established a coaching school near Bath Cricket Club. Jim Roebuck decided he was going to kill or cure his son's cricket fixation and enrolled him – an action, as Roebuck described it, which should not be mistaken for encouragement. The father was banking on his son being deterred from playing after getting hit a few times by the hard ball. This slightly conspiratorial plot backfired, Elizabeth says: 'Later, Peter [Wight] told us, "One day your boy could play for England."' Jim, the long-redundant backyard coach, was in all likelihood disappointed. He was convinced his son could be an outstanding barrister and harboured concerns that his personality was less suited to the sometimes brutal domain of male sport.

Sportswriter Rob Steen criticises this calculated action of the father. 'They take him off to the nets and get him hit to put him off cricket. Why would you do that? When you are exposed to that level of cruelty, however civilised they doubtlessly were as an academic family ... That was one thing that really struck me.'

The would-be cricketer himself felt that it was tough love taken to extremes but that the motivation and approach of his father was correct: 'Better find out immediately whether the lad had the stomach for a fight, otherwise a lot of time and money could be wasted.'

When a fifteen-year-old Roebuck captained Millfield against a team from Wales, his parents witnessed *his* hard-nosed approach. One of the visiting batsmen survived an appeal. Roebuck, says Elizabeth, reacted with a by-now typical pedantry. 'Peter was in the middle of the pitch, cap thrown on the ground, saying "He must be out – I know the rule." Jim and I went to see what was going on. It was during our lunchbreak. Boss was walking around the boundary. He was terrified of what might happen.'

A walk-off ensued. Eventually young Roebuck took his team back on the field on one condition: that when the match was over, the umpires would check the rulebook. 'You can guess who was right,' says Elizabeth. 'We were so embarrassed, but to him you must keep to the rules.'

His parents imbued him with certain left-wing values, and Millfield, being co-educational, was not among the most prestigious or expensive of schools. 'The Marlborough lot were the toffs and Peter hated them,' Elizabeth recalls. 'He vowed never to lose a match against them – and he didn't.'

He was in talented company. The Millfield team of 1970 contained five future first-class cricketers, one of whom also played rugby for Wales, plus a future England hockey international and others who went on to play cricket at Minor Counties or county 2nd XI level. His own batting technique was sound, if lacking in power due to his small, youthful frame, and he bowled fizzing, looping leg-spin. Word spread: at thirteen he debuted for Somerset's seconds in a game against local rivals Devon.

The cricket dream was now something to actively pursue. It took on an added resonance in family life. 'Our schedules were governed by cricket,' says Beatrice. 'We would have our Sunday lunch at extraordinarily early times like 11.30 a.m. so that Peter could get picked up to go to Taunton because he was in the 2nd XI.'

Elizabeth would prove to be a staunch supporter. 'If he wasn't picked in the team, or batting in the right place, his mother wanted to know why,' recalls veteran Somerset player and coach Peter Robinson. 'There was a game in the 1970s when Closey [Brian Close] was captain. Brian Rose came in on the Saturday morning and wasn't fit so I ended up playing. Roeby was in the 2nd XI down in Devon and didn't get called back. His mother was on the phone asking why wasn't Peter playing. She was very keen on his cricket. I never met his father.'

After finishing at Millfield, Roebuck studied law at Emmanuel College at the University of Cambridge, graduating with first-class honours in 1977. He rejected the possibilities this presented – too stuffy, too inhibiting, too formal – and instead chose the relative career brevity and remunerative mediocrity of life as a cricket professional. The following excerpt from a letter to an Australian friend, written in 1982, says much about Roebuck and his scorn for establishment values:

> I did my law degree in Cambridge – got a first class
> degree, & never had the slightest intention of doing
> Law … You see I have done exactly what I wanted to –
> with one exception. First, partly through insecurity
> (need to prove yourself) and partly through my rampant
> competitive streak I first had to prove to the beggars
> that I could beat 'em at their game, if I wanted. I did that

at Cambridge – then I threw it all away – to show, well
the game was not worth playing.

If this is an accurate representation of the student Roebuck's motivations – and there is no reason to believe otherwise – he was prepared to go to considerable lengths to make a statement. His brother Paul, who also studied at Cambridge, remembers being told by one of the university porters that his brother was 'the most astonishing student he had ever come across'. At the same time he was on Somerset's books and batting in the top order for Cambridge in first-class fixtures. To meet all his demands he would rise at four o'clock during summer term to commence studying, and after wading through four or more hours of that he would have breakfast before heading to Fenner's, the university cricket ground, for the day's play – 'without fail', according to that same porter. Afterwards he would return to his rooms for supper. It was lights out by 8.30 p.m. every single night.

All this to achieve a qualification he had no intention of employing; having climbed the mountain, he did indeed throw it all away. Fellow students rose to the top of their profession and can today be found plying their craft at the Old Bailey and in courtrooms around England. Roebuck's life would revolve ever after around cricket. It was not so much an attraction for the sport's traditions, for the camaraderie, or for the potential for fame. Rather, he believed cricket was more than a game, it was about character – a point 'surely now within the grasp of even the dimmest intellectual'. He said some enter sport's fray because of a lack of alternatives but those who deliberately choose that course must make it work in order to justify their existence. Read over, it is a grim and severe line to take.

Despite the earlier coaching attempts by Jim and unstinting support of Elizabeth, ambivalence about their son's chosen vocation – cricket over law – was expressed. The Roebucks knew the law was a gilt-edged option for their son, a forum in which he would surely shine. While there are well-documented stories of those who took the road less travelled and triumphed, they are vastly outnumbered by the less visible tales of failure and disappearance without trace. Their son's passion for the game played by flannelled fools had been burning since solitary days and nights of Owzthat in the attic. Yet it differed from the sheer joy of sport that has fuelled the ambitions of others through the years. The psychology of Roebuck's choice appears to have been far more complex. 'It was a requirement,' he declared, 'of my character.'

* * *

Now in her late eighties, Elizabeth Roebuck is robust, spirited and good humoured. Although bruised by the controversies that had scarred Peter's life, his family members in England were in no way prepared for the horrible news of his demise. They were physically removed from the traumatic event and struggled (still do) to determine the exact nature of events. But they swear by his integrity. They remain defenders of his name and reputation. While Roebuck had told some close friends his mother was dead, Elizabeth is unequivocal in denying that he cut himself adrift. If communication between them was less than it used to be, she insists that was her son wanting to spare his family the risk of media scrutiny, brought on after he was found guilty of assault by that court in Taunton. 'His life changed in 2001,' Elizabeth says, 'because of what we call a miscarriage of justice.'

'Contact was sporadic,' she admits. 'We were expected to remember birthdays and Christmas, although we stopped his phone calls on Christmas Day because it got too chaotic.' In fact Roebuck shied away from Christmas celebrations, explaining to one friend that his father used to lock himself in a room for the festive season.

'We would have intermittent emails,' says Beatrice. 'He was very proud of the achievements of the people he sponsored and Mum and I were part of his circulars, so we'd get updates like that. Mum would get phone calls but ours was mostly email contact. It was lovely to have his little comments every now and then. I mean, we could have spent our lives following him around the world and tuning into the ABC and subscribing to the *Sydney Morning Herald* but that was his world and his job and we had ours.'

If the idea of a family relying on 'circulars' and maintaining contact via media dispatches suggests remoteness, Beatrice insists her brother cared deeply. 'He was always asking if people were all right. In later years it was "how are Mum and Dad?" and "have they got enough money to live on?". He was very caring towards us. He would have done anything for us, and we would for him. And we are for him now.'

When Paul, who has been based in Latin America for some years, was enduring a difficult period in his mid-forties, sometime around 2008, Peter emailed him: 'Dear Paul, I hear through Mum that you are having a hard time. Let me know if I can help in any way. Sorry, I haven't been much of an elder brother to you. Peter.'

'I replied,' says Paul, 'that he had been a wonderful older brother to me.'

Elizabeth too remembers a letter. This one was sent after the 2001 court case. 'It said, "Sorry Mum – have I let the family down?" It was about the publicity. I said he hadn't let us down. He had stood up and was counted and the justice let us down.'

The contradiction between recollections like these and what Roebuck had told close friends about his family triggered surprise and concern, leaving even those who held him in highest esteem to wonder. Harsha Bhogle's is a voice well known to millions in countries wherever cricket is played. His first venture into radio commentary in Australia coincided with Roebuck's debut season as an ABC regular in 1991–92. The pair formed a firm friendship, Bhogle writing a foreword to Roebuck's autobiography and admitting to being in awe of his friend's skill as a writer. He says the notion of familial fracture is particularly confusing viewed through Indian eyes. 'There was something there that we didn't know,' says Bhogle. 'Peter always said he didn't have a family and we discovered afterwards that he did and that he was actually in touch with his mother.'

Rohit Brijnath, who also saw Roebuck as a beacon and mentor, and who Bhogle describes as 'the best Indian sportswriter by a long margin', says: 'In India there's a great need to encompass everybody into the bosom of your family. He was a solitary person. I would ask him about his family and why he didn't have a stronger relationship with his family as perhaps I had, for example. But Peter drew lines. He would take you so far and then not allow you to go any further, not reveal himself.'

Even Roebuck's adopted African family appear to have learnt little of their patron's background. 'He didn't used to speak about his family,' says James Gwari, a member of the Pietermaritzburg household. 'It was a sensitive topic for him. He told us that he didn't get along with them. The way he went on about it, it was like he hated the English. That's why he went to Australia.' Justice Hakata, another house member, says: 'He would talk about us on air when he was commentating the cricket. He would refer to his sons. But I never heard him talk about his own family.'

Many who spent time working with Roebuck in Australia and England could relate to this. Asked whether family was ever mentioned by Roebuck in his presence, Australian writer Gideon Haigh's reply is a flat: 'Never.'

'He rarely if ever spoke of his family,' says Mike Coward, 'and was mystified that others, me in particular, knew of the family circumstances of other members of the press corps. That I should know the names of wives, partners and children bewildered him. Such talk did not engage him in any way. In the few conversations that might have strayed to background and family, I gained the impression his family had little understanding of him and little or no appreciation of his pleasure in living primarily in South Africa and Australia.'

Nevertheless, his love and concern for his mother was evident in his writing. Of Elizabeth's commitment to Jim and decision to marry him, he wrote in a matter-of-fact manner that she gave up a scholarship, took on her partner's Catholic faith and '... otherwise carried on in her own indomitable way'. It cannot have been easy, Roebuck intimated, given his parents' contrasting natures. 'Her cheerfulness sat uncomfortably beside his morbid pessimism.'

Elizabeth remembers of the father and son's relationship, 'He and Jim would sit and go at it hammer and tong, having a debate about politics, or economics. They weren't quarrelling. Just having a debate.' Beatrice concurs: 'Our father would quite happily provoke a conversation and see who nibbled. Conversations, debates – sometimes arguing for the sake of arguing.'

But it cut deep. Roebuck reacted against the intensity, shying away from the pressure of his father's urgings. If the son was left bruised, it may be reflected in his repeated and insistent view that every boy must, at some time, take a stand against his father. While not an unfamiliar refrain in the area of male psychology, for Roebuck it was a matter of certainty and urgency. Male offspring of two notable Australians, both of whom attended Cranbrook School when Roebuck taught and coached there, heard the message in strong terms.

One was James Packer who, according to Roebuck, was instructed that sooner or later he would have to fight father Kerry or forever live in his shadow. The other was Nick Horne, son of the author and public intellectual Donald Horne. Nick recalls a letter Roebuck wrote him from England in which 'he talked about my father's autobiography, *The Education of Young Donald*. I'd read it several times, seeing it as a kind of template for how I should live my life; he [Roebuck] pointed out that I was different to my father and had my own life to lead. The idea that sons should move out of their fathers' shadows was a constant theme in his mentoring of young men.'

From a relatively young age Roebuck appears to have practised what he would later preach. He rebelled against his father's cricket coaching and it clearly put distance between them. But human psychology is rarely so simple that such a backlash is the end of the story. In this case, the adult Peter Roebuck came to re-enact and reflect some of the qualities he had earlier rejected in his father. Stories of Roebuck's own rigid perfectionism abound, told with bemusement by those on the receiving end or who were mere witnesses.

Jim Roebuck died in 2008. His second son described him as having 'remained a tormented man, lost somewhere between frustration and fury'. The father, though, was more charitable in return. While the character analysis mentioned previously acknowledges his son as someone who might be seen as 'odd', Jim goes on to explain him as an 'unconventional loner, with an independent outlook on life, an irreverent sense of humour and sometimes a withering tongue'. He refers to him as 'kind and tolerant ... tough and austere and responsive neither to bribes nor threats ... tough on himself'. The last of these qualities, Jim Roebuck wrote, caused his son to be 'harsh in his judgement of others, especially the self-indulgent'.

They are words generally reflective of a father's pride, and they describe Roebuck in terms absolutely identifiable to those who knew and admired him.

As for Jim Roebuck's comparison of his son with Don Quixote, perhaps the father was making an observation about his son attacking imaginary giants – 'tilting at windmills' – as Don Quixote did. Many who knew Roebuck, particularly the man of later years, speak of his belief that he was obsessively pursued. That he had made enemies is not in dispute.

But it remains a matter of conjecture whether they cared about him as much as he about them. If his anxieties and suspicions were correct, then who knows what inner turmoil this caused. But if he was wrong, then perhaps Roebuck's fixation with them did indicate a tendency to rage at the light.

In the end, he saw betrayers and detractors around every corner. In the last email to his family, he expressed a longing to come home.

2

SUMMER'S TEST

'There must be some fascinating stimulation in
the game to make so many of us, so ill-prepared
for turmoil, risk its ugly changes.'

- IT NEVER RAINS, **1984**

There's a beautifully framed image of Viv Richards reaching out to touch his batting partner Roebuck on the shoulder, in an almost paternal gesture of reassurance, during the Benson & Hedges Cup final of 1982. Bony, awkward, Roebuck stands in total contrast to the muscular, majestic West Indian. Roebuck gazes downward, shoulders slumped. With his thin-rimmed spectacles and apologetic air he looks somehow miscast, as though he has strayed onto a stage and forgotten his lines.

Although Somerset would triumph over Nottinghamshire that day at Lord's, Roebuck was scrapping – as ever – up against the likes of Hadlee, Hendrick, Rice and Hemmings, international players all. Through gritted teeth and with pokes, prods and deflections, pushes to leg and the odd flourish, Roebuck brought up a half-century. It had taken him twice as many balls as Richards but then it nearly always did. More to the point, their unbroken 105-run partnership would see Somerset home with plenty of overs to spare. The apologetic figure had won.

Later in life he reflected with pleasure on the occasional triumph but during his career the ever-present shadows of the many struggles lost consumed and often pained him. 'It's strange that cricket attracts so many insecure men,' he once noted. 'It is surely the very worst game for an intense character. There must be some fascinating stimulation in the game to make so many of us, so ill-prepared for turmoil, risk its ugly changes. Otherwise we'd never tolerate its bounce of failure. And it is mostly failure, even for the best.'

Every innings, according to Roebuck, was an ordeal. His diaries and accounts reveal persistent doubts and an endless fight against the pitfalls of his chosen occupation. 'In a way it's madness me being a professional sportsman,' he wrote in a private letter in mid-1983, 'it expects things of me I cannot easily provide.'

Stuck for much of his time at Somerset between the brutal power of Richards and the belligerent risk-taking of Ian Botham, he could be forgiven for harbouring such misgivings. Yet his technique was sound, the product of relentless fine-tuning. He was, as Mike Brearley put it, 'the Larry Gomes of Somerset', a reference to the sheet-anchor role Gomes played so reliably for West Indies. It could be said that in sport as in character Roebuck was more gifted than he ever admitted. The self-loathing and agonising that was exposed on the page – never so nakedly as in *It Never Rains* – betrayed a view of his own game that fell far short of his considerable abilities and achievements. And this was not some feigned attempt at characteristically English self-deprecation. One diary entry ran: 'I'm stuck in a swamp, being sucked down and waving my arms around in desperation, hoping that someone will notice.'

'He could be a complete pain in the arse and a lot of it I put down to cricket,' says his ex-Somerset teammate Nigel Popplewell. 'In *It Never Rains* there's a chapter where we go to Lancashire in 1983 and he just has a complete wobbly. Now, he usually threw one of those around Weston-super-Mare, so the beginning of August. Coincidence, Weston-super-Mare, lack of form ... whatever it was, he'd have a real lack of self-confidence at some stage during the season. When he was depressed like that he was difficult.'

This was a man who made a thousand runs in a season nine times, weathering all manner of conditions and defying quality opponents. It couldn't put paid to the recurring bouts of gloom. 'My one frustration with Pete,' says Vic Marks, 'and I had this with Tav [Chris Tavaré] as well, is I often thought they were better players than they allowed themselves to think. Pete would agonise every season, "How am I going to get a run?", and I would say, "Pete, you'll get 1100 runs at 37." And by and large, he'd get them.'

Resolve played a major part in his durability and effectiveness. This was, after all, a profession of his choosing, not calling. The relentless practice ethic instituted at a tender age by his father no doubt contributed, likewise a pointed appreciation of his family's humble circumstances. Plus he belonged – and knew it – to that not-so-exclusive club of players for whom natural dexterity extends only so far. Best, in the circumstances, to put an intense, energetic disposition to work; this was a man striving not so much for perfection as acceptance. The dread of failure propelled him to push valiantly against it, leading to murmurings of self-obsessive traits that would never really leave him. Zealous tenacity, in a sport where collective harmony is the ideal, is more respected than admired. At times in the Taunton dressing room, Roebuck was more a case study than a teammate.

He worked doggedly at the technical aspects and remained a fitness devotee throughout his playing career, at odds with the less taxing expectations of the era. 'I must have thrown thousands of balls at him,' says Peter Robinson. 'He had such wonderful powers of concentration as a batsman. We all talk about "ugly runs"; well, there was no one better at it than Pete.'

He was never more aroused and alert than during confrontation with an eager foe – Leicestershire's Jonathan Agnew, for example. 'It's easy to look at Peter as scholarly, a quiet chap, but that's not Peter,' says Agnew. 'He was gritty and would give a bit back in the middle, which is how it should be. He wouldn't be cowed. He was in his own little world, aware he had these stellar batsmen behind him so he always had to prove himself.'

'When I was in some situations with him in a match,' says Somerset wicketkeeper Neil Burns, 'my respect for him grew. He was someone who was prepared to fight hard. It was like, we're two men out here, we've got a job to do, just get on and bloody do it. He was someone who basically worked out how he was going to absorb the pressure of a fast bowler.'

An acute awareness of his workmanlike capacities could drive Roebuck to heightened powers of resistance, days when rash play with bat in hand was anathema. There was a famous innings, late in his Somerset days, against Allan Border's 1989 Australians. Swept aside by the pace and bounce of Merv Hughes in the first dig, Roebuck resolved not so much to fix bayonet but shield when Somerset batted again. He defended stoutly for 289 balls and nigh on six hours. While out there, the thought occurred that some less than flattering portraits written of the brittle Aussies over preceding seasons may have awakened stirrings of revenge against the *Sydney Morning Herald* correspondent. Despite what Hughes and Carl Rackemann threw at him by way of bowling and gratuitous advice, Roebuck remained undefeated and secured a draw. It later prompted one of his best lines: 'Border seemed to find my batting dull and he had a point.'

* * *

As with so many parts of Roebuck's life, there was contradiction and paradox about his batting and captaincy: capable of long innings and a regular maker of centuries, yet encumbered by self-doubt; attacking and at times reckless as a captain, stolid and dull with bat in hand. 'Watching Roebuck was like being at a requiem mass,' said Jim Laker, somewhat churlishly, after enduring a slow Roebuck knock at The Oval in 1985. The most contrary aspect of all was the flourish of his pen, a vibrant and occasionally florid departure after years of grinding down opposition bowlers with stodgy defence and minimal risk. The contradictions flowed into his personal and social life as well, for there was a breaking of rigorous and self-imposed shackles in certain, trusted company.

In his early days he contrived to hit a plastic ball against a wall on the landing below the flat in Scarborough and play the rebound. Thereafter, spare waking hours were spent in the company of brothers and sisters on the concrete forecourt of the garage. Typically older brother James was doing the bowling.

From the age of eight, sessions at Peter Wight's indoor school lasted two and a half hours each Saturday. He played junior club cricket with Bath initially, Lansdown later, then Street. Jim took up the cause at home, hanging a ball on a string and working with his son for an hour a day to perfect his range of strokes, even if that arrangement was not a happy one. He was by no means tall or strong enough to hit boundaries, but sceptical coaches and teammates alike were soon stirred by his rigid application and the wickets claimed by his leg-breaks.

At Millfield he was called up to the first team, and on summer breaks played club cricket. He took a wicket on his county 2nd XI debut, playing a dozen or so more matches for them over the next few seasons. During this period he formed an immediate bond with Vic Marks. Both youngsters were initially wary of a brusque, rambunctious lad from Yeovil by the name of Botham, whose manner and potent talents they soon warmed to. Roebuck's batting was by now taking precedence, after a growth spurt, and the foundations for a professional career were laid. Perhaps inevitably, the weight of expectation he felt – whether self-imposed or conveyed with brooding intensity by his father – left him a little at odds with less cluttered, less complicated teammates. He'd had a taste of captaincy at Millfield, later observing of this time: 'A tendency to overreact emerged, an inability to wait until things turned around.'

At Somerset came encounters with people, other than Marks and Botham, who would go on to play significant roles in his life. Brian Rose was in and out of the 2nd XI, so too Peter Denning and Mike Tarr, who would later draw the illustrations in *It Never Rains*. County veterans Brian Langford, Roy Palmer and Roy Kerslake – so much a part of Roebuck's Somerset experience in the years to come – were winding down their playing careers, while Peter Robinson, a loyal supporter in testing times, was midway through his. Appearing as a teenager at this level meant mixing with older, worldlier men, absorbing their salty language and match-hardened tricks of the trade, and seeing first-hand the shifting dynamics of team politics.

By 1974, his first season on contract, Roebuck had played fifteen games in the seconds for a top score of 78. After a quiet start that season he hit his straps with 339 runs for four times dismissed in a five-week purple patch across July and August, including a new highest score of 81 not out. Rewarded with a first-team debut at the age of eighteen, Roebuck impressed straight away, opening the batting against Warwickshire at Weston-super-Mare and sharing a 104-run partnership with Derek Taylor. In a sign of things to come, the number four bat that day was an elegant and confident West Indian – Isaac Vivian Alexander Richards – who made it look all too easy in a short and sweet knock of 41. Brian Close, charismatic and tough, was Somerset's skipper, a good quarter of a century older than Roebuck. Close would eventually make way for Rose, ushering in a new, emboldened era.

'We had a happy summer as young pros in 1974,' says Marks, 'knowing we would be going up to university that October. We used to have to do some groundstaff work. There was an epic game against Hampshire where Both had his teeth knocked out by Andy Roberts and went on to win the game for us. And Pete and I were operating the scoreboard and we got so excited we made a complete bollocks of it. People were shouting at us to get it right. There was total chaos. It was Both's first dramatic entrance into the game and we were excited to see one of our peers doing this.'

The next stage of Roebuck's cricket progression took place at Cambridge. Far more taken with cricket than his chosen course of study, he nonetheless struggled to come to terms with the quality of attacks the university encountered, undergoing searching examinations from Roberts, Imran Khan, Sarfraz Nawaz, John Lever and Derek Underwood. In 1975 he endured a run of low scores and was in the doldrums after failing in Swansea against a modest Glamorgan line-up. Walking out in the second innings in a decidedly more attacking frame of mind, he hit an assured 146 not out, his maiden first-class ton, and followed that with 158 against Oxford three days later in the varsity match. 'Oxford had a chucker called Cantlay,' recalls Scyld Berry, who caught the end of Roebuck's innings. 'He was quite quick for a student and Roeby just lashed him through the off side. His wonderful driving through the off side that he had when he was young … The similarity was often made with Peter May.'

Roebuck described his effort in the varsity match as the innings of his life. Hooking Imran off his nose and into the Lord's pavilion gave him enormous pleasure. Two big hundreds in three days was quite a statement from an emerging player, and duly noted. He played out the rest of that season in the County Championship for Somerset without ever threatening to scale such heights again, although an unbeaten 81 in the final game, against Glamorgan once more, guaranteed future interest from the county's hierarchy. 'I knew of him since he was thirteen at Millfield,' says Rose.

The steady progress wobbled over the next two years. There were occasional highlights but his batting, whether for Cambridge or Somerset, struggled to live up to the comparisons made with eminent batsmen of yesteryear. A savage blow to the head from an Andy Roberts bouncer at Fenner's in 1976 didn't help matters.

Roebuck was carted off to hospital, only to return and have his cap knocked off by the same bowler. A photo exists of Roebuck holding a cloth to the swelling, one eye already bloodshot.

For a while after that bowlers peppered him with short stuff; the cricketers' grapevine feasts on whispers of susceptibility. Not for the first time, the young man refused to cower. He would not be easily deterred. It was a watershed moment, a reckoning that he had much to learn. Methodically and repetitively, he rebuilt his technique. 'By hook or by crook I was going to survive in that often unkind game,' he mused. The fear of failure burned more deeply than fear of being struck again.

Somerset stuck by him. After returning from university with his first-class degree, his first full season as a county pro in 1978 was judged a modest success. There was an unbeaten hundred against the touring New Zealanders at Taunton and a string of crucial cameos in one-day competitions. He was gaining ground. Rose thought it wise to use Roebuck as a buffer between the two explosive talents – Richards and Botham – and the arrangement worked admirably, their freewheeling batting complemented by Roebuck's ability to soak up whatever opposition bowlers could muster. Against Gloucestershire in May he and Botham added 129 – with the increasingly burly all-rounder making 86 of them – while in July against Leicestershire he and Richards put on a game-changing 136, Roebuck contributing 50.

'I batted Viv at three, Roebuck at four and Both at six,' says Rose. 'Batting Ian higher than six was always slightly disruptive, whereas with Pete Roebuck I could take the dog for a walk. He was that sort of batter.'

Mike Brearley, captain of Middlesex at the time, agrees, suggesting the threat posed by Richards and Botham in tandem was not matched by the reality. 'Peter often did a good job batting between Richards and Botham, keeping them from batting together. Their partnerships, which would always be alarming to opposition bowlers and to people hanging out their washing in neighbouring gardens, were not I think all that productive.'

An odd incident is recalled from this time when Roebuck was seeking a foothold in county cricket. Competition for places was keen; the promise of contract renewal or threat of release (or banishment to the 2nd XI) could see two players fighting it out. A talented young Somerset batsman, Phil Slocombe, had burst onto the scene during the mid-1970s but his performances fluctuated thereafter. By 1980 it was perceived that either he or Roebuck would secure the final spot in the batting order. That season Roebuck's form was ordinary but Slocombe's was disastrous. The moment of truth arrived against Glamorgan in late August. To his horror, Roebuck was dismissed cheaply and trudged off, forced to watch the rest of the innings. Slocombe came in at number six and began cautiously. Then, with his score on 10, facing little-known spinner Neil Perry, he popped a ball up close to the wicket. Roebuck, unable to contain his glee, was heard by teammates to cry 'Catch it!' from the pavilion. Slocombe was caught by Ezra Moseley, dropped for the next match, and didn't play another Championship game for the best part of twelve months. Roebuck was unapologetic. 'It was dog eat dog,' he wrote in *Sometimes I Forgot to Laugh*. His place was secure.

These were glory years for Somerset. Under the imaginative stewardship of Rose the county won a fistful of titles, a feat made all the more meritorious given Somerset had not a single trophy to its name prior to 1979. The county's Championship history was decidedly mediocre; despite the odd placing somewhere near the upper part of the table, Somerset had never consistently pressed for the highest honour since their readmittance to the first-class scene in 1891. Things got so poor in the 1950s that they contrived to land on the foot of the table four years running. New resolve was instilled under Close in the 1970s, and Rose's subsequent appointment was an inspired one. The Somerset dressing room at this time can only have been a fascinating cauldron. Such kaleidoscopic diversity: joining Richards from the Caribbean was Joel Garner – all 6 foot 8 inches of him – and complementing them were the tempestuous local lad, Botham, taking all before him, the more cerebral Oxbridge set, and a fleet of younger players starting to shine. Somerset would climb as high as third in the Championship but it was in the one-day arena that Rose's side excelled.

In some respects Somerset's repeated bids for silverware coincided with a golden era in domestic one-day cricket. Sponsorship increased, prizemoney surged. The BBC televised a match every Sunday throughout the season and the local cricketing landscape was populated with the world's greats: Gordon Greenidge, Zaheer Abbas, Glenn Turner, Javed Miandad, Clive Lloyd, Mike Procter, Andy Roberts, Richard Hadlee, Imran ... to name some. Then there was Somerset's famed West Indian duo. Matches were often billed as showdowns between overseas pros.

Sunday afternoons at the county ground in Taunton became immensely popular, with lockouts and nail-biting finishes not uncommon. One of the best was the Gillette Cup semi-final of 1978. Somerset hosted Essex – Gooch, McEwan, Fletcher, Denness, Lever, et al. – and officials were forced to shut the gates almost two hours before play was due to commence. Countless fans milling outside were later let in. Richards was in fabulous touch and played a blinder, adding 103 with Roebuck. Essex were left chasing 288 for victory, considered a huge total in those days. But with Gooch at his imperious best and Fletcher immoveable Essex kept coming. In a heart-stopper, seven runs were needed off the last three balls. With the crowd at fever pitch and the tension on the field palpable, Somerset panicked – fumbled byes, a no-ball, overthrows. Only a run-out by skipper Rose off the last delivery saved his side, much to the rapturous delight of the thousands flooding onto the field.

Rose then took his troops off to Lord's for the final but the occasion proved one obstacle too many and they fell somewhat limply to Sussex. With Richards and Garner in rampaging form Somerset went one better in 1979, collecting both the Gillette Cup and Sunday League, and added further one-day trophies in 1981, 1982 and 1983. United by ambition and enjoying a huge swell of support, the players mixed well on and off the field. Potential divisions along the lines of background, education, political leanings or race were not countenanced. Richards affectionately labelled Roebuck 'Professor' and, for his part, Roebuck would later research names for Richards' children. 'He had no problem at all in the Somerset dressing room,' says Engel. 'He was accepted as highly eccentric in that most bizarre of environments, part of the mix in both cricketing terms and personality.'

Cricketers, Roebuck liked to pronounce, generally stand somewhere to the right of Margaret Thatcher. Fellow travellers on the county circuit may well have lapped up soccer pools, page three girls and a flutter on the nags but Roebuck was elsewhere: the theatre, for one, buried in literature for another. Politics was also front and centre. He along with Marks and Mike Brearley campaigned with Labour MP Derek Wyatt to prevent the British

Lions tour to South Africa in 1986, a less than fashionable cause at the time. A few years later he bequeathed his life insurance to the African National Congress. 'They accepted him being a little bit different and within county cricket it's probably not that easy when you're very bright,' says former Sussex captain John Barclay. 'First-class honours degree at Cambridge and you're in a dressing room where 75 per cent of them read the *Sun*. It must have been quite a delicate balance. Cricket throws up that disparity of intellect.'

Later Roebuck would claim the seeds of dissent were simmering in the background, but for several heady years it all held together for Somerset's brigade of increasingly colourful characters.

'We had a lot of fun,' Rose says. 'Back then we didn't have managers or coaches around our neck, so it was left to the captain to manage things. When Viv started out he was with me in the 2nd XI, and Both started at the same time, so did Vic and Peter, we all knew each other. Pete Denning was my batting partner. If you had what you would call "personalities" it was easier to manage. I would either ignore it or confront it. Mostly, I ignored it.'

* * *

For an insular man, these days of acclaim did not sit easily. Roebuck's game was steadily improving but, paradoxically, his spells of depression and spiralling self-doubt intensified.

After a relatively bare summer in 1982, he made more than 1200 runs the season after – which included brief exposure to the captain's role – then burst through the barriers in 1984. While England's best were crumbling before the might of West Indies, Roebuck racked up 1702 runs at 47.27 as an opening batsman.

He'd begun the season in outstanding form, with 145 against Boycott's Yorkshire and 152 four days later against Oxford. 'I always thought he was one of the best batsmen never to play for England,' says Kerslake. 'Superb technique, rarely hit the ball in the air. He was never going to be a Botham or a Richards but he got his runs with cricket shots.'

It got better. Across a fifteen-day period in late June and early July he compiled four hundreds in four consecutive Championship matches: this from a batsman who, stretching back ten years, had reached three figures on only six previous occasions. He hit a new best score of 159. A series of collapses and other calamities beset the national side, on the receiving end of a West Indian pace barrage of Marshall, Garner and Holding. Roebuck kept piling up runs, and may have been unlucky to be overlooked. Scrambling for inspiration, England's selectors used twenty-one different players across that summer's five Tests – all of which England lost – as the likes of Warwickshire's Andy Lloyd, Kent's Chris Tavaré and Hampshire's Paul Terry got the nod.

'I would have thought,' says Scyld Berry, 'he would have played for England in 1984, when it came down to Mark Nicholas, Paul Terry or Roebuck. If he'd been a junior Peter May that would have appealed to selectors, rather than putting on the hairshirt and becoming a leg-side nudger.'

Other factors may have been at play. A personality perceived as eccentric, or at the very least disengaged from the rolls and tumbles of teammates, didn't help. Lapses of form or crises in confidence triggered the sort of intense soul-searching and mood swings that could be disconcerting in a team setting. And Roebuck had been unashamed about his tangles with depression, baldly portraying his foibles and frailties in print. Neil Burns compares

Roebuck's intensity with that of a couple of later Australian batsmen, Michael Bevan and Steve Waugh, and talks of the need to switch between fervour and relaxation, according to context. 'I'm not sure Pete was able to find contexts which enabled him to relax and unwind. Perhaps because he had such an incredible mind, the idea of him slowing down and resting was anathema to him. He needed a high level of stimulation.'

So the England selectors may have been wary. 'For all his strengths,' says Robinson, who was by now Somerset's coach, 'he was somehow insecure – "I can't play today, I've got a mental block".' Robinson recalls an occasion when Roebuck, selected in the first team, was found walking across the oval at Wellingborough School where the second team was playing. Asked what he was doing, Roebuck appeared exasperated: he wasn't up to playing, he claimed, because he couldn't focus. 'There were phases,' says Marks, 'when he was down and not scoring many runs and he'd say, "I can't play the next game." He wasn't malingering and we were playing a hell of a lot; the right thing to do was to listen to him.'

Within the Somerset cocoon, an attentive approach was required. Robinson remembers inquiring often and genuinely about Roebuck's welfare. So does Roy Kerslake. 'People like Roy,' says Marks, 'were always coming up to me and asking, "How's Pete – is he all right?" Because Pete could be distant and moody. Even back then people identified that there was potential that he could do himself in. But at the time I thought he's not really brave enough to do that.'

Kerslake, notably close to the players, had risen to become a steadfast and popular Somerset chairman of cricket. 'I always thought there was that thing with Peter where you weren't quite sure how he was going to be that day.' He and Robinson had been involved in Roebuck's development since early on. They marvelled at his determination at the crease, were privy to his absent-mindedness, felt concerned about his lapses into depression, and got occasionally annoyed by his myopic tendencies. 'My wife would help when he'd gone to Australia,' says Kerslake. 'We used to clean the place and let it during the winter for him. We'd go over there and he'd literally walked out – the bed wouldn't be made, dishes still in the sink, fridge still full. He'd just gone, leaving the house for six months. What sort of person is that?'

Robinson was a staunch ally, then and later in life. Roebuck would state in his autobiography that Robinson 'remains my only friend in Somerset' – at once both a heartfelt commendation and a despairing reflection of just how low he thought his standing was. It was something of a one-sided friendship and it says much of Robinson that he stayed loyal. 'In some ways you'd say he was bit of a user,' Robinson says. 'The season would finish and he'd be off to Australia. He wouldn't say a few days ahead, but the day before leaving he'd ring me and say, "What are you doing tomorrow? Can you give me a lift to Heathrow?" So we'd get to Heathrow and he'd give me a chequebook with all of the cheques signed. He'd say "call in, get my post, and anything that looks like a bill, pay it, and stuff that you think you ought to send to me, send it." This went on for years.'

Despite that, Robinson laments Roebuck's loss. The bond they shared was forged over countless cold mornings at the county ground in Taunton, Robinson filling and refilling a bucket of balls so Roebuck could face the bowling machine. More than that, Robinson and his wife provided something of a protective cloak. Roebuck would regularly call over at their house, yearning perhaps for some domestic warmth, some contact with people he could confide in. 'Pete used to leave his car for people to use during the winter. He was generous to those he felt he could trust. I still felt if I was in trouble I could turn to him for help. He was just a very bright person who was mixed up somewhere. I often think, what if he had somebody who was there, if he had the right partner? … He just had too much time to think, in a way.'

To opponents, Roebuck was merely unconventional, yet another peculiar figure in a sport known for its roll call of eccentrics. 'He was very bright intellectually but, if I'm honest, not so bright socially,' says John Barclay. 'He'd be fine with me, fine with those he knew. He didn't endear himself socially and instinctively to the rest of my Sussex team. But he was a good egg, very honest.'

It was Roebuck's teammates who bore the brunt of his introspection and doldrums, just as they could be buoyed by his searing wit and fondness for debate. Marks roomed with Roebuck on the county circuit for more than a decade. He of anyone knew the strengths and frailties of his friend and, as was the norm at certain junctures in the English season, things went awry.

'There was a trip back from Sussex one time,' Marks recalls. 'I was in the car with Pops [Popplewell]. Pete was driving. He was in a dark period and we'd played dreadfully. We got to Worthing and at some traffic lights he stopped and out he went, gave the keys to Pops, and said, "You drive home – I'm walking." We said, "Come on Pete, come back with us", and we tried to encourage him back. "No, no, off you go," he said. So the lights turned green and we buggered off. He overnighted in Salisbury in a B&B.'

Being outspoken on social and political matters set him further apart from the lager-and-chips types in the dressing room.

Then there was the manner in which he batted – 'the sort of figure', wrote the *Age*'s Peter Hanlon years later, 'that fired a zeal in opponents to either get him out or knock him out'. Middlesex fast bowler Mike Selvey found bowling to Roebuck irritating: 'I think it was his curious, quizzical stance, his back arched as if his body shape was posing a question, and the fact that if you tried to talk to him when non-striker he would turn away rather haughtily.'

His friendship with Mike Tarr soured and was severed in the years after their collaboration on *It Never Rains*. Tarr was an artist. Despite a modest record for the Somerset 2nd XI he had stayed close to the club and Roebuck, who 'became a frequent visitor to our house', Tarr says. 'But he was always only able to discuss cricket and his part in it. A couple of evenings were ruined by his inability to show social graces in terms of accepting there were other people in the world beyond him. He would refuse to talk about anything other than his own agenda, to the point of it being excessively rude. On one occasion he asked if my wife and children could go into the garden so he could discuss important cricket business with me, such as whether Viv should bat at number three or four. People who have extra intelligence, of which he was one, tend to lose sight of the world around them; he just didn't see how the world worked.'

Intriguingly, after his initial assignment as team leader in 1983 – a period when Rose had stepped down and Botham, Richards, Marks and Garner were on World Cup duty – Roebuck was moved to divulge: 'It's forced me out of my shell and made me more concerned for the welfare of others.' It's an odd statement from someone well into his tenth first-class season, especially one who had come to rely so heavily on his peers to furnish him with support during descents into gloom. He was not blind to fluctuations of fortune or the rise and fall of a dressing room's atmosphere; all manner of life's myriad dealings could and would affect an individual's spirit. They certainly did his.

The Roebuck captaincy experiment of 1983 worked. 'It invigorated a lot of us,' says Popplewell. 'Pete was absolutely fantastic. It was against his natural personality to jolly everyone along but he did it really well.' And the runs kept coming. There were 1255 of them in 1985 and 1288 runs at 47.70 in 1986, his first year as officially appointed captain. Going by the numbers it was methodical, almost clinical, stuff. Behind the scenes, as the cricket world was about to find out, it was anything but.

But that trouble could wait. In June of 1986 he came face to face with a coldly furious Richard Hadlee at Trent Bridge. Roebuck, by now a rising columnist, had deigned to criticise Hadlee in print. Hadlee was in the form of his life, fresh from scything through Australia's batting during the antipodean summer. On this day Roebuck was rendered hapless by Hadlee's first, piercing delivery. Amazed, he discovered the ball had somehow missed the stumps. Hadlee peppered him, struck him on the body, extracted edges that simply would not go to hand. Roebuck dug in, hung on, then flourished as the Notts attack wilted. Midway through the next day, declaring Somerset's innings closed, he walked off with a mammoth 221 not out beside his name. He soon after noted with not undue satisfaction that the competition's best bowlers appeared to expend more energy targeting him. 'I take it as a challenge and as a compliment,' he told the press, 'when I see how they look when they've got my wicket.'

3

COUNTY IN CRISIS

'It was obvious that any captain agreeing to the
release from his squad of two, eventually
three, such popular and gifted champions was
signing his own death warrant.'

- SOMETIMES I FORGOT TO LAUGH, 2004

There he stood, a bespectacled and angular figure leaning against a doorframe, seemingly unmoved.

Typically apart, Roebuck was witness to the pitch and sway of arguments that would make or break an impasse that had rapidly become a conflagration. In excess of 3000 members poured into Shepton Mallet on a gloomy day in November 1986 to vote on two motions that would ultimately determine Somerset's future. Wisely, perhaps tellingly, Roebuck had elected not to speak. But a parade of others took to the podium, including bumbling club chairman Michael Hill, knockabout 'rebel' Peter Denning and, most persuasively, the recently retired Nigel Popplewell.

The first of the motions was a vote of no confidence in the general committee and was overwhelmingly defeated. The second – a call for the committee to stand down and face re-election – went the same way. The rebellion was crushed. But according to many who were present, and to Roebuck himself, there was little sense of jubilation or vindication. The only winners were maladies; discontent, bitterness and regret carried the day.

The club's mid-year announcement that it was dispensing with the services of Richards and Garner, in the knowledge that comrade-in-arms Botham would most likely depart as well in sympathy or protest, had divided the cricket world. As writer and club historian David Foot saw it at the time, the decision was 'courageous, far-sighted, crazy or insensitive'. Hill had publicly advocated for Botham to stay but admitted the club would just have to wait and see. One committeeman – preferring to retain anonymity – told the press the club would not be blackmailed by Botham's blustering. On the other side, former captain Roy Kerslake weighed in by declaring the club's supporters saw the decision as 'wicked'. The battlelines were being drawn. Almost immediately, Roebuck was deemed to be the instigator of the move.

'Old Somerset never had anything like this in the past,' says David Frith. 'It was spiky counties like Yorkshire and Surrey that were always scenes of civil war. And there was this bespectacled, puny, innocent-looking fellow who was their captain, the instigator against the mighty Richards and Garner with Botham in tow. It was David against three Goliaths, an astonishing situation. I had my own problems with Richards so I understood what it was all about: it was a little old dressing room dominated by superstars. Garner was a lovely man, but Richards and Botham were world superstars in this provincial little hut and the rest of the blokes must have felt like they were just apprentices. It was an awkward situation and it wasn't going to change unless someone got rid of Richards, and that was unthinkable.'

The Boycott-related intrigues and infighting that had so dogged Yorkshire during the 1970s and '80s paled by comparison. Just how a dispute over whether to release or retain two overseas players escalated into lifelong enmities and threats of violence defies belief to this day. Accusations were hurled, friendships cut. 'The '85–86 period dragged a lot of us down,' says Peter Robinson. 'It was a terrible time. I remember seeing a wreath on the field. I mean, you've got people *now* not coming to watch Somerset because of it.'

To those supporting the move, Richards was past his best and increasingly jaded by the treadmill of county duties. Further, his Test and one-day international commitments meant he would be spending more time away from Somerset in the coming years. Garner, thirty-three, was struggling to slip into top gear, troubled by niggling injuries, and had raised the possibility of bypassing Championship matches altogether in 1987 in favour of one-day cricket. As for the elephant in the room – Botham – he had long since generated more headlines for off-field antics than on-field deeds. He was, ran the party line, a major distraction in a team attempting to rebuild; the side no longer contained the wise heads and stronger personalities to curb or at least cope with his behaviour.

'It was an odd situation,' says Brian Rose. 'I was caught in between two storms because I neither agreed properly with one camp or the other one, so I was not very popular for a few years with either camp.'

One wunderkind, New Zealander Martin Crowe, was mooted as the replacement for both men. Crowe had impressed all and sundry during an initial stint with the county in 1984. He was a superstar in the making, and proponents of the radical move could point to the clean-cut Crowe's exemplary conduct, team-oriented enthusiasm and coaching of younger players. In stark contrast, Richards and Botham were perceived to be far removed from their merely mortal teammates and a law unto themselves. Garner, a quiet and humble man, did not present the same concerns but was intrinsically linked to Richards. There was the ever-ready whiff of drug usage to boot, a heady cocktail of rumours and innuendo and reputed late-night escapades that were confirmed, in part, by Botham's admission of cannabis consumption in May of 1986 and Richards' refusal to take a drug test at a game against Gloucestershire in Bristol. But Richards and Botham were hardly isolated examples. In truth, far stronger substances were widespread on the circuit.

Timing was also a crucial factor. Somerset's performances had been steadily eroding and the dressing room was descending into a fractured, tense pit. Set against internal frictions spilling onto the field, the club's one-day glories seemed like mocking mementoes of an altogether richer, more innocent era. 'We stopped playing for each other,' says Popplewell. 'After we'd had the success that we'd had, the desire to keep winning was slightly lost. We just stopped performing collectively ... ran out of puff. In the hothouse of life on the road little things get blown up but could I see the seeds in 1985 of what became behavioural issues in '86 and '87? No, you couldn't have seen it coming.'

A side featuring Richards, Garner and Roebuck accounted for Dorset in the first round of the NatWest Trophy but then crashed out to Lancashire two weeks later. Worse, in the Benson & Hedges Cup the side managed a solitary win from four matches.

Somerset finished a creditable sixth in the Sunday League – traditionally a strong point – but results in the Championship were disastrous. Following a last-placed position in 1985 under Botham's captaincy, the club could climb only one rung higher under Roebuck in 1986, winning three matches in five months. Divisions within the playing group became apparent as poor results on the park ratcheted up tensions off it. Tempers were fraying. Vic Marks remembers the atmosphere as 'poisonous'.

Yet the case against the move seemed just as compelling. The star power of the mighty trio was unquestionable. Ridding the club of such illustrious names was akin to sacrilege, came the charge. Ray Wright, the club treasurer, told the *Times*: 'When people ring the ground on a match day they ask two questions. They want to know if the game is on. And then they want to know if Ian Botham is playing.' Richards, Garner and Botham were world-class players who had thrilled crowds for a decade or more. Capable of match-winning turns at the drop of a hat – on the biggest days and biggest stages – they stalked cricket grounds with an immeasurable presence. 'Going there [to Taunton] was quite intimidating,' Jonathan Agnew remembers.

The three giants had performed reasonably across the 1986 Championship season. In between disciplinary hearings and ducking reporters, Botham averaged 44 with the bat in a dozen appearances, a figure somewhat abbreviated due to his drugs ban. His 22 wickets were expensive, although for England he claimed a wicket first ball of his Test recall (following the ban) against the Kiwis. He then clobbered a half-century.

Garner's county haul stood at 47 wickets at 23.21, although his final month in Somerset colours was forgettable: 7 wickets in his last five Championship appearances. He hadn't taken more than 50 wickets in a season since 1981 and to insiders it was evident that he wasn't moved to strive for extra effort under Roebuck's leadership. 'Remember, Somerset won all of those one-day competitions thanks to Viv and Joel – and Both a bit – but the holy grail, the County Championship, was never won by Somerset,' says Scyld Berry. 'How are you going to do it? Joel has to run in. Joel didn't want to run in; you could tell from his run-up when Joel was keen.'

Richards topped 1000 runs for the season but averaged close to half what he had averaged during a stellar 1985, prompting David Miller of the *Times* to insist his game had 'sharply declined'. True maybe, though the England bowlers who took a pounding during his 56-ball Test century in Antigua earlier in the year may well have proffered other opinions. Yet he was clearly distracted at times, moody and preoccupied with the suggestion that Crowe would be replacing him. Any talk of Crowe was taboo in the dressing room, a difficult subject to avoid given New Zealand were touring the country and their star batsman was flaying England's bowlers. Yet Richards could still turn it on; in what proved to be his final Championship appearance for Somerset he simply oozed class with 53 and 94 against a star-studded Essex line-up. In his very last game for the club, a Sunday fixture against Derby at Taunton in the middle of September, he stroked his way to an effortless half-century.

Oddly, throughout the year Roebuck had appeared as close to Botham – in print at least – as ever. A series of interviews and articles and the release of a joint publication had Roebuck in turn defending, explaining and praising the man who would become his enemy. On the eve of Botham's appearance before the Test and County Cricket Board following his drug revelations, Roebuck told the press: 'Ian is a part of the team and family of Somerset, and we don't intend to turn him away.' A *Time Out* cover story penned by Roebuck that appeared during Botham's suspension was even more emphatic:

> In truth, this prodigious and maverick cricketer is a player England cannot do without. It is nonsense to say that he cannot or will not fit into a team. It is nonsense to suggest that his lack of discipline spoils an 11 and undermines the captain. If Botham is wanting discipline then the fault lies as much with the weaknesses of his leaders as with him.

Odder still was *It Sort of Clicks*, a book that went on sale four weeks before Somerset announced the decision to release Richards and Garner. It was marketed as 'Ian Botham talking to Peter Roebuck' and appeared a year later than planned. In it Roebuck constructed a series of themes with suitable introductions and Botham's first-person responses provided the detailed accompaniment. The contents ranged from Botham's most memorable innings to his tussles with Aussies, from the superiority of the West Indians to his thoughts on bowling and life at the top of the cricket tree. While much of it was a platform for Botham to repair an image battered by off-field infamy, Roebuck's searing honesty when articulating character assessment was one of the book's redeeming features. 'He is an unusually lonely man,' Roebuck wrote, betraying candidness hitherto rarely witnessed in this genre's typically fawning nods to sporting heroes. Botham's spell as England captain and, later, Somerset captain was laid bare in similar fashion:

His England captaincy brought four defeats and no victories. He lost form and his team lost faith in him. In some respects, Ian is a slow learner. His captaincy was instinctive, often superb, but his judgement of character and treatment of others was poor ... In September 1983, Ian succeeded Brian Rose as captain of Somerset. It was a position he desperately wanted ... But Ian could not communicate his vision, he wanted it simply to happen. Nor did he show his younger teammates that he wanted his team to do well. They hadn't witnessed his triumphs of the past. They only saw this legend who didn't want to bowl, couldn't talk to them easily and took reckless gambles. They saw his anarchism not as hilarious but as destructive.

The book did sufficiently well for a reprint to be commissioned. That gave Roebuck – although not Botham, as the pair were no longer cooperating – first opportunity to air his thoughts on the so-called Somerset Affair. 'Till the final break-up,' Roebuck wrote, 'Ian and I enjoyed a curious relationship in which we'd laugh in private and yet fight about the cricket.' He stood by his version of events, that the club made the call on Richards and Garner and although it seemed likely Botham would react combatively, such a response should not sway the administration's thinking. He described Botham wading into the ensuing debate cavalier-style, as though swatting balls from Lillee and Lawson à la Headingley in '81. He made no secret of Botham's hostility towards him, citing the 'Judas' placard Botham hung above Roebuck's spot in the Taunton dressing room. Yet, despite the hostility, Roebuck mused that Botham's stance was somehow honourable: it displayed his determined sense of loyalty.

Curiously, Roebuck surmised the matter would soon be done with. On the 1986–87 England tour of Australia their paths crossed several times and, according to his account, communications were cordial. He was there as a correspondent for the *Sunday Times* and *Sydney Morning Herald*; Botham was there to retain the Ashes and bludgeon Merv Hughes and company in the process. The tour ended with both men divided yet, in Roebuck's mind at least, the battles of the past had not 'entirely destroyed our relationship'. In the years and events to come, how quaint these words must have appeared to the man who committed them to print. How they must have mocked him.

Earlier, upon his appointment as captain to replace Botham, Roebuck had also tried to woo Richards. In a letter Richards reproduced publicly in an attempt to embarrass Roebuck, he urged: 'As far as I'm concerned, you are part of the buildings and the furniture at Somerset and so are Vic and Ian ... I hope that you'll be able to play with us until those legs turn to jelly, because I think that you and I and Ian and Vic are Somerset players right down to our bootstraps.'

Support from Viv would have been cherished by Roebuck for team harmony reasons as much as any. In print he had described Richards as an emotional cauldron and said 'anyone who is not a little afraid of him does not know him'. He had also written an account of Richards smashing a bat to pieces in an episode of rage. Marks, too, had observed Richards' influence over many seasons and took umbrage at suggestions he stifled the careers of younger players. 'What got to me, and this had nothing to do with Pete, was that there was a seam of players in that team who latched onto Viv as a kind of excuse for underperforming,' says Marks. 'A little seam of batsmen saying "we can't play with Viv, he's so overpowering, he's so moody, it's impossible for us to play to our potential", which I thought was bloody bogus at the time. And then you look at their performances post-Richards and they're exactly the bloody same.'

* * *

'The debate was about the future of the club,' says Popplewell, 'but the whole focus got too polarised about personalities and Pete got dragged into that as some sort of pariah figure who was orchestrating everything.'

From the outset, the notion that Roebuck had hatched some Machiavellian plot stuck fast. According to Botham, Roebuck wished for a side full of young players so he could mould them in his image. This dynamic of mentor and follower evokes parallels with other aspects of Roebuck's life, from his adulatory students at Cranbrook to the house he later established in South Africa. At Somerset, where Roebuck cast himself as a sage, others saw a lesser talent attempting to impose his will over those whose cricketing deeds far overshadowed his own capabilities. 'He wanted to dictate how that side played, more than most captains,' recalls Marks. 'Pete wanted to be that leader who had a group that would follow him. He cherished that hugely.'

Initially at least, the club's position was formed by Hill and Brian Langford, a former captain of Somerset who was head of the cricket committee. Robinson remembers Hill being especially taken with Crowe, urging 'If we don't get hold of Crowe now we'll never get him.' Robinson also recalls walking around

Weston-super-Mare Cricket Club with Langford, discussing options and possible consequences, and the debating that went on between Roebuck and club president Colin Atkinson. Hill called Roebuck to an impromptu cricket committee meeting on 21 July where the matter came to a head, with opinions canvassed and opportunities for everyone present to weigh up the merits of ridding Somerset of Richards and Garner. Remarkably, despite strong differences of opinion and a whispering campaign arousing suspicion within the playing ranks, news of this meeting and the surrounding discussions was not leaked.

Upon learning of the club's intentions, Roebuck faced an extraordinary dilemma: concur and be part of the most controversial determination in Somerset's history or, as captain, use his powers of intelligence, reasoning and influence to dissuade the club from acting. It was a decision he wrestled with protractedly. He was nothing if not aware of the possible consequences. Ultimately, it could be said, enmities were precipitated that forever after plagued his waking hours and fuelled obsessions, some have claimed to the point of paranoia, that ultimately contributed to his horrible ending.

'He confided in me, as his friend,' says John Barclay. 'He said "We have a real problem." Pete had a certain vision that Martin Crowe would come forth as the real potential future. I remember being outside the pavilion at Taunton, saying "Look, Pete, weigh up the situation … Are you sure you've got the stomach for this fight?" I remember saying, "It's going to be quite a battle, because you're up against real heavyweight performers who have massive support behind them, which you won't really have." But I didn't take sides; it was none of my business. It's very dangerous to take sides, rather like when a marriage breaks up.'

Roebuck also confided in Marks, Rose and, as he put it in *Sometimes I Forgot to Laugh*, an 'artist friend who lived near Taunton'. That was Mike Tarr. Tarr carried on a vigorous debate with him over the course of the affair until matters came to a head at the Shepton Mallet meeting. Thereafter, they barely spoke again. 'During the conflict there were many meetings on either side and, although we disagreed, he and I kept in touch,' Tarr recalls. 'I believe he was taking the stance not out of concern for the future of Somerset cricket but because he saw an opportunity to get rid of Richards and Garner, and Botham would follow, because these players were, for him, impossible to deal with as captain. In many ways he was jealous of their prowess and acclaim.'

Roebuck writes about their dialogue with a disdainful air, suggesting Tarr – whom he still didn't name – let him down by breaching a confidence. 'The whole situation was a victory for bad management,' Tarr says now. 'PR jumped in, had seen the way the wind was blowing, and changed his attitude towards the whole affair. At the Shepton Mallet meeting I was, among others, asked to speak on behalf of the rebels. I pointed out that up until a short while before Peter had been attempting to get rid of the secretary and expose the committee. I knew this because we had discussed it previously. When I spoke to the assembly and pointed this out, Peter took umbrage, saying I had broken a confidence.

'This, I have to admit, I had done and I can't say I feel particularly good about it to this day. I realised it would affect our friendship but by this time I had given up on him because of his behaviour towards Viv and the others ... Subsequently he vilified me in the press, in his autobiography and everywhere else as far as I know. This didn't really bother me as I felt it was the behaviour of a spoiled child. He never realised that if you treated people badly, life was more than likely to come around and kick you in the teeth.'

A decisive meeting was held on 8 August between the club's management and cricket subcommittees. Votes were cast and a ratification of the earlier decision was passed by nine votes to three. On 22 August the club's committee endorsed the decision and management was urged – by Roebuck – to notify the affected players forthwith. Botham's reaction was not countenanced and he was soon offered a two-year contract. 'There was a real tension building up to it,' says Marks. 'On the night of the significant committee meeting we were all at a party at Nigel Felton's house. That's when Pete came up and said "We've done it – I could've saved them but I couldn't bring myself to." Thereafter, and I can't remember too much because I've probably blanked it out, there was no real communication.'

Roebuck forever claimed the notion had not been entertained before chairman Hill invited him to attend the special cricket committee meeting in July. For one, he and Crowe hadn't spoken for the best part of two years and Roebuck had no idea the gun Kiwi had been in contact with Hill, expressing his intention to join Essex in 1987. Given Somerset held the rights to Crowe's registration, the ball was firmly in the club's court; the Test and County Cricket Board rules of the day dictated that Somerset could keep Richards and Garner and lose Crowe, or release the West Indians in favour of Crowe. Hill had clearly defined thoughts on the matter. 'The notion of Crowe was floated by Michael Hill and Pete went along with it,' says Marks. 'He had the power to dictate which way they swayed.'

The public announcement came as England were hosting New Zealand at The Oval. The previous afternoon, Richards and Garner were summoned to the county ground and informed of their respective sackings by Langford and Somerset's chief executive, Tony Brown. Richards was furious. Later he would tell the press: 'When you have two workhorses and shoot them in the back, I think it's evil. You don't treat animals in this way. I was blindfolded, led up an alley and assassinated.' Despite the melodrama, some sympathy could be afforded him; amid mounting tensions before the decisive vote, Langford had sought out Richards to assure him his contract for 1987 was secure. To ensure transparency, Langford notified the committee of this and felt compelled to vote against the release of the West Indians. Even his attitude hardened, however; he soon labelled Botham a bully and told the press a number of young players were refusing to sign contracts until the departure of Botham and Richards was confirmed.

Aroused by the scent of battle, Botham stormed back to Taunton and circled the wagons. He immediately called a meeting of the players and pointedly did not invite Roebuck. He told those assembled of his intention to leave the county and accused Roebuck of treachery. 'Botham felt it was an absolute betrayal,' says Rob Steen. 'He thought mateship should come before everything else, regardless of how good or bad it did the team. He would have lost face had he backed the committee.'

Richards did confront Roebuck – angrily. Roebuck was labelled 'sick' and 'devious' and a 'terrible failure', Richards going on to assert that this action was Roebuck's revenge on the world. He also rounded on Hill and Langford as they attempted to speak to him during his final Somerset appearance, sending them packing with a volley of verbal abuse. Even the mild-mannered Garner claimed assertions of disruptiveness by the star players amounted to character assassination. He later said of Roebuck: 'I've never met a man who has read so much and knows so little.'

In between it all, Vic Marks kept a cool head and took over the leadership when Roebuck was injured, sparing the club the embarrassing task of asking Richards – the official vice-captain – to take over. 'Viv was distraught and Joel was hurt … Both was rampaging around. I told Pete "I would not do what you're doing" but I was not going to end our friendship on this basis. I was one of the few still talking to all parties.'

After the stunning news broke, an assortment of former officials and players and a bloc of current members rallied to oppose the decision. Life member Bridget Langdon, Dr David Challacombe – the club's long-time honorary doctor, whose dislike of Roebuck was intense – and 'Dasher' Denning headed the so-called 'rebel committee' (something of a misnomer, given their motivation was to keep the West Indian pair in the West Country, thereby maintaining the status quo). Denning, opening partner of Brian Rose during the halcyon years, was one of those initially consulted by Roebuck. At the time Denning had appeared somewhat ambivalent, but he resolved to join the rebel camp, publicly uttering that Roebuck had caused more trouble in the dressing room than Richards, Garner and Botham put together.

Behind the scenes, the popular figure of Roy Kerslake emerged to articulate the rebels' stance. He had served the club in various capacities since making his first-class debut in 1962. Chairman of cricket as Somerset claimed its string of one-day titles, he was highly regarded among players and fans alike. The day after the sackings, both Richards and Garner telephoned him. 'I hadn't been involved in the club for four or five years but I was still friendly with them,' says Kerslake. 'I said "I don't believe it." I would have done all I could to keep them. I was very disappointed when they left. But I hadn't been involved and didn't know if there had been problems in the dressing room.'

* * *

Roebuck was only thirty years of age, yet already a veteran of the county, someone who had alternately beguiled and bedevilled the Somerset scene. He thought himself 'caught between warring factions for neither of which he much cared'. He tried to claim it was a purely cricketing decision and sentiment had to be cast aside. No one was listening. His striking intellect, incisive writing, physical appearance, awkward batting style, idiosyncrasies, and lack of anecdotes and backslaps at the bar had marked him as a man apart. Without a more visible target – Hill was considered an amiable benefactor, and Langford had voted to retain the West Indians – the rebels and their supporters fixed Roebuck in their sights.

'He had death threats,' says Peter Robinson. 'In a way, he took all the flak within the club. No one associated Michael Hill with it … It was [seen] that Roebuck was the instigator of it all.'

Right away he was warned that should he be moved to reveal less seemly aspects of Botham's private life, his own affairs would be up for scrutiny. The ghouls of Fleet Street duly descended. In the week before Shepton Mallet three investigative tabloid reporters staked out Taunton. In a sense, they never left.

Illustrating the tenor of the time Botham, some twenty years on, was moved to write that he could have happily watched Roebuck drown in the river behind the Taunton ground without feeling the need to pull him out.

Perhaps inevitably, Roebuck's family was sucked into the conflict. Various family members still lived in Street, roughly halfway between Taunton in the west and Shepton Mallet to the east. The family had welcomed the likes of Popplewell and Richards into their home over the years. Elizabeth Roebuck remembers Richards as a 'lovely young man'. Beatrice says, 'The Judas poster went up and there was a huge amount of media. It was a very hostile environment. Mum received a family death threat, which she crumpled up and shoved in the fire. It was the start of [Peter thinking] "I need to keep the family out of this". It was all pretty vicious.'

Elizabeth Roebuck expresses heartfelt admiration for her son's stance: 'I received vitriolic letters and death threats. Peter knew he was putting his head on the line. He tried to say it was all cricketing matters and the committee tried to say it was for cricketing reasons. Had he not done what he did, he would not be the strong character that I admire so much.'

* * *

For her part, Elizabeth Roebuck believes there were wider issues at play that had nothing to do with releasing Garner and Richards or Botham's support of them. She contends the bitter division from others, resisting change, was in part fuelled by match-fixing, or to be more accurate, spot-fixing. She claims that Peter confided in her at length about players who were making large sums of money from gambling and those who were left in the dark. Further, the players were aligned with a certain set of supporters who would inexplicably cheer – most rowdily during afternoon sessions after a few drinks – following the bowling of a no-ball.

'I'm trying to tell you something here,' she says, 'so you won't be chasing shadows.' Someone else told her 'If ever anybody wants to know … go and look at certain people's bank balances.' She also contends that these private revelations of her son were broadly vindicated upon the release of the Condon report into cricket corruption in 2001. The report's findings certainly suggested something had been rotten in the state of England:

> It started with friendly fixes in the UK in the old Sunday
> leagues. Over a weekend you'd have a county side playing
> their county match and then a Sunday league match
> and there would be friendly fixes, not for money but for
> manipulating places in the leagues. These friendly fixes
> quickly became more sinister, probably in the Eighties.

Roebuck made only veiled references to match-fixing in the English domestic game. In a piece he wrote for the *Natal Witness* in 2007, he stated: 'Every county indulged in lob bowling, arranged declarations and so forth. Nor were fixed matches unknown.' Later in life, in response to Lord Condon and in the midst of other match-fixing scandals, he had many opportunities, in many jurisdictions, to lay bare the cupboard if Elizabeth's contentions were true, but he never did.

* * *

Mike Tarr, still attempting to persuade Roebuck to throw his lot in with the rebels in order to throw out the incumbent committee, recalls Roebuck saying he was disappointed the club's management had left him to fight the battle.

Yet many who observed Roebuck's conduct during these turbulent months thought him energised by the cut and thrust of proceedings. 'Although Pete and I were very close,' says Marks, 'we were very different characters – he liked a bit of confrontation. It was traumatic and ugly but he was buzzing with the whole political, combative element.'

A week out from Shepton Mallet, Roebuck finally waded into the public arena, defiantly spelling out his manifesto. In a wide-ranging interview with Ivo Tennant of the *Times*, he reiterated his agreement with the club's decision and made clear the distinction between instigating the move and merely going along with it. Somerset's record was simply not good enough, he told Tennant. The club needed modernising and its on-field woes had been worsening for years. He cited the merry-go-round of captains. He would not be drawn into making personal comments, despite Richards labelling him in the same newspaper as 'selfish' and 'cranky' the day before the interview took place. And, in a typical Roebuckian aside, amidst the animosity and rapidly transpiring events, he admitted out of the blue, 'I am not sure if socially and in terms of character development, cricket was the right career for me.'

* * *

So came the day of the meeting. It would, in a sense, and inadvertently as far as he was concerned, vindicate or condemn Roebuck. He had told the *Times* he would walk away from cricket if the rebels won the day, and few doubted his conviction. As the thousands of members poured into the Bath and West Showground, surrounding roads choked with traffic. Local and national press were in attendance, likewise a multitude of TV cameras. 'There was a traffic jam outside Street,' recalls Elizabeth Roebuck. 'All the little people were going to the meeting because they were ardent, ordinary Somerset members.'

It was, strangely, a polite and somewhat subdued scene. Despite previous antipathies, opponents mixed easily as the hall filled. Roebuck was spotted in friendly enough conversation with a number of parties who had actively voiced their dislike of him and what he stood for. As members took their places, sipped tea and nibbled on sandwiches, the meeting began. The format was simple: five nominated speakers from either side and fifty minutes for alternative speakers, limited to no more than two minutes each. Roebuck positioned himself away from others and listened impassively.

Two legal entities, John Foley and Roy Kerslake – nominated by the rebels to reassume the club secretary's role – spoke against the committee. They were backed by Denning and another retired player, Graham Burgess. Foley, a barrister, did the rebel cause no favours by calling for decorum then drawing a comparison between the committee's conduct and that of Libyan dictator Colonel Gaddafi. Burgess portrayed the divisions among the players as being wholly caused by the committee. Denning cut a likeable figure but failed to convince. Mike Tarr gave vent to his opinion of the affair, much to Roebuck's chagrin.

Former player Jimmy James spoke for the committee, as did, and tellingly, Len Creed. The bookmaker from Bath had discovered Richards while holidaying in the Leeward Islands in the early 1970s. He had agitated for Richards to come to Somerset, and his testimony now carried considerable weight. Both men warned of the dangers of the tail wagging the dog. Otherwise, the official arm of the club lacked bite, exemplified by the fumbling of chairman Hill who spilled his notes on the floor as he rose to deliver his address.

The crucial intervention came from Nigel Popplewell. He had retired from first-class cricket at the end of 1985, aged twenty-eight, to concentrate on his law career. 'I didn't really follow what was happening in 1986 but obviously I was still close to the players,' Popplewell says. 'I had no intention of speaking at the meeting and it had nothing to do with Peter. What I saw in the press was a complete polarisation of views. The people who were saying Viv and Joel should have their contracts renewed were saying they were perfect people who had behaved perfectly, and the people who were supporting the committee were saying, no, they've behaved reprehensibly. It was a disgraceful polarisation. I felt I had something to add because I had seen what it was like and could speak as an expert witness. If I was acting on behalf of anybody, it was the younger players of the club whose future depended really on Martin Crowe coming back.'

His two minutes of testimony destroyed whatever chance the rebels had of carrying the day and overthrowing the committee. Dressed informally and speaking from the floor, Popplewell spoke in a flat, even tone about the 'dreadful' state of dressing room relations. He said he was in despair halfway through the 1985 season because the attitude of Richards and Garner towards county cricket differed considerably from everybody else's yet they expected nothing less than '110 per cent commitment' from the rest. He went on to assert that they only tried when it suited them. The coup de grâce was his recollection of team harmony during Crowe's stint in 1984.

The impact was devastating. Many members sympathetic to Kerslake and Langdon cast their vote and walked out, knowing they had been soundly defeated. The committee, unable to convincingly articulate what was in essence a sensible cricketing decision, had found an unexpected ally whose presence and delivery far exceeded anything they could muster. Accordingly, the voting was a whitewash: the vote of no confidence was lost 1828 to 798 and the call for the committee to stand down was defeated 1863 to 743. Botham later described the results as 'close'.

'I hadn't realised at that stage the strength of feeling there was that Peter was orchestrating this,' says Popplewell. 'Everybody said Peter was just trying to get a team he could run, that he didn't want significant and slightly difficult personalities in the mix, but I never saw that. In a way it was nothing to do with him, nothing to do with whoever was going to be captain. It was a question of what I had seen in the dressing room and, indeed, what other players had seen but weren't prepared to say.'

If the result was a sort of vindication for Roebuck, he was perceptive enough to realise the cost had been 'enormous'. There was little sense of celebration. 'When it was all over I think a lot of people rated him quite highly,' says David Frith. 'I think it was a very brave thing to do. The after-effects were that certain people would never talk to him again. But I would suspect that he would feel pride whenever he looked back on that for the rest of his life. He was unquestionably the leader of the revolt. I thought it was a great performance.'

On the other side of the world Botham, part of the England touring side playing a warm-up game in Perth against Western Australia, heard the news from his mother (who'd attended the meeting) and immediately made good his threat to quit Somerset, adding 'I'd just love to take them apart every time I come across them next summer.' He said he had no axe to grind with Crowe but Somerset's actions were 'disgusting'. Upon learning Roebuck was in London, preparing to fly down under to cover the Ashes, Botham suggested he would be a lot safer if he stayed put.

As we know, Roebuck shrugged off that threat. Over the course of that Ashes series he sought out Botham away from the public eye on at least one occasion. He was unsuccessful in gaining any sort of response. But in Adelaide, Botham asked him into the England dressing room after hearing news that a Somerset player was ill and the club wasn't doing enough to help, only for Roebuck to call Taunton and discover the news was false. A week after that Adelaide game, in the company of Australian paceman Mike Whitney, Roebuck and Botham chatted again, this time in Canberra in the wake of the Prime Minister's XI game.

Six months later, on the cusp of the 1987 county season, Roebuck told assembled media that he and Botham had 'talked amicably' during the tour and he was hopeful of a thawing in relations. He said Botham would be welcome anytime in the Somerset dressing room: 'In the heightened emotion of the time friendships were broken. But it would be great if Ian could come back here and feel wanted. Personally I'd like to see it.'

When notified of Roebuck's comments, Botham dismissed them unequivocally. There would be no thaw. Marked by difference in habit, appearance and custom, Roebuck would now be forever labelled as the man who sacked Richards and Garner and tipped Botham out as well. 'Lots of people wouldn't have taken on the enemies he took on,' says Michael Atherton. 'They are bad enemies to have.'

In an extensive piece written by Ivo Tennant for the *Cricketer* magazine on the twenty-fifth anniversary of the split, both men reflected on the circumstances. Roebuck wondered why his reputation was so poor in England and believed his 2001 conviction for common assault was partly to blame, though in any event '... that was driven along by the rebels'. He further opined that he should have left Taunton right away and that 'Botham did things in that period and afterwards that I will never forgive or forget – never'. Botham was just as obstinate, claiming weak people allowed Roebuck – 'a very strange person' – to determine the outcome. 'I have no regrets over what happened.'

At the end of his 1986 county commitments, Vic Marks relocated to Perth for the southern hemisphere summer to ply his trade for Western Australia in the Sheffield Shield. He was unaware the rebels had earmarked him for the vice-captaincy (with Richards taking over the captain's role from Roebuck) should they be successful in unseating the committee. Upon returning to Somerset, Marks quickly had to come to terms with what had unfolded – the committee still in place, Roebuck as captain, and Richards, Garner and Botham gone. 'Pete had to go out and sign new players, a motley group, and I remember coming back from Western Australia feeling a bit odd, going into the dressing room and shaking hands with about four new players who I'd probably played against a few times.'

Unsurprisingly Botham, bound for Worcestershire, attempted to ferment further discontent. 'Beefy tossed out the notion of [me] going to Worcester,' says Marks. 'I don't think I was ever going to go but I didn't really look forward to the '87 season hugely as it was a dressing room that was barely recognisable. Pete was very keen for me to stay; if I'd gone it would have been an expression of disapproval. So there I was, the old guard, vice-captain, and I supported him as best I could. I think Pete was always looking for approval for that decision and I never really gave it to him. I still felt a decade later he was seeking a rubber stamp from me saying "you got it right". I still don't think it was the right way to go. It was an incredibly divisive time.'

Brian Rose has given the matter considerable thought over the years and believes the fallout was avoidable. He says now, with the benefit of hindsight, the two overseas players should have been consulted and a scenario put to them of where the club needed to be in two to three years. He believes such consultation would have motivated Garner, at least, to retire willingly. 'I think Peter in his heart thought he was doing the right thing,' says Rose, 'but he needed more people around him to put him in a slightly better position to do it, and perhaps not that year.'

For Scyld Berry, who was covering the story and privy to Roebuck's intentions: 'The critical element was whether Crowe was fit enough to bowl. It was worth getting him in to replace both Viv and Joel if he could still bowl. He was a Mark Waugh type; he could be really quick. It was reasonable to expect he could have done the jobs of both men, and better, and without the decadence in the dressing room. But I think he had an injury ... If Crowe couldn't bat and bowl it would have been best to stick with Viv and Joel.'

In a cricketing sense, the outcome was mixed. The turnover of players 'created big problems', thinks Rose. 'It took a decade to get over. We had to go and sign experienced players from other counties. The club was desperate.' Ultimately Crowe, due to a back complaint, bowled just thirty-three overs and went wicketless. But with 1600-plus runs and six first-class centuries he displayed a genuine mastery of English conditions with the bat. If there was another silver lining, it was the fill-in role of a certain young Australian – Steve Waugh – who played several outstanding knocks in Crowe's absences, including a brilliant 111 against an unrestrained Sylvester Clarke at The Oval.

'At that age,' says Waugh, 'I was just concerned about playing cricket. It was there, it was festering, but I never really delved into it ... Peter briefly talked about it one time, saying Joel was fantastic but Viv and Beefy were their own men and dragged the team apart, so he wanted to change the culture.'

Faced with enormous pressure and savage criticism, Roebuck responded not by retreating into his shell but actually freeing his own play up. He hit ten sixes in the course of the 1987 season. He displayed a range of shots previously unseen by many of his teammates. He averaged a tick under 50 and his name featured among the heaviest scorers in the land. Always hard to budge, he was now in lofty company, judged one of *Wisden*'s five cricketers of the year for his deeds that season. 'He was a fantastic batsman,' says Waugh, 'and should have played Test cricket for England. I saw him get 165 at Weston-super-Mare against Malcolm Marshall and Marshall wasn't holding back. It was a flat wicket but his technique was well and truly up to the task of facing the best bowler in the world. He was definitely as good as the players who were playing for England at the time.'

Not everyone agreed. 'The brutal answer is that he wasn't good enough,' says Atherton. 'He was a crabby, not fluent player – a bit like me I suppose – but found ways to get runs. I don't think he was good enough to be an international player in his own right, but he could have perhaps played the Brearley role.' The last point is intriguing, a nod to the man-management and tactical acumen of Mike Brearley, who despite averaging less than 23 with the bat was revered for inspiring his charges – notably Botham and Bob Willis – to great feats against the old enemy, Australia.

There was a humiliating early exit from the NatWest Trophy, bundled out by Buckinghamshire, to deal with, but the side reached the quarter-finals of the Benson & Hedges Cup and again performed solidly in the Sunday League. And oddly, despite winning one fewer game than 1986's inglorious tally of three, Somerset – minus Richards, Garner, Botham – climbed five places in the County Championship.

Richards spent the season in the Lancashire League, playing for Rishton, and Garner came back to England too, turning out for Oldham in the Central Lancashire League. But with suspect knees his career was on the wane. He played his last Test in Christchurch in March 1987 and rounded out his career with five Shell Shield matches back in the Caribbean. For all the hue and cry about Somerset releasing Garner, he would play in just eleven more first-class fixtures before calling time. Richards continued enjoying the fruits of international competition, and even made a triumphant return to county cricket with Glamorgan in 1990, aged thirty-eight, striking seven centuries for his new club in a long, dry summer.

As for Botham, the huff and puff didn't quite match the output. His fourteenth Test century – in Brisbane against Australia in November 1986 – was to be his last. The summer after, for his new club Worcestershire, he averaged under 30 with the bat and over 40 with the ball. Against Somerset, at Taunton, in a rain-affected match with time only for one innings, Vic Marks remembers standing behind the umpire at the start of his run-up, feigning wobbly knees as he prepared to bowl to his friend and former teammate. Botham would not be drawn into such folly. He laboured his way to a determined 126 not out, a point to prove in an otherwise pointless encounter, and his only Championship hundred of the summer. 'There is a picture of Pete and Both out in the middle, not talking to one another, and I'm floating around,' says Marks. 'Both was back. Pete was very tense.'

The next summer was Roebuck's third and final season in charge. For a man who went out of his way to portray himself as almost completely without ambition, his leadership displayed noticeable hallmarks of an absolutist. It was suggested by Marks and others that he wanted to dictate how the side played more than most captains and was keen to have devotees, to appear in control, and to be able to make decisions that would not be queried. After one game there was a run-in with Waugh – 'It was all over in ten seconds,' Waugh says. 'That was Peter; he had his own way and he didn't back down from it ... I respected him as a captain.'

Some went so far as to assert he craved acolytes and the opportunity to preach to adoring followers – driven, in Botham's eyes, by a 'fanatical desire to rule Somerset'. Others are more subtle in their interpretations. Neil Burns, one of the new signings, as wicketkeeper-batsman, to replace Somerset's famous trio, says: 'He was clearly a deep thinker about the game. You could argue he was consumed by it. I think he got very frustrated when players wouldn't buy into his plans or didn't have the skill to execute them. He may have been a better captain at a higher level, or at a lower level ... but man to man, at a first-class level, I think there were some people who just found his manner too brusque.'

At the end of 1988 he stepped down without fuss to clear a path for the more amiable Marks. And for all the angst caused off the field during his stint as Somerset captain, Roebuck's name came to be tossed around in certain circles as a potential skipper of the Test team. What was good for Brearley, went the line, may have been good for Roebuck. It is hard to imagine the malignant antipathy triggered by the split at Somerset hadn't marked Roebuck's cards for good – that, and a growing perception that he lacked the Brearley touches of empathy and restraint. An incisive cricket brain was beyond doubt, but his tendency to lose patience and act, albeit completely free of pretence, the man apart gave rise to an impression of detachment.

Yet by the 1989 Ashes series there was a push for his inclusion in the Test side. Allan Border's Australian squad had been labelled the weakest ever to tour England but Waugh, Taylor and Jones had other ideas, amassing huge scores and setting up the swing of Alderman and seam of Lawson. England chopped and changed in increasing panic and despair, picking twenty-nine different players on the way to a humbling 4–0 series defeat.

Five separate opening combinations were tried. Seasoned county performers like Barnett, Moxon, Curtis, Robinson and Stephenson were conscripted to fill the breach. All failed, miserably. Only Curtis and Robinson had averaged more that season than Roebuck, who was now partnered at the top of the Somerset order by prolific South African Jimmy Cook. Roebuck's resistance in the second innings of the tour match against the dominant Australians had not gone unnoticed either. 'He was the only guy who stood up to us in '89,' says Lawson. 'He was not going to get out.'

But he still wasn't selected. In his moving obituary of Roebuck, Marks remembered: 'In 1989, with the national side in chaos, the coach and captain at Somerset were asked to suggest a replacement for the Edgbaston Test against Australia. We recommended Roebuck, who was in superb form; the selectors opted to recall Chris Tavaré.'

To his immense credit, Roebuck displayed not a hint of bitterness. Tavaré, having lost the captaincy at Kent, was by now sharing the Taunton dressing room with Roebuck. He consoled Roebuck after being informed of his own selection but Roebuck was decidedly matter of fact, stating the more accomplished player had been duly rewarded. Tavaré, for his part, was none too thrilled at being redrafted.

Botham, of course, was still around, although he was selected in only three Tests against Australia that summer and misfired badly, averaging 15 with the bat and 80 with the ball. But Roebuck, seen neither as an establishment man nor rubbing shoulders in the boys' club, remained determinedly – and to his detractors detestably – a man apart. 'His personality was so far at one end of the spectrum that he couldn't fit in,' says Waugh. 'That was the era of Gower, Lamb, Botham ... They were a tight-knit group, fun-loving cricketers who played and socialised in a certain way and Peter definitely didn't fit into their way of life.'

It would be the closest he came to participating in Test cricket. 'I wouldn't cross a bridge to watch Peter Roebuck play,' says Rose. 'But he was super-effective and he had a fantastic record. He reached the standard at one stage where he was competing with the likes of Chris Tavaré ... I'd rather have had Pete Roebuck batting at four for England than Chris Tavaré.'

* * *

By way of overdue recognition, or because of a dearth of candidates, Roebuck was instead offered the captaincy of an England XI for a one-off, short stint to the Netherlands squeezed between the fifth and sixth Tests. It would be another unusual episode in his eventful life. He led a side containing a number of experienced hands sprinkled with likely prospects. Future England captains Nasser Hussain and Alec Stewart made the trip, accompanied by established all-rounder Derek Pringle and fringe Test player David Capel. In a peculiar turn of events, and rubbing salt into the wound of a terrible summer for English cricket, Roebuck's charges lost the first game by three runs.

As Roebuck was apt to point out subsequently, the match was conducted on an artificial pitch and England's innings was played out in semi-darkness. 'I always felt very sorry for him when he was made captain for that trip,' says Agnew. 'It had been a complete stinker of a summer for England and Roebuck got the short straw. They even lost there; it was one of those horrible moments.'

The natural order of things was restored the following day as the Dutch were put to the sword. The legion of pressmen, however, sharpened their pencils and painted the expedition a disaster. Roebuck was pilloried. Indeed, England manager Micky Stewart raced around to each journalist imploring them to ignore anything Roebuck had said.

'At the time, the press got it into their heads that Roebuck was the next England captain,' says Matthew Engel. 'Graham Gooch had been made captain, who the chairman of selectors Ted Dexter had described – in his capacity as a journalist for the *Sunday Mirror* – as having the charisma of a wet fish. There was nobody else and suddenly there was an idea that Roebuck was the obvious candidate. All of the newspapers at the time were pushing Roebuck. Now, I don't think this had any basis in fact whatsoever, but it was given credence by his appointment to captain in Holland. So Roebuck got the job then a meltdown happened when they lost. He was giving a press conference afterwards and

Micky Stewart was strutting over going, "What's he saying?!" It was clear they had no intention of appointing him captain. And they were right; he would have been eaten alive.'

All quite possible, but Engel also noted at the time: 'There were a couple of tricky public situations, and Roebuck handled them masterfully, with a sureness of touch that has eluded every England captain for eight years.' It mattered not a jot. Off went a one-day squad to contest the meaningless Nehru Trophy in India, then a Test squad was dispatched to the West Indies, and at the tail end of the English winter an England 'A' side toured Zimbabwe. Roebuck was not included anywhere. He went back to Australia instead.

His final Championship game came late in season 1991 against Yorkshire, fittingly at the county ground at Taunton. Roebuck took guard against bristling young paceman Darren Gough, hit him backward of square for six, played out a draw under captain Tavaré, and promptly retired. There was little fanfare. A legion of older hands had come and gone, friends and foes from all those yesterdays. Marks had retired two years prior, Rose two years prior to that. Crowe had not played county cricket since injury restricted him to five matches in the second season of his return to Somerset. Botham was at his second county club, shortly to join a third. Richards farewelled Test cricket that year, signing off with 60 to his name at The Oval. New, emboldened faces were pushing things along. So it is with cricket and so it will always be.

* * *

In those fraught, frantic months of 1986, this lean and unfashionable figure triumphed over those who would attempt to bully him. 'He had the intellect, combined with the drive and passion, to do what he believed was right ... Quite rare things to coincide there,' says John Barclay. 'Lots of people would have brushed it under the carpet – anything for a peaceful life – but Pete wasn't that sort of person.' His part in the affair remains, to this day, a matter of conjecture. According to Roebuck, the animosities stemming from what happened were relentless. The question remains as to whether the campaign against him was material and unceasing, or whether it was a matter he was endlessly preoccupied with and, some might say, tortured by. 'If we accept the effect of '86 was not on Richards, Garner and Botham,' says Engel, 'it was on Roebuck, and it destroyed him, one has to think that the paranoia was really derived from *they will find out the truth.*'

For Nigel Popplewell, the man many say determined the outcome at Shepton Mallet, the day still carries a certain resonance. '"Both",' he says, 'had clearly been strongly loyal to Viv and Joel and, I'm not blaming him for this, his perception was that I'd stitched his mates up and "I'm going to resent you for that". Whereas Viv, who I've seen a number of times since, has always hugged, shaken hands, and there has been no side to it at all.'

Popplewell had little to do with Roebuck after 1986.

The season after he walked away from Somerset, 1992, Roebuck had an approach from Geoff Evans, the secretary of Devon, wondering whether he might like to come and play with them. When the captain Nick Folland reiterated the offer Roebuck agreed, upon the laying down of certain conditions: he would play without payment, he would not stand in the way of younger players, and he would prefer to bat down the order and work on his bowling instead.

It paved the way for a fruitful, mutually satisfying decade. The Minor Counties Championship was a largely amateur affair featuring consummate old pros and up-and-coming tyros. In Roebuck, Devon had a wily campaigner still burning with competitive intent, and in Devon, Roebuck's eccentricities were embraced and his impatience tolerated with good humour.

Each English summer, back from Australia, Roebuck took up residence in Exmouth. When Folland, a batsman, departed for a two-season tilt at first-class cricket, Roebuck took over the captaincy for seven remarkable summers. Prior to his joining them, Devon had claimed the Minor Counties Championship just once, in 1978. Under Roebuck, playing a breed of attacking, colourful cricket, they won four successive titles. His own game had scarcely diminished. In two of those title-winning years for example, 1996 and 1997, he picked up 47 wickets (at 15) and 40 wickets (at 17) while averaging in the low 60s with the bat. This from a man batting well down the order, or not padding up at all in the case of modest run chases, preferring to give a chance to lesser-qualified teammates.

The eccentricities, too, remained. Roebuck's outbursts would become the stuff of Devonian folklore. 'Peter's captaincy was part-theorist and part-emotional wreck,' recalls Devon teammate Gareth Townsend. 'He was a mixture of everything; sometimes he would come up with facts and measured responses in matches, sometimes he would lose the plot and you would have no idea where he was coming from.'

Roebuck had the grace to admit later that of the many stories hawked around relating to his captaincy, all of them were true. Infractions in his eyes invariably brought about some kind of recrimination, such as instructing a non-bowler to come on and deliver an over or two, or, famously, against Cornwall, ordering every fielder on the leg side to swap places with every fielder on the off side. By chance, a run-out was managed and a delighted Roebuck took responsibility, claiming his act had created confusion. Among his troops, such actions created a mixture of amusement and bemusement. By his own admission, the friendships forged and team's success kept him in the game far longer than he had anticipated.

Even then, one of his Devon admirers noted, while he loved the camaraderie and jocularity of the team dynamic, it had to be built around him as he felt insecure if in an environment he had no control of. Yet he was held in affectionate regard, an elder statesman devoted to the cause of the team and to cricket. Peter Robinson recalls Roebuck would go out of his way to tell him what wonderful people the Devon folk were. He demonstrated care and concern for the younger players and was a source of constant technical advice. His ability to conjure victories inspired faith, albeit mixed with confusion depending on his latest spontaneous tactic. Further, he could lead from the front when required, rapidly accelerating the scoring with a sense of adventure that he'd kept so methodically under wraps at Somerset.

'At Devon, they knew some of Pete's flaws and that he could be an oddball, but they loved him,' says Marks. 'They soaked up all that cricketing knowledge. In a curious sort of way, I'm sure that was the happiest time he had on a cricket field, captaining a team that recognised he had something massive to offer them, that delighted in his eccentricities, laughed at him – and with him. That was the perfect combination.'

When he bowled, it was frenetic. 'Each ball,' recalls Townsend, 'he would live as the equivalent to a soap episode: exasperation,

ABOVE: R.J.O. 'Boss' Meyer: educationalist, entrepreneur and first-class cricketer. Founder and long-time headmaster of Millfield School, his influence on Roebuck was profound.

ABOVE: The Millfield Senior Colts team in 1969, with Roebuck back row third from left and inset.

BELOW: Junior Somerset representatives with revered former player and coach Bill Andrews in August, 1969. Roebuck, second from right, was already something of a cricketing prodigy and would make his county 2nd XI debut a few weeks later, aged just thirteen.

ABOVE: Roebuck the elegant, driving crisply through the off-side for Combined Universities, albeit bedecked in Somerset apparel, in the summer of 1976. (PATRICK EAGAR)

ABOVE: Somerset's star-studded side at Taunton in 1981. The line-up included five internationals: Botham, Garner, Marks, Richards and Rose. (GETTY IMAGES)

MIDDLE RIGHT: Roebuck in 1982. His various eccentricities were becoming common knowledge on the county circuit.

BOTTOM RIGHT: Heady days, post–Gillette Cup win over Essex in 1978. Roebuck was 'Pete lad' to Botham and 'Prof' to Richards.

ABOVE: A section of the County Ground at Taunton, circa 2001. Roebuck used the facilities to coach his 'youngsters' long after he left the club. (CRICKETPIX)

MIDDLE LEFT: Roy Kerslake, Somerset's popular cricket chairman, and Vic Marks (seated) watch Gavaskar batting at Kent in 1980. Roebuck's mind is elsewhere.

BOTTOM LEFT: Happier times in the Caribbean for Botham and Roebuck, on a pre-season tour for Somerset in 1982.

ABOVE: Roebuck the nudger, congratulated by Viv Richards upon reaching 50 in the Benson & Hedges Cup final against Nottinghamshire in 1982. He had taken twice as many deliveries as the Master Blaster to make his half-century, but wore down the likes of Richard Hadlee, Mike Hendrick and Clive Rice. (GETTY IMAGES)

RIGHT: Somerset under Botham pictured at Hove before the NatWest Trophy quarter-final against Sussex in 1983. (GETTY IMAGES)

ABOVE: Roebuck evades a searing delivery from Geoff Lawson against the touring Australians at Taunton in 1985. He carried his bat in the second innings as Jeff Thomson ripped through the fragile Somerset line-up. (PATRICK EAGAR)

ABOVE: The cracks appear. Roebuck (with an obscured Brian Langford) watch Botham's return to cricket – in Somerset's 2nd XI – following his drugs ban in 1986. (CRICKETPIX)

RIGHT: Roebuck as captain in 1986 with Botham and Garner. (PATRICK EAGAR/GETTY IMAGES)

Somerset may sack Botham

LONDON, Monday: England all-rounder Ian Botham, who has threatened to quit Somerset over the English county's sacking of West Indians Viv Richards and Joel Garner, may also be axed.

Some Somerset members are so furious over Botham's ultimatum to leave if his Caribbean friends are not reinstated that they are calling for the two-year contract offered to him to be torn up.

"He is splitting the county in two, so we should get in first to make it clear loyalty is two-edged," said a member who did not wish to be named.

"We paid his wages while he was suspended for pot smoking and stood by him while other allegations were flying round, but all we have got back is a kick in the teeth."

ABOVE and LEFT: The 'Somerset Affair' in late 1986 split the county, dominated headlines, forced Richards and Garner out and sparked enmity between Botham and Roebuck.

BELOW: The opener walks off. His county cricket record stands at 17,558 runs at 37.27, with 33 centuries. Named one of Wisden's cricketers of the year in 1988, he was considered unlucky not to have played Test cricket.

(CRICKETPIX)

Angry Botham leaves Somerset in no doubt

By SCYLD BERRY

AN HOUR before yesterday's start of play in Perth a familiar figure entered room 1302 of the

is over, cricket is a game played by 11 men or persons. In this respect the county was surely correct. World-weary superstars

brings the worst out of English batsmen. Who knows whether it is high living the night before or the fact that they are accustomed to

panic ... he was like a ticking bomb waiting to go off at the easiest cause. We played against Oxfordshire in an important two-day championship game and after thirty minutes he brought himself on. After his third ball – steam was coming out of his ears as the ball was doing bugger all off the pitch – he proceeded to sit down on the wicket, roughly on a length, and shout out, "What's the point of life? What's the point of life?", as he bounced the ball on the pitch. For a full minute he sat there and no one said a word – it was hilarious. An hour later he had taken 9 for 12.'

With a comfortable life now established as a columnist, author and broadcaster, these were contented days. But they couldn't last. The ghosts of '86 still circled, Roebuck suspecting a conspiracy at most turns. Tabloid dirt merchants snooped, Botham sniped, rumours swirled. Roebuck bit back, sometimes on the pitch and sometimes in print, and not always to his credit or benefit. News that he had been arrested on charges of indecent assault in 1999 pleased his enemies, who were all too numerous. He resigned the Devon captaincy and shut up shop, playing only a handful of fixtures in the early 2000s, having been reinstated as leader upon Folland's withdrawal. His last hurrah came in 2002. In a three-day match against Berkshire at Torquay he cleaved a six and two fours in a mad rush to chase down 202 in only 21 overs on the final day, his cherished Devonians falling seven runs short. A fortnight later they were beaten in an ECB County Cup Final at Worcester. That was it. He made a short speech afterwards and left without fanfare.

Four days after Roebuck died, the man who cajoled him into his second cricketing life reflected on what reaching out to him had meant for the county. 'His positive example as to how the game should be played made a huge impact,' wrote Geoff Evans.

'After masterminding the most successful period in the club's history, Peter decided to retire from all cricket at the end of the 2002 season, leaving behind a dressing room devoid of discord.

'May peace now be granted to an extraordinarily gifted, troubled soul.'

4

THE FATEFUL FEUD

'African schools are far more robust than their
English counterparts ... chastisement is part of
the programme.'

– SOMETIMES I FORGOT TO LAUGH, 2004

On the day in Melbourne of the 1992 World Cup final – in which Botham was playing, Roebuck writing and commentating – an attempt was made to persuade Roebuck to open up about his nemesis.

Tim Lane remembers:

'It was Roebuck's first summer as a regular on the ABC.
Over a couple of years in media boxes before then I
had scarcely spoken a word to him. I'd seen him as
a rather forbidding figure. When I became aware he
was to join our ranks I was intrigued. The experience
of becoming his colleague was a pleasant surprise. He
wasn't easy company but he was stimulating, he left

you wanting more of him, and as time wore on we often debated issues on air. My experience was that he always enjoyed a joust. In fact he told me a number of times that 'friends' liked our on-air sessions together. I took it to mean that he, and they, approved of our occasional differences. Maybe this was partly because he inevitably came out on top, but what it told me was he didn't want to be pandered to.

Sometimes, such as over the Australian players' industrial dispute in 1997–98, our differences had an edge to them. He was a professional cricketer who believed in the nobility of his fellow workers fighting for a better deal. I saw it through the eyes of an Australian cricket fan. It seemed to me, rightly or wrongly, that a national sporting team had a responsibility to represent those of the nation who were invested in its fortunes, and to use their affection as a form of leverage in a pay dispute amounted to emotional blackmail. After that, Roebuck made reference in a column to people on the other side of the argument to him having watched too many Charlton Heston movies.

On the first weekend of the 1992 World Cup, West Indies were demolishing Pakistan at the MCG and Roebuck was in trouble with a toothache. Seeing his distress, I absented myself from the cricket and drove him to Royal Melbourne Hospital, a fifteen-minute trip. We got to the dental section and I offered to wait and take him back. Without a word, he jumped out of the car, closed the door and headed inside, not a word of thanks, not then or later.

The evening before the final was the infamous occasion when comedian Gerry Connolly impersonated Queen Elizabeth and Botham and Gooch walked out in disgust. I put it to Roebuck that Botham may have been grandstanding. Knowing the bones of the Somerset story, I was curious to see his reaction, but he didn't bite at all, didn't take the bait. Maybe he felt he didn't know me well enough for that, or quite possibly there was a sense of honour involved, in that he wouldn't engage in gossip, wouldn't backbite in a private corner, but rather save it for a public forum.

It did not take long for Roebuck to join Botham at the hip in mutual loathing. Of course, they had to confront one another on the cricket field, Roebuck as captain at Somerset, Botham as Worcestershire's new recruit. 'We had some traumatic games thereafter,' said Marks. 'There was one game where (Graeme) Hick got 405, but there was also the game when "Both" came back. There is a picture of Pete and Both out in the middle, not talking to one another and I'm floating around. It was a rain-affected game which ended in a draw but Both was back. Pete was very tense about the whole thing.'

In 1990, before one of Roebuck and Botham's last matches against each other as on-field rivals, Somerset versus Worcestershire, there was a public humiliation set up by Chris Lander, a *Mirror* journalist. Lander called Roebuck to say Botham was done with the feud and wanted to bury the hatchet. Roebuck approached his nemesis with hand outstretched and was duly rebuffed. Botham had no inkling of Lander's plan but a photographer was dutifully present to record the moment for posterity. It would not be the last time that the gregarious and popular Lander – sitting somewhere between jester and bidder on behalf of Botham, whom he referred to as 'The Legend' – would be involved in this tale.

Botham then flew out to Australia to play in the Sheffield Shield, lured to Queensland on a lucrative, multi-sponsor three-year deal. Crowds soared and his performances at first matched the lucre. Off the field, soon enough, mayhem took centre stage. He and Dennis Lillee (during his brief comeback for Tasmania) were accused of vandalising a dressing room in Launceston and fined. Reports of friction in the camp filtered out and Botham was fined for abusing spectators in Melbourne. Then things really got out of hand. As the Queensland team flew to Perth for the Shield final against Western Australia, Botham intervened in an argument between Greg Ritchie and Allan Border with a combination of profanities and a headlock on a passenger who took umbrage. He was arrested in Perth and had to be bailed out of the cells. Convicted of assault in the wake of the final, which Queensland lost, Botham's contract was terminated soon after. He told reporters that he 'couldn't give a stuff' about the conviction and later likened himself to the outlaw Ned Kelly. Ever the quixotic character, Botham jetted off to Europe to begin his next fundraising effort for leukaemia research – in the Alps, with elephants in tow.

Back in England, *The Sun* burned its Botham bridge. The tabloid sacked Botham as a columnist and embarked on an editorial rant, describing him as a foul-mouthed slob and a bullying lout. Roebuck, who had also spent that summer in Australia, gave his two cents' worth: 'Botham is convinced he can deny responsibility for misconduct by pointing to great deeds he has performed. That wouldn't wash in a court of law and it must not wash in cricket either.'

It demonstrated a Roebuck tendency that reared, for effect or otherwise, through much of his writing career: sweeping, instinctive statements on character; finger wagging; pointed adjudicating on supposed necessary remedies. If the tone adopted wasn't exactly moralising, it did frequently border on a schoolmaster's plane. It was a tendency that worked for and against Roebuck. Readers loved the sharp, snappy asides and bristling denunciations but detractors increasingly took aim at Roebuck's own struggles to stick to the higher ground he so trenchantly took in print.

After that it was tit for tat. Botham called Roebuck a 'sad case'. When Roebuck's name was mentioned as a possible England tourist to the West Indies, Botham poured scorn on his chances but did say he would enjoy seeing Roebuck struck by Malcolm Marshall. Presented by his superiors at the *Sydney Morning Herald* with the opportunity in late 1994 to review Botham's ghostwritten autobiography, Roebuck could barely contain his glee at such easy pickings:

Ian Botham portrays himself as immature, spiteful and arrogant. His greatest trick has been to convince people of his standing as an anti-Establishment hero. Rarely has a cricketer been so protected by those in power. Alas, his memory is faulty, too. Perhaps I've been unlucky. Perhaps this book does contain accurate passages, it's just that I never found any of them. Seldom can so great a cricketer and entertainer, a man who helped to take the game into the pubs and to the people, show himself in so poor a light.

In *From Sammy to Jimmy*, the epic Somerset official history he authored, Roebuck wrote with a cold, acute edge and recounted the split in naked terms, describing Botham as living in a fantasy world, hungering for power, and spoiling all and sundry with an ego enlarged and aggressive intent unchecked. The frankness leapt off the page. It was compelling stuff. The enmity intensified, although for all of Botham's macho posturing, there was little risk of physical harm. A youthful Botham may well have thrown a punch at Ian Chappell but such red-misted belligerence wasn't intended for Roebuck. There were other surreptitious and more damaging courses to take.

Perhaps unsurprisingly, Chappell became a firm ally of Roebuck's. 'Pretty quickly we realised we had a common denominator and that was Botham,' Chappell says. 'His dislike of Botham was even greater than mine and that takes some doing, because I would have him at the top of the list of people I dislike.'

* * *

When not sidestepping his bête noire at cricket grounds around the world, Roebuck was building a life on three continents. Maintaining his presence in Taunton was in hindsight an odd decision, surrounded by people he perceived as adversaries intent on his ruination. But his writing gathered further acclaim, particularly in the *Sunday Times*. He undertook numerous trips to South Africa and later Zimbabwe, intertwining coaching stints at schools in Bloemfontein, Harare and Bulawayo with fact-finding missions and incisive reporting. Summers down under meant reconvening with trusted friends in Sydney and whistlestop tours from Ballarat to Bowral covering all manner of cricket matches.

He 'chased the sun', as Darshak Mehta, chairman of the LBW Trust – a charity providing scholarships for disadvantaged children in developing, cricket-playing countries – puts it. Already well established in Australia, he put down firmer roots with the purchase of a house in Bondi and put steady credits in the bank as a full-time cricket writer. His analyst's role on ABC Radio took him far into the realm of public consciousness in an adopted country. His clipped delivery was heard in lounge rooms, cars and on beaches. According to many, this was the most satisfying chapter of Roebuck's life; for a man rarely described as content or restful, the post-Somerset days granted him a decade or so's respite, free of controversy and featuring spirited flights of fancy.

His sojourns to the subcontinent produced a flowering of mutual admiration with some of the great sportswriters of India and Sri Lanka, men and women who were for the most part relatively unknown outside their own lands. Friendships with Sharda Ugra, Haresh Pandya and Rohit Brijnath gave him a depth of insight into India's family, cultural and cricketing fabric that could be so easily overlooked by correspondents of the gin and tonic variety. Earnest, genuine encouragement for the likes of Dileep Premachandran gained him a warm admiration that lasted until the end.

These trips also produced direct philanthropic opportunities. A foster daughter, Malabika, in Kolkata was the first of many such interventions in cricket-playing nations. He encouraged colleagues to help; 'send her useful things like clothes and books' he urged Pandya at one point. The hot, dusty climes, boisterous scenes and obsession with cricket in India captivated him. Conversations were sought with railway attendants, sweets sellers, gatekeepers. Other eminent members of the media corps shunned close-ups with the native inhabitants; Roebuck often took crowded trains from cities to outposts in order to trigger such encounters. It stimulated a wider, more nuanced perspective than most western writers could obtain.

He therefore gained confidences, from both the learned and lowborn. A discreet check via a trusted source in Chennai provided Roebuck with the verification he needed to buttress Special Commissioner K.K. Paul in his corruption case against Hansie Cronje. Knee-jerk, jingoistic shrieking in Cronje's defence was coolly swatted away as Paul's credentials were established. Roebuck went for Cronje's throat accordingly; other writers followed thereafter. Some would say in later years his sympathies for India's charms and challenges outweighed a critical glare when necessary. He was prepared to overlook the juvenile on-field antics of Harbhajan Singh, for example, signalling Australia's bully-boy tactics were the greater sin. His condemnation, however, of the corruption and myriad prejudices of Board of Control for Cricket in India (BCCI) heavyweights and IPL cronies was typically forthright. And his voice remained revered throughout the subcontinent. 'A philanthropist, an avuncular counsel to young writers, an idealist, and the conscience-keeper of the game – that was Peter Roebuck,' wrote Rohit Mahajan.

* * *

Back in Taunton, as was the case in Bondi and later Pietermaritzburg, his home was opened to the short-term hosting of promising cricketers. They typically came from South Africa or Australia and rent was a matter of negotiation. Lawns were to be mowed, chores done. They were mostly school leavers and placed with local cricket clubs. Few would go on to stake a serious claim in the game although one, Omari Banks, went the journey, representing Somerset for two seasons and West Indies in ten Test matches.

The regime accompanying his hosting of them was uncompromising. At a certain point (exactly when remains unknown) came an unforeseen shift in mindset. Roebuck had admitted in 1990 to his friend Toby Jones that he was 'awfully right-wing' in his approach to education. But few who knew him could envisage a subsequent belief in corporal punishment. In his own homes, however, he began to both espouse and practise it. Such acts were not, as some have charged, an intrinsic or historical part of Roebuck's nature, sexual or otherwise. In an environment at Cranbrook where corporal punishment was second nature to many of the masters, Roebuck demurred; nothing ties him to any act of physical punishment while teaching or coaching there. 'He was old school,' says former Cranbrook student and lifelong friend Fabian Muir. 'He did believe it added value, but whether that's a great way to motivate people I'm not sure. He maintained that there was agreement that if they're not up to scratch, it was an option. But I went to a school [Cranbrook] where caning was rife and I can't remember a single incident of Peter caning anyone.'

Nigel Popplewell, who had been a housemate of Roebuck's in Somerset days, says: 'The whole thing struck me as slightly odd – that people who had been brought over had allowed themselves to be physically abused. But if that's what happened, it's reprehensible and cannot be condoned in any circumstances. There was no inkling of that side of him when I was sharing [a house] with him or playing alongside him.'

Yet at some juncture in the 1990s – and speculation inevitably points to the environments he experienced in schools in South Africa and Zimbabwe – Roebuck embraced disciplinary measures that were rapidly losing favour elsewhere, if not already dismantled and frowned upon. In the hyper-charged, sexualised landscape of the UK, Roebuck's adoption of caning was at best a woebegotten stake in times past, a craving for corrective measures that straightened attitudes and jolted youth out of inertia. At worst, it was a risky slide – in early middle age – that took advantage of youthful and economic vulnerabilities in order to satisfy darker impulses. Either way, he left himself wide open to charges of impropriety, particularly given Roebuck's use of the practice occurred outside the structure and scrutiny of an institution.

Ominously, the Fleet Street dirt merchants were already lurking. Veteran journalist Conrad Sutcliffe, who chronicled Roebuck's career at Devon and remained a friend throughout testing times, says he was aware of allegations of journalistic skulduggery well before any hint of wrongdoing by Roebuck. Reporters doing the bidding of Chris Lander offered inducements as rumours circulated. For his part, Roebuck claimed any discipline he handed out was agreed on beforehand: 'I'm raising lions, not pussy cats.'

It was a questionable defence, then and now. For one, he walked in the path of self-made teachers, a family devoted to the premises of learning and its uplifting promise. Nowhere did his own experience reflect a greater good from being a recipient of physical punishment. Rather, in his autobiography he makes brief reference to shedding tears during the first hiding he copped as a child. Yet in the latter stages of the same book he commends the strict methods of African schools, admiring the fact that 'chastisement is part of the programme' and noting how this resonates in the formation of character.

If there was no shadowy inclination on Roebuck's part, then his disciplinary practices were poorly conceived and left him exposed to accusers seeking retribution. 'He could deceive himself along the R.J.O. Meyer notion that "I am the educator here, such is my capacity here that I can use whatever means because in the end it will benefit you",' says Vic Marks. 'There was an element of deception there, but I suspect an element of self-loathing as well. There were moments of acknowledgement that he'd fucked up in terms of how he had behaved.'

His sister Beatrice strongly disagrees with this notion. 'In the UK,' she says, 'you do not touch a child; UK education is up to the age of eighteen. These people were older than eighteen. With Peter, I subsequently found out that it was part of his belief, his education structure, that discipline was important to success, and for him corporal punishment was acceptable. It was part of the process and, for some of us, it was part of our growing up.'

In 1999, over the course of an English spring, three promising South African cricketers came to stay in Roebuck's Taunton house. The first, Keith Whiting, was from Johannesburg. Nineteen at the time, it was his first substantial period away from home. Roebuck immediately put the young man through an intensive fitness and coaching program, including dawn runs and indoor nets. On his first morning Whiting dropped well behind Roebuck during a run and was subsequently caned. Under oath at a later date, he said Roebuck had told him: 'I'm going to cane you now. Then it will be over and I will forgive you and, if I don't cane you, I will feel differently about you.'

Roebuck wrote in his autobiography that the caning was administered 'with a stick from a bunch he [Whiting] had brought home'. It conveys the possibility of a ritualised aspect.

The other South African youths, Reginald Keats and Henk Lindeque, were also nineteen. Keats copped the same treatment as Whiting and did not take kindly to Roebuck's corrective measures. Lindeque, too, was caned. Further, Roebuck on one occasion requested Lindeque to drop his shorts so Roebuck could inspect the welts, which he did, briefly. Whiting later testified that Roebuck had also asked him to show the marks left by the cane. Upon revealing the nature of life in the household to a visiting cousin, Keats and the others were encouraged to move out. Whiting informed his parents and Richard Lines, the secretary of Bishop's Lydeard Cricket Club where Whiting was playing. Lines acted quickly and helped move the youths and their belongings. Roebuck came home to find his place empty, an episode he describes in his autobiography. It makes for uncomfortable reading.

The guest cricketers did not return and the end of the summer passed without incident. Lines, however, was friendly with Botham and news of the punishments and unusual behaviour spread. According to Roebuck a number of 'bitter and longstanding enemies', including former Somerset players, then weighed into the fray and a complaint was made to Avon and Somerset police. He later disclosed to Ian Chappell that Botham was the driving force. 'Peter,' says Chappell, 'told me Botham has got some very dicey friends, and it makes sense to me because Botham is a bloody coward – he loads the gun but he never pulls the trigger.'

Journalists confirmed to Roebuck that those involved met

with Lander and Botham, with Botham reportedly delighted at the revelations. A story was contrived. They were able to convince one of the South Africans, Whiting, to go on the record, which meant Lander had something for his paper, the *Sunday Mirror* of 12 September 1999. (Lindeque was later persuaded to make a complaint to police a year after Whiting and Keats.) Thereafter, Lander's influence ended; he died of cancer within months of the article's publication. The journalist who put the piece together, Rupert Hamer, was killed in horrific circumstances in 2010, covering the conflict in Afghanistan.

CRICKET CAPTAIN IS ACCUSED OF SPANKING PUPIL

'Roebuck gave me 12 of the best as punishment because he said I was unfit'
By Rupert Hamer

CRICKET star Peter Roebuck is being investigated by police over allegations that he assaulted a young player.

Roebuck, 44, who captained Ian Botham, Viv Richards and Joel Garner during Somerset's glory days, is said to have used a cane and then his hand on 19-year-old Keith Whiting's backside. Keith, from Johannesburg, said the 'punishments' were administered during fitness training while he was staying at Roebuck's bungalow in Taunton.

He said: 'We had a race and Roebuck beat me. He said my fitness was not up to standard. He said, "Go fetch the cane, there is one in the garage." I went out to get it and found one lying on the floor, with three or four others nearby. When I got back to the lounge he gave me 12 of the best, six with the cane and six with his hand.'

Keith added: 'I was scared and lonely and very vulnerable. It was the first time I had been away from home. I was very confused.'

Keith said he was caned again after batting practice a few days later – and was also struck with a cricket bat after returning home late from a nightclub …

Last night bachelor Roebuck, in Sri Lanka covering their test match against Australia for a newspaper, refused to comment.

It was perhaps fortuitous for 'bachelor' Roebuck that he was in Sri Lanka. A *Mirror* stringer was duly dispatched but unable to persuade him to speak. Mike Coward met Roebuck there: 'There is no doubt that he changed after charges were brought against him in England. He reached Kandy in a state of considerable distress, feeling he was being hounded by the British tabloid press who were intent on bringing him down.'

Journalist and photographer Mark Ray was also on that tour. He and Roebuck were not close but they got on well and worked for the same media organisation, Fairfax. Roebuck had surprised Ray twelve months earlier with a phone call at home – the first of its kind – after they returned from covering Australia's tour of Pakistan. There, Ray had contracted dysentery and became terribly sick. Roebuck rang for an update and to offer his best wishes, a gesture Ray appreciated while finding it somewhat out of keeping for Roebuck. In Sri Lanka, he confirms, Roebuck was agitated at the accuser who went to the *Mirror* but Ray did not feel he was making excuses. In a moment of candour, and to Ray's dismay, Roebuck told him: 'I feel suicidal.'

Fortunately, Roebuck and Coward were able to take advantage of a sizeable break between Test matches and head into Sri Lanka's breathtaking hill country. They were joined by Pakistani cricket writer Qamar Ahmed and for a few days at least Roebuck was beyond the reach of those he imagined were intent on destroying him.

Back in the UK the following spring he was arrested, taken by police and interviewed. He was living in Exmouth by now and gave an interview to a local paper, the *Herald Express*, in which he claimed he was the victim of a long-running smear campaign. Roebuck placed the blame for the allegations against him firmly at the feet of enemies he made during the Somerset Affair, stating: 'I am at the point where I have had enough. Perhaps it is time I wrote a book and told my side of the story.'

Events turned farcical, tabloid flunkies doing their utmost to track down past visitors, with payments offered to anyone prepared to damn Roebuck. None were forthcoming. Interpol put aside matters of terrorism, organised crime and drug trafficking to interview some of Roebuck's former house guests. Nothing came of it. Some twenty months after he was initially arrested, Roebuck was formally questioned again in May 2001. Taunton police locked him in a cell before outlining charges of indecent assault. All bar one of his print media employers suspended him.

The tide of public opinion in his homeland had long since turned. Post-retirement, Botham's charity work continued unabated and he was a fixture on the long-running BBC show *A Question of Sport*, displaying a dexterity and deftness before the camera that surprised his sceptics. 'Botham has been able to change his image down the years,' says Rob Steen. 'Roebuck did in Australia, but not here. Roebuck wasn't perceived in English quarters as a particularly likeable person, whereas if you are on the right side of Botham he's a good lad to have around. Botham was the biggest sports star in England. He was a massive figure. You didn't cross Botham.'

* * *

A great friend of Roebuck's, Charles Bott, now a London-based Queen's Counsel, warned him on the eve of the ensuing court case that a belief in corporal punishment left him vulnerable. He advised Roebuck to retain a lawyer as, remarkably, he had not done so to that point in time. The legal firm Roebuck engaged suggested he plead guilty to a lesser charge, common assault, to which he reluctantly agreed.

At Taunton Crown Court in October 2001, Roebuck was dealt a devastating blow. Judge Graham Hume Jones pointedly admonished the defendant, stating he had abused his power and influence over the young South Africans, who he said were vulnerable due to isolation from family and friends. The prosecutor, Ian Fenny, told the court Roebuck deployed a harsh fitness program as an excuse to castigate his charges. 'It may well be,' said Fenny, 'that Roebuck deliberately took these boys on an arduous run so he could create the environment in which he could mete out punishment.'

It got worse. One of the complainants testified: 'I did not consent to any assault but he is a dominant person who makes you feel that you must do as he says.' Given the age difference and status of Roebuck this was difficult to dispute, although he maintained forever after that physical punishment was consented to, agreed upon, and expected. Next Fenny revealed the most disturbing part of the allegations: 'Roebuck then pulled the boy towards him, in what appeared to be an act of affection. He then asked if he could look at the marks on the boy's buttocks, something which he in fact did.'

This proved impossible to defend. Roebuck's lawyer, Paul Mendelle, instead made reference to his client's track record with young people. He also stated that Roebuck spelled out to each visitor that corporal punishment was part of his methodology, and that his client assumed the South Africans came from a culture where such recrimination was accepted. In addition, Mendelle said twenty-five out of twenty-nine boys who had stayed with Roebuck for cricketing tuition had supplied written testimonials.

The judge was unimpressed, summing up:

It was not appropriate to administer corporal punishment to boys of this age in circumstances such as these. It seems so unusual that it must have been done to satisfy some need in you. These were talented young men with high ambitions. They were far from home, far from their families and were keen to come under the tutelage of a person like you, being highly respected and well known in the cricket world. So, not only were they in your care but you had power and influence over them and that power and influence was abused by you. You used your position to abuse these boys and humiliate them.

Roebuck's impressive statements of support and earlier plea of guilty to three charges of common assault did not sway the judge. He was sentenced to four months in jail on each count, with the sentences suspended for two years, and ordered to pay £820 in costs. It was a shattering verdict and the humiliation effectively finished him in England. He visited a few friends and then flew to Zimbabwe, intending to resume his life in Australia afterwards. 'He was so disgusted with the legal process over here that that was it, the final nail in the coffin,' says his brother James. 'It pushed him to move permanently to Australia.'

'With the issues he had, I suppose people abandon you,' says Peter Robinson. 'But I never did. With all of his troubles I used to go and see him. He was very upset. He never conceded [that he'd done the wrong thing] … I just surmised that was the way he was brought up. I didn't go to the court that day but straight after he came to my house. My wife made him a sandwich and he said, "Right I'm off." He went straight to the airport.'

His parents knew next to nothing of the matter. 'He hadn't had any discussions with his parents – they were living in France – and he was half hoping they wouldn't get to know about it,' says Marks. 'It perplexed him what they might think. He was just desperate to get to Australia, get on with life in a place where he was appreciated and not pursued.' He had telephoned his brother Paul, a lawyer at the time, asking for advice; otherwise, and inevitably, other family members discovered the misadventure via newspapers or else were eventually informed. Beatrice Roebuck acted as messenger for the family and was requested by Peter not to alert their parents. At a later date she did let them know. 'There were never any recriminations or shock or horror,' says Beatrice. 'He didn't think he had done anything wrong.'

Roebuck's family, too, are victims of the whole sorry business. Impassioned defenders of his reputation, they believe that were it not for the criminal proceedings he would have spent considerably more time with them in the ensuing years. Instead contact, although not cut off, was sporadic. His family members remain convinced of his innocence and highly sceptical of less salubrious interpretations of his actions.

'And what do we mean by corporal punishment?' asks his mother, Elizabeth. 'A whack sometimes? Nowadays parents can't even do that. All this fuss ... I know he looked at their bottoms but he said, "I had to make sure I wasn't doing it too hard." It's a clan Roebuck approach, in that we don't awfully care about what the rest of the world think about us. We do, hopefully, what we think is right at the time. But these were young men – Peter only took them on once he'd seen their parents – and I have to qualify that with this particular group he hadn't met their parents. The rule was that they had to hand Peter the cane and that was a symbol that "yes, I have broken the rules and I have agreed that this is the quickest and easiest punishment". It was a nothing.'

His friend and ABC colleague, Geoff Lawson, formed a similar view: 'He was charged with disciplining somebody. God, when I was going to school you got the cane pretty regularly. There was no accusation officially of any sexual misdemeanours [but] there was that generalisation that if he did that, there must be something more to it. There never was anything more to it.'

* * *

He returned to England in 2002, part of an earlier agreement to captain Devon for one final summer. What happened next typified what lay in store. A spat in print with *Telegraph* and *Spectator* writer Michael Henderson got personal in the Lord's pressbox during the Benson & Hedges Cup final in June. Some of those present suggest Henderson merely voiced, 'Well, he shouldn't have spanked those boys, should he?', well within earshot of a clearly infuriated Roebuck. Earlier, as he and Henderson traded barbs in the press, Roebuck had declared 'for sixteen years I have been putting up with this rubbish from Ian Botham and his lapdogs'. Henderson no doubt felt aggrieved at that label. His recourse personified what Roebuck would contend with by way of scuttlebutt and snide asides forever after.

'From 1986 onwards there was a different set of circumstances to Peter's life,' says Beatrice. '[Peter felt] there was a viciousness and an oppression because [of those] who didn't like what had been done. Peter left and was barely over here again.'

Matthew Engel feels sympathy for the sentiment but does not believe the matter carried as much weight with Botham as it did Roebuck: 'He's a good hater, Botham, but I think Roebuck would have occupied 1 per cent of his mind whereas Botham would occupy 99 per cent of Roebuck's mind. After Botham, the paranoia kicked in.'

Notably, of the eight pages devoted to the punishments and court case in *Sometimes I Forgot to Laugh*, Roebuck made no mention of the most damaging claim: that he had asked to see the welts on the young men's buttocks. He may well have stood by his methods around corporal punishment but this conduct seemingly went well beyond any intention to modify behaviour. It remains a troubling, disquieting note.

What's more, he claimed to have not realised that pleading guilty equated to an acceptance of everything in the victims' statements. 'Roebuck's description of that is the most extraordinary business in the whole book,' says Engel. 'I've never come across such bollocks. This is a man with a first in law saying: I didn't realise that if I pleaded guilty it meant I'd done it. This is insane. How could anybody mishandle it the way he did? So arrogant that he didn't get proper legal advice, and incredibly stupid to not realise what the consequences were. It beggars belief.'

Of course, more serious offences have been committed without recourse to the law and, as one of the victims, Henk Lindeque, said upon learning of Roebuck's passing: 'He did warn us he had hard ways and in many senses that's not a bad way to look at life, especially in cricket.' Philosophically and generously, Lindeque expressed sadness at the news. 'I have moved on and come to terms with it. It's not something that ruined my life.'

A case could be mounted that it ruined Roebuck's. The headlines splashed around the cricket-playing world – the rumours, the speculation, the denigration of reputation. There was enough spice in the sexual misconduct allegations to result in wholesale public shaming. Roebuck was peculiar and unorthodox, and that made him an easy target. His perceived enemies had influence. He broadcast opinion and judged the actions of others, thereby motivating plenty to rub their hands together at the prospect of seeing Roebuck pinned in the dock. Even the fair-minded Malcolm Speed, who was CEO of the Australian Cricket Board, admits the shellacking Roebuck had dished out in print to him and his organisation motivated feelings of distrust and dislike. 'I wasn't unhappy to read he was having a hard time of it, put it that way,' Speed says. In later years they enjoyed an odd but meaningful friendship.

After some initial angst, Roebuck's relationship with various

Australian employers remained unchanged. 'The ABC had hate mail,' Jim Maxwell recalls. 'There was a fair bit of hate mail to [ABC producer] Peter Longman and some pressure. I remember discussing it with Longy and saying, "As far as we're concerned he's doing a wonderful job for us and you have to be the judge of whether or not he's a fit and proper person." It would have been discussed up the chain, Roebuck's suitability to continue, but we stuck with him and thank goodness we did.'

Jonathan Agnew was taken aback by that decision – it confirmed in his mind Roebuck had a different relationship with Australia than with the UK. Geoff Boycott had been stood down by the BBC after a French court convicted him of assaulting a former girlfriend. Agnew was commentating for the BBC on the 2002–03 Ashes series when, driving to Adelaide, it occurred to him to tune in specifically to hear whether or not Roebuck was being used by the national broadcaster. 'In the minds of the greater population in England, who would be inclined to back Botham and Richards, his image did suffer. You can't hide the fact that there was a conviction against him and I remember being really surprised that he was on the radio. If it had have been in England, that would have been it.' Fortunately for ABC listeners it wasn't, and the wonderful rapport Agnew enjoyed on the air with Roebuck continued for years to come.

Already bruised by the Botham-led vitriol of the Somerset Affair, Roebuck was now permanently scarred. In his mind, the campaign being waged in retribution was relentless. Vic Marks listened to him detail this grievance but thought the prospect unlikely given how much time had elapsed. Marks did not want to get involved. But he does remember his friend claiming he had been set up.

Agnew's take on the rumours and scuttlebutt were: 'Because Botham hated Roebuck with a passion, there was always a danger that what you heard might have come from Botham. There would have been that thought in the back of my mind, that he was being smeared. When Botham falls out with somebody, he falls out. It's like him and Ian Chappell … they never say a word. Have you seen Chappell and Botham together? It's dreadful, it's horrid, and it's pathetically childish on both parts frankly. I mean, for god's sake, but that's the level to which Botham does take a falling out.'

Roebuck confided in Harsha Bhogle, sitting him down, pouring out his unhappiness and distress at the court's finding, and laying the blame with his enemy Botham. 'He thought Ian Botham was behind it all,' says Bhogle. 'He said, "I think I know Botham is behind it and they're trying to trouble me." And I thought: here is the irrational side to an intensely rational thinker. I didn't tell anybody, I didn't let it colour my feelings on Peter. He was very convinced that the court case and the actions against him were instigated by a group close to Ian Botham.'

Mike Coward was also privy to Roebuck's concerns at the time, being a genuine confidante who held and retained an awareness of Roebuck's vulnerabilities. Their exchanges took place well out of the public glare and revealed a plaintive, embattled state. 'In conversations he made it clear to me that he was deeply hurt by what happened in England and was consumed by an overwhelming sense of injustice,' says Coward. 'He had been misunderstood and had received the wrong legal advice to the charges brought against him. He regretted taking the advice to plead guilty. He believed forces opposed to him during the tumultuous period at Somerset years earlier were behind this attempt to bring him down. He made it patently clear to me that he would never again go through such an ordeal.'

Roebuck now saw the vengeful hand of Botham in every shadow. Irrespective of its veracity, this reckoning of conspiracy would consume him. Towards the very end of his life, as the hours counted down to his untimely demise, he posted what proved to be a final, pithy summation that was guilty of the very charge he knocked Botham for all those years before: 'Am not perfect but think the good outweighs the bad.' Simplistic in expression, jarringly sad given what was to unfold, it seemed to grasp at accounting for a life that preached and practised so generously a noble path but delivered evidence at times of something less worthy.

Ultimately Botham could be convinced that his youthful transgressions paled in the face of extraordinary philanthropic and sporting accomplishments. He could point to his great deeds. He is a knight of the realm. In the immediate aftermath of being accused of his most serious transgression, Roebuck turned away from the world.

5

A UNIQUE VOICE

'Ignoring blatant threats, bullying, misuse of funds,
unlawful procedures, naked racism, intimidation
of critics and so on and so forth – all the ghastly
weapons of the all-consuming state.'

– Roebuck on Zimbabwe, *ESPN Cricinfo*, April 2008

Of the many pieces that constituted the Roebuck puzzle, his innate skill with the pen divides opinion least. 'He had a felicity with language,' says Rohit Brijnath, 'an ability to write these beautifully sharp, cogent sentences, an ability in two sentences to capture something profound, an ability to capture an essence of players, people and places.'

Peter Lalor of the *Australian*, not drawn to Roebuck socially, was nonetheless another admirer of his written work. 'He would never look like he was watching the cricket that much,' says Lalor. 'He would cock one eye at it and then somehow have this amazing analysis. He was a beautiful writer, had a real poetry to it, and he wrote quickly.'

There is a view, expressed most freely among members of the English press corps to which he once belonged, that things changed. 'I believe he was one of the most gifted writers on cricket there has ever been,' Engel says of the younger Roebuck, 'but he lost something along the way.' Engel describes Roebuck's 2004 autobiography as nothing short of a cry for help. 'When I review books I try to find whatever good I can. But I can't explain how someone who wrote *Slices of Cricket* and *It Never Rains* could have produced something that had he been married, it's the sort of thing a wife would say, "Very nice dear, now put it away and let's forget all about it – with luck you'll feel better." Because that's what it is. I couldn't recommend it to anyone.'

Scyld Berry agrees on the matter of the younger Roebuck's output. 'What wonderful humour in his earlier writing, when he was young and innocent and the world was fresh, as witty as any cricket writing has been. He had insights like nobody else has had ... insights of a poet.' But Berry, like Engel, believes he saw Roebuck change: 'A bit like John Arlott, Roeby didn't like equals. He and Roeby liked acolytes or worshippers. I would criticise him, tell him where he'd gone wrong. He didn't want anyone in his life doing that.'

Roebuck's work was assessed more critically by those of his native land than elsewhere. While this was perhaps influenced by his decision to disavow himself of England, those who had known Roebuck in his first incarnation were unarguably in a position to observe him over a fuller length of time. It is also a matter of fact that they were observing the work of an opinion writer whose outlook changed as he himself changed his physical and, consequently, his philosophical position. As for the view that the quality of his work diminished, English writers are not alone. As demand for his work grew, and perhaps because his non-cricket commitments were doing likewise, Roebuck overcommitted. When he should have been downsizing, according to Gideon Haigh, he headed in the opposite direction.

'He was writing, always writing, for someone, somewhere,' says Haigh. 'Was he hiding behind his writings? I think we all do that to a degree. In Peter's case, though, there was something compulsive about his industry.'

India, with its ever-growing cricket market, was part of the problem according to Harsha Bhogle. 'Towards the end I think he wrote too much,' says Bhogle. 'He tried too hard to be a big name in India. Everything you opened there was Peter Roebuck.' It is not an unfair comment; Roebuck's observations and judgements could be found in the *Hindu*, in *Sportstar* magazine and, earlier, on Rediff.com and in *India Today*.

Yet throughout he was capable of capturing a moment: 'Glenn McGrath looks like a monk, periodically behaves like an enraged chook and bowls like a Swiss clock.' Of Pakistan's Shoaib Akhtar he suggested: 'He belongs to the wild and woolly school of pace bowling. Those expecting him to spend time drinking milkshakes and visiting libraries are doomed to a life of disappointment.'

And, just two weeks before his death, a column in praise of the appointment of John Inverarity as Australia's chief selector began: 'Silver-haired, sagacious, serious but not solemn, ancient yet modern, steeped in the game but much else besides, a leader but not a ruler, Inverarity is a superb choice ...' Whatever the overreach and overexposure, Roebuck at his best was a glorious wordsmith.

This was evident in his first book, 1982's *Slices of Cricket*. Comprising a series of essays and character studies, it appeared when Roebuck was barely halfway into his first-class career.

Then, in 1984, came *It Never Rains*, his diary of a county cricketer's season. Compiled during the tail end of Somerset's glory years, it was as groundbreaking as it was well timed, for he shared a dressing room with three of the world's greats – Botham, Richards, Garner – and the book made for fascinating and intimate reading, at once a glimpse into the author's own fragile psyche and a study of superstar sportsmen whose qualities and peccadilloes were dealt with in equal measure.

It Never Rains remains striking for its insights into the author/cricketer's late-season psychological meltdown. In late July of 1983, the summer that he kept his diary, Roebuck revealed:

> Almost every season I sink into a trough of despondency which lasts sometimes a week, sometimes a day.
> For some reason I seem unable to last from April to September without a bout of morose self-examination. I can sense a growing upheaval within and I'm afraid it will not easily be stilled.

The downward spiral, he explained, usually coincided with poor form, though not on this occasion. 'And yet,' he forebodingly conceded, 'it is building.' It seemed tied to an innate sense of worthlessness, an inexplicable yet very real pessimism to do with self-identity and his effect on others: 'It still seemed a worthless existence, an empty experiment with a character which did nothing for teammates and ignored the acres of ability which could contribute something more constructive.'

The malaise occurred during a stretch of nine days on the road and away from home. 'Most bad things that happen to a cricket team happen on away trips,' he observed. In the middle of four days of cricket against Lancashire, he climbed into his car on a Sunday evening and in torrential rain resolved to head for home. Not far down the M6 motorway, realising the 'senselessness of it all', he stopped at a service station and rang his sometime unofficial counsellor at Somerset, Jock 'Falstaff' McCombe. Whatever was conveyed was taken seriously enough for McCombe to leave Taunton and head north, arriving at the team hotel shortly before midnight. The pair talked into the early hours. The book's account for the following day reads:

Monday 1 August
No entry.

Roebuck subsequently reconstructed that unrecorded Monday, noting the purpose of the book was to 'fully reflect my experiences as a cricketer'. The next day, after consulting with Viv Richards ('He was impressive, finding words and ideas to match his passion') and Vic Marks ('We agreed that not only should I retire but he should, too!'), equilibrium was restored. Ultimately Roebuck concluded that 'what I had lacked had been that sardonic sense of humour which offers a shield against the severest blows'.

The authors sought guidance from a Melbourne-based member of the Australian Psychoanalytical Society. It was suggested to us that Roebuck, during this period, was struggling to maintain not only his usual functioning but also his characteristic persona of control. The threat of lack of control, perhaps primarily of his innermost feelings, was looming.

The question as to what he perceived as 'the severest blows', and whether they related to cricket's demands or to something deeply personal, is unanswerable, although cricket was pressing down on him: 'I've dedicated myself to being good at cricket and simply cannot do it, which is immensely frustrating. What's more, in my efforts to succeed I become irritable and tense, characteristics I rarely show in my winter's teaching in Australia.'

The security of a career in the law had been forsaken for a game played in full public view. And he was – in his mind – failing. Few such raw first-person accounts of a sportsman's inner life can ever have been committed to print. Neil Burns read the book well before becoming a teammate of Roebuck's, when he was a cricket-obsessed youngster. 'Over the last thirty years I've come to see what a good book it was,' he says. 'But as a young schoolboy dreaming about becoming a professional cricketer I did find it quite a strange book. Perhaps he wasn't as good a cricketer as he wanted to be and the game was some form of torture, whereas writing and broadcasting gave him more of a platform to be exceptional.'

A future England captain in Michael Atherton was also reading him. 'I remember reading his early books,' says Atherton, 'and thinking there's not many people around who can write like this.'

Whatever torture showed in Roebuck's writing, he wrote with authority and wry humour. While still in mid-cricket career he sent letters signalling his availability to England's competing cricket magazines: the long-running *Cricketer* and David Frith's more recent creation, *Wisden Cricket Monthly*. Frith was aware of Roebuck's early forays into writing and was impressed. 'I grabbed him as I recognised he was no ordinary writer.'

Later Frith would invite Roebuck to write a foreword to his remarkable tome on cricketers who have committed suicide, *By*

His Own Hand. 'I thought there's no one better than this chap,' says Frith, 'because he has written about his dark days, where he has been seriously perturbed, and although he says he's through it and there'll be no return to those dark times, here is a thinking man who will probably do the foreword proud.'

Frith's work was published in 1991. Roebuck's contribution addressed, among other observations, the notion that he, too, might one day join the ranks of those whose fates were catalogued. 'Since *It Never Rains* some people have predicted a gloomy end for this writer,' wrote Roebuck. 'One colleague said so to my face in 1986. It will not be so. The art is to find other things which matter just as much, which stretch you just as far.'

When Frith updated the book a decade later, he sought a fresh interpretation for the new edition and invited Mike Brearley to contribute a new foreword. 'Roebuck and I weren't talking anymore,' says Frith. 'I'd see him in the pressbox and he was a changed man. He not only belonged to the *Cricketer* but he was on the escalator, moving fast, writing for newspapers in more than one country.'

He'd pitched his services to the *Sydney Morning Herald* as an occasional columnist, and by the Ashes summer of 1986–87 he had engineered a six-month contract with the Fairfax chain of papers, thus becoming a summer staple in Australia's two biggest cities via the *Herald* and the *Age*. He also wrote an old-style tour account of that summer's Test series, *Ashes to Ashes*, his fourth book. For those who would later pour scorn on his conversion to all things Australian, a gentle reminder from within its dusty pages might suffice as a rejoinder: 'Melbournians have a reputation for surliness. Though the streets are wide to accommodate the trams which still breeze through it, though the city itself appears to be interesting, the people are reputed to be pale, wasted and dreary. Experiences so far support this traditional view.'

He was the third cricket contributor for Fairfax, joining reporter Mike Coward and columnist Bill 'Tiger' O'Reilly. A couple of years on, when the legendary and irascible old leg-spinner O'Reilly penned his last column, Roebuck was perfectly placed to succeed him. 'He was the only person,' says Scyld Berry, 'who could step into Tiger's shoes and do even better.' It was not an inheritance Roebuck took lightly; he rated O'Reilly and Harold Larwood as the two greatest cricketers he had met.

Coward and Roebuck would soon become friendly rivals when the former took on a columnist's role at the *Australian*. Whatever rivalry existed, Coward had the deepest respect for his opposite number: 'At his best he was a great writer who had a large and loyal following.' It was a head-to-head contest between two men of exquisite writing skill, one a former player, the other a career journalist. If there was either advantage or impediment in this for Roebuck, according to Coward he claimed neither. 'He did not like me saying that as a columnist he came from a playing background whereas I came from a journalism background,' Coward recalls. 'He refused to accept the distinction. But to me who had acted as a copyboy and a cadet before becoming a fully-fledged journalist the distinction was obvious.'

Roebuck's difference and talent were now on full view in Australia, at a time when some would say his work was at its best. The by-product of a radio career came later. Not well known is the fact that Roebuck had been heard in Australia during an iconic cricketing moment four years before that door opened. Long-time *Test Match Special* producer Peter Baxter had eyed Roebuck as a possible ball-by-ball commentator, and he had done some occasional work in England. Baxter subsequently realised Roebuck's real talent was as a summariser and employed him in that role for the BBC's coverage of the 1987 World Cup final at Eden Gardens, which was also carried by the ABC. As a commentary change was being effected in an overmanned, undersized Kolkata box, with Henry Blofeld struggling to shoehorn himself into the commentator's seat, the first ball of an Allan Border over just happened to be the delivery that cajoled Mike Gatting into a moment of reverse-sweeping madness. The dismissal to which England's failure to win the World Cup would be largely attributed was thus broadcast by Roebuck. It would be some time before an Australian audience heard his voice again.

As well as being a long-time regular in the media gallery, Jim Maxwell was an old boy of Cranbrook, so he and Roebuck had a connection beyond cricket. In late 1991 he invited Roebuck to join him for a commentary stint during a Sheffield Shield match. It was a masterstroke; Roebuck's knowledge of the game and powers of communication were immediately apparent. With India due for a five-Test series and a World Cup to follow, a packed broadcasting schedule lay ahead. Come the first Test in Brisbane, Roebuck was part of the team as a couple-of-times-a-day contributor. Initially a casual arrangement, it would continue for twenty years.

Maxwell takes pride in the recruitment of Roebuck, whose death, he admits, left a void unfilled to this day. 'He has been hard to replace.' Like others who worked with Roebuck, Maxwell appreciated his breadth. 'He could talk about anything in an analytical and informative way. You could throw him a line, not knowing what was going to happen. The one I always remember is when I said, "What is it like to be an Australian?" There was a pause. Then he said, "Being an Australian is sitting up the front in a taxi." I thought it was a great line.'

There was, though, a faintly uneasy attitude towards the newcomer among one or two team members. Perhaps it was based on old-school values. Roebuck had not played Test cricket. He was a Pom. And he was … different.

'He forgot all about the animosity between us,' Frith recalls, 'by approaching me at the Gabba one day and saying he was doing a book on great innings. He knew I'd written a book on Archie Jackson and could I tell him about Archie's 164 on Test debut in 1928–29? I said, "Sure, even better, I know the book is in the office here", so I went down, got the book and handed it to him. He beavered at it all day, gave it back to me, may have said thanks but certainly didn't give any acknowledgement in his book for the research on the Jackson innings, any more than he thanked anyone else for their help on all of the other innings he wrote about. And I thought this is a selfish man, a man who is not as intelligent as I thought he was, and it was plain rude.'

Agnew remembers a BBC and ABC social get-together during an Adelaide Test when Roebuck, unusually, joined them. 'We were in a tavern,' says Agnew. 'Peter was opposite me and Caroline Short, who was the Radio 5 Live producer, was on my right. Peter got involved in one his typical hand-waving, full-on emotional discussions, probably about nothing very important, and he's hit a carafe of red wine that's gone straight over Caroline. I mean, all down her. He didn't flinch … he did not even blink. Didn't look at her, didn't wring his hand. Just carried on, completely ignoring the chaos that's going on. Caroline got up, I got up, there's red wine everywhere and he didn't even notice. I thought that was extraordinary. I'm not sure what it tells you except that most people wouldn't behave like that.'

Numerous others who worked with Roebuck over the years have their own stories. Yet many of these same people were fond of him and would regard his behaviour as not so much rude in the conventional sense, more that of a person strangely detached from life's normal polite transactions.

Since the retirement of Alan McGilvray the ABC's radio coverage had lacked a centre of gravity. By contrast, TV's Nine network had former national captains Richie Benaud, Ian Chappell and Bill Lawry, with Tony Greig and a galaxy of stars in support, thus combining star factor with the highest authority in the land. Among ABC staffers there was now a view that Roebuck was bringing an elusive X-factor to their coverage. True, he had not played at the highest level, but his articulateness and expanse of knowledge made him like no other 'expert' the ABC had ever employed. He had a big-picture view of the game's place in the world and a surgical ability to dissect its issues. His commentary elevated the discussion of cricket on the ABC. Colleagues could bounce ideas off him, challenge his opinions with their own, and discuss the game and its players in a way that was never predictable or boring. Also, he had an astute ability to manage the potential conflict of interest inherent in serving two major employers. He could cover the news issues of the day skilfully on radio then come up with a newspaper angle fresh enough to have the broadcasters kicking themselves for not having thought of raising it.

Nor was he about to defect. A Test cap was a prerequisite, and Test captaincy desirable, for inclusion on Nine's team. A Pom who had not risen beyond county cricket other than captaining a national 'A' team to defeat against the Netherlands would not rate a second thought. At any rate, Roebuck had little interest in commercial TV's lure, once writing of those within it: 'These people know where their bread is jammed.' As a matter of course he refused all pre-recorded TV interviews, even for the ABC, because he was not prepared to put his words in the unpredictable hands of editors.

Roebuck's radio work put him in the mainstream. The Fairfax broadsheets and the ABC have long served a particular market in Australia – generally regarded as the elite end – but cricket broadens the national broadcaster's listenership like few other of its services. Roebuck now crossed demographic divides. If he was different, it was a difference that made him compelling listening. 'He was insightful, always had something interesting to say, thought-provoking, with a twang of humour and I relished working with him,' Agnew says.

According to Haigh, Roebuck's radio work eventually outstripped his writing. 'The best of Peter in later years was on the ABC. His mind was so fertile and his delivery so felicitous.' Mike Coward saw it the other way: 'I thought Peter a better writer than broadcaster.'

As with his writing, Roebuck's broadcasting caused an Anglo-Australian polarisation. His commentary was attacked for its anti-English tone and increasingly Australian sound. Those who had known him first as an Englishman swore to hearing an audible metamorphosis. To Matthew Engel it was shamelessly contrived: 'A mature adult, whose accent would fly all over the place while on air … He would adopt this completely fake Australian accent and sometimes there was some South African in there as well. I can only take it as a sign of great insecurity.

He was a brilliant broadcaster ... But you don't hear Christopher Martin-Jenkins or Jonathan Agnew breaking into Strine because they're broadcasting a series [in Australia].'

As for Frith, he readily admits he did not like the sound of Roebuck's voice anyway. 'I'm perhaps in the minority,' he says, 'because I'm well aware that right across Australia he was a very popular performer. Maybe I'm being too severe on him, but he had a dark voice, a creepiness, and I'm not being wise after the event. It perturbed me.'

And there were others, Frith recalls, who felt the Aussie Pete thing was a bit much. 'I remember David Gower having a chip at him, saying "You think you're Australian now do you?"'

Roebuck's robust views, in print and the electronic media, on big issues made him the most influential commentator during one of Australian cricket's greatest eras. It is easy to imagine such a figure being derided as an Aussie-bashing Pom, but that was rarely if ever Roebuck's style. As his English critics noted, he championed the Australian way and reserved his most trenchant criticism for the players of his native land.

'If you read some of the things he wrote about the English team, of which I was a part, there was an undercurrent of dissatisfaction,' says Atherton, who came to the view that Roebuck suffered a form of global identity crisis. 'Part of that, I felt, was because of his relationship with England. It didn't seem like a straightforward relationship to me. He quickly picked up an Australian accent and referred to us as "Poms".'

This view of Roebuck – the disenchanted Brit who could barely find a kind word to say about England – was widely held among the English press. Rob Steen, while suggesting it was a relationship breakdown to which both parties contributed, thinks many of his colleagues were unforgiving. 'Some of the stuff he wrote about English cricket really pissed off a lot of English writers,' says Steen. 'I could see where he was coming from, to be honest, but most of my peers didn't feel the same way. The distance between him and England became huge. I think he resented the old world, the old life, and he resented a lot of the cricket writers. And there was probably resentment coming back from over here because he had attained this position as the voice of cricket.'

Over twenty years Frith witnessed what he saw as a growing sense of hubris:

> He was no longer shy and withdrawn, he wore that ridiculous great straw hat, he offended old-timers like me by standing up in the pressbox and you couldn't see the play. So suddenly this innocent young fellow, who as a teenager had been standing at the crease, playing for Somerset seconds and looking like a question mark with his curved spine and straight legs ... he was no longer someone one felt sorry for or supportive of. I began to resent his very presence because he wasn't being very nice to some of us. The ambition was beginning to stick out of every aperture.

Australian players and media colleagues were inclined to see things differently. The younger incarnation of Roebuck was unknown to them and, besides, he was frequently pointing out that his adopted country was his preferred option. Not that he shied away from identifying its shortcomings. But he did so with a sense of ownership. 'Australia has many fine people and fine things,' he declared in a 2010 column, 'not least the ability to get on with life come hell or high water and look every man in the eye. However, our country also has a dark side that includes a racism that cannot be denied and a fondness for grog that goes beyond taste.'

One Australian player with whom he forged a connection was his ex-teammate Steve Waugh. As the young all-rounder struggled to cope with his premature elevation to the national team, Roebuck remained an ally. As early as the opening Test of Australia's 1988–89 series against West Indies, with his maiden century still half a year away, Roebuck said in answer to a question about Waugh's ability, 'I think he's a great player.' The admiration was mutual.

'There was only one journalist I read,' says Waugh. 'I would always read his articles because it was one way of actually learning about my own game and captaincy. I didn't always agree with it but if he said it then maybe it would influence what I was doing, or I would look at other options.'

In the mid-1990s Roebuck's work took on a new force as he tackled a succession of major issues with full-frontal ferocity. The first occurred in the summer of 1995–96 when Sri Lanka's rubbery-jointed off-spinner, Muttiah Muralitharan, announced himself to Australian crowds. On the opening day of the second Test, Murali was no-balled by umpire Darrell Hair and the repercussions continue to bedevil cricket twenty years later.

The physically imposing and opinionated Hair had officiated at the Singer Trophy tournament in Sharjah a couple of months earlier. Along with fellow umpires Nigel Plews and Steve Dunne, he expressed concern at Muralitharan's action to International Cricket Council (ICC) referee Raman Subba Row. Subsequently,

Hair was in the middle while Murali bowled in a World Series one-dayer on 21 December at the SCG. He took no action. Now, on Boxing Day at the MCG, Australian cricket's day of the year, he called Muralitharan seven times during his fourth, fifth and sixth overs. Many Australian cricket watchers believed Murali's action was dubious and felt Hair acted courageously. But Roebuck, who had previously held Hair's umpiring in considerable esteem, saw it differently. His front-page commentary the next day implied grandstanding on Hair's part: 'Perhaps Hair has been brave. But his action was also public and certain to catch headlines. Some men like to wear their courage on their sleeves.' In the same article, Roebuck's criticism of administrators contained no such qualification:

> Cricket has permitted the public humiliation of a player. Indeed it was almost an execution. It is not a performance I'd care to witness again. There is no sport in it ... and it was not done quietly, in some hallowed corner of cricket officialdom, with the senior men of the International Cricket Council studying film and gravely reaching their verdict. It was done, instead, in front of a crowd of 55,239 on the first day of a match scheduled to last five. It was done when he [Murali] was playing for his country. It was done in a foreign land.

Roebuck's suggestion that dubious bowling actions should be dealt with away from the gaze of a crowd foreshadowed precisely what would follow. That this has enabled suspect bowlers to proliferate, only adding ambiguity to matters, is hard to dispute. But Roebuck stuck to his guns. In a 2010 tribute to Murali he wrote: 'Unsurprisingly, and despite hoots from the old guard, cricket went in search of a better way of dealing with throwing, long its thorniest issue, and emerged with a process as opposed to devastating rejection.'

Roebuck made a bigger call. Such indignities, he stated, were more likely to be inflicted on coloured players. To those who honestly believed Murali stretched the law, this was highly inflammatory. 'He was telling the world the ICC has got it in for Asian chuckers,' Frith says. 'He played years and years of first-class cricket but you don't need to have played first-class cricket to realise Muralitharan threw the ball.'

The question of Murali's world-record 800 Test wickets will be argued over for decades. Whatever one's view, though, the bowler and Roebuck found backing from the game's most powerful ally. Late in his life, the man who had counselled Australian umpires to act on chuckers in late 1963, shortly before umpire Col Egar's call ended Ian Meckiff's career, put himself in Muralitharan's corner. 'I believe Hair's action – in one over – took the development of world cricket back by ten years,' said Sir Donald Bradman. 'For me, this was the worst example of umpiring that I have witnessed, and against everything the game stands for. Clearly Murali does not throw the ball.'

Another cause to stir some of Roebuck's most provocative commentary was player remuneration; he had been a professional cricketer and was proud of it. So passionate was Roebuck's crusade on the Australian players' behalf during their 1997–98 pay dispute that he mounted a blistering attack on Australian cricket's two senior administrators. One of his many columns on the subject demanded that Denis Rogers, the chairman, and Malcolm Speed, the CEO, both resign. Speed, who had picked up the reins only a few months earlier, was shocked: 'I hadn't met him, didn't know him, he was Sydney-based, I was Melbourne-based, but he attacked the board's position, criticised me, criticised the chairman, in typical Peter Roebuck fashion where he didn't hold back. It was a very bitter attack.' So much so that the Australian Cricket Board gave serious consideration to a defamation action.

A barrister turned career sports administrator, Speed says that while pursuing such an action would not have been wise, Roebuck's commentary was 'over the top. He was often over the top. We were upset about it, Denis in particular, Bob Merriman in particular. We had some good advice about it from a very well-regarded QC who said if you can prove these things are untrue there's a defamation action.'

Curiously, at a later date Roebuck chanced upon Speed and his wife and greeted them effusively. And when Speed in his role as ICC chief executive butted heads with recalcitrant cricket chiefs over the Zimbabwe issue, Roebuck was firmly in his corner. 'Of the contemporary writers when I was involved,' says Speed, 'Peter and Christopher Martin-Jenkins stood out as the two I would go out of my way to read. Peter had a great understanding of the social setting of cricket.'

One of his journalistic strengths was an imperviousness to the reaction that unflinching commentary could provoke. 'I follow the Bill O'Reilly school of thought,' he wrote, 'which is not to cross paths with players, umpires or officials. It's not my job to be popular with them and I write to the game and not to them.'

A memorable instance of his indifference to backlash occurred in early 2007 when Michael Clarke returned from a New Zealand tour to attend to his troubled relationship with enfant terrible Lara Bingle. At that stage the pair were engaged, their partnership disintegrating under the public's gaze. Bringing the approach of an agony aunt to a highly conspicuous real-life situation, Roebuck maintained that Clarke, Ricky Ponting's deputy at the time, would have to rid himself of Bingle if he were to ever captain Australia. That same morning, Roebuck phoned a former colleague and inquired as to his view of the column. When it was put to Roebuck that what he'd written was unlikely to be well received by feminist readers, or by women generally, he was completely unfussed. He said he was well acquainted with a couple of Bondi shop owners who had made their opinion of Bingle clear to him and he had, therefore, no qualms about his assessment of her.

Roebuck's sources always were a matter of mystery, typically spoken of with an enigmatic gleam in his eye. There were clearly some good ones and they were not run of the mill. 'I remember he sat me down at the Madras Cricket Club in Chennai,' says Harsha Bhogle, 'and told me about match-fixing. He told me about bookmakers in Dubai, and Azharuddin, and offers made to various people, who was clean and who wasn't. I said, "Peter, how do you know all this?" He just said he knew. I put it at the back of my mind.'

That was in 1998. Roebuck initiated another intriguing conversation just as that match in Chennai was beginning.

Tim Lane recalls:

It was the first time ABC radio had broadcast a Test series from India and it was done on a shoestring budget. Jim Maxwell was technician as well as lead commentator, while our analysts were Roebuck and Coward whose travel was funded by their respective newspaper chains. As for Jim's sidekick, he didn't even have his own clothing, my bag having mistakenly remained in Kuala Lumpur after the first leg of our flight from Sydney.

That first morning was steamy at Chidambaram Stadium and the box provided to the ABC lacked the usual sense of organisation we were accustomed to. There were problems before a ball was bowled. India won the toss and making their way out to the middle were the openers, Navjot Sidhu and Nayan Mongia, with me straining to work out which was which, under their helmets, and Roebuck perched next to me while we awaited our cue, Maxwell standing in a corner with a mobile phone to one ear, ready to deliver us a theatrical flourish upon being given the word from ABC master control in Sydney.

In my mind was, I think, a piece of advice given to me in my earliest days of broadcasting: never treat a microphone as if it is anything other than 'live'. But Roebuck chatted.

Roebuck: It's a murky world, Tim.

Lane: What ...

Roebuck: ... also needs to be ... have his [a senior Indian player] name cleared. It'd be a very good thing if there was a proper investigation of all these matters in both countries.

Lane: Jeez ...

Roebuck: Interesting, isn't it?

Lane: Mmm.

Roebuck: Thousand rumours. But they ... you must have proper police investigations. The whole bloody trouble with all of these things in the first place is there's been no proper police investigations. There's just one now in Pakistan.

Lane: Yeah, yeah, plainly. I heard a referee who was in Australia recently was questioning an umpire ... an umpire's integrity. Won't name him into the microphone.

Roebuck: No, no quite.

Only later in the day, when instructions arrived that an on-air apology be made, did we become aware of what had transpired – our conversation, which began with Roebuck suggesting Mongia was a player under suspicion, had gone live to parts of regional Australia. Three days later our exchange was detailed, under a headline 'Caught Napping', in the *Indian Express* with the name of a senior player deleted. The senior player was Mohammad Azharuddin, who would be banned for life by the ICC and BCCI in December 2000 – nearly three years after Roebuck accidentally named him on air. Mongia was named in the report by India's Central Bureau of Investigation which led to the ban, accused of assisting Azharuddin. Roebuck was way ahead of the curve.

Ian Chappell used to share observations and information with Roebuck on match-fixing and believes he knew more than most. 'Occasionally I'd throw out a name to him and see what bounced back,' says Chappell. 'He had contacts ... he was the original font of information. He knew quite a lot about fixing and I was never in any doubt that if I asked him a direct question I'd get a direct answer.'

Greg Baum thinks Roebuck's writing attracted information that remained inaccessible to most. 'For a guy who didn't easily make acquaintanceships even,' says Baum, 'he always seemed to have a lot of people around him, or going to him. And that can only be because of the power of his writing, the power of his commentary.' Perhaps it was also due to the impression of courage and morality that lay within both his print and broadcast work.

Roebuck was staunchly supportive of the investigative efforts by India's police and outraged at the Clouseau-like image attached to them by the western press. This lined up with his view of cricket's imperial establishment nations and their supposedly racist underbelly. While he may sometimes have been prone to hyperbole on such matters, in India he was greatly admired and appreciated.

'Very few western writers took the time to understand India and its cricket,' says Rohit Brijnath. 'Because Peter went to small towns, because he spoke to everybody – not just journalists – because he listened to people on the street ... he ate the dust of India.' Thus, says Brijnath, any criticism by Roebuck of Indian players or administrators was perceived as being without agenda and carried a weight virtually no other western writer achieved.

Roebuck's writing about India and its place in the game had bigger influence than perhaps even he realised. The great batsman Rahul Dravid tells of the anticipation he felt as a youngster waiting for Roebuck's next piece to appear in *Sportstar*. 'I had read what Peter had written before I got the chance to meet him,' Dravid recalls. 'Growing up and reading some of his books and articles it was like – "Wow" – he was a phenomenal writer. One of the things which attracted Indians and Sri Lankans to him was you suddenly felt there was fairness in his writing about the subcontinent.'

However well intentioned his support of Asian teams, it is generally felt that in January 2008 Roebuck went too far. His call for Ponting to be sacked as Australian captain following a bitterly fought Test against India in Sydney was largely seen by his closest colleagues as a misjudgement. Coward puts it in the category of Roebuck's 'pompous and needlessly provocative' moments. This was a match in which anger and taunting went both ways and an accurate apportioning of responsibility remains difficult. The Australians, claiming Harbhajan Singh racially insulted Andrew Symonds on the third day, lodged a report. As the off-field dispute escalated after the match India threatened to abandon the tour.

What remains undisputed is that in the heat of the moment, Ponting's Australians reacted aggressively. 'We play a hard game, but when someone plays a hard game against us we're inclined not to like it,' Allan Border noted afterwards. Tension ran high on the final day as the home team pressed vigorously for victory; too vigorously, in Roebuck's estimation. Labelling it 'a rotten contest', he accused Ponting and his team of abrogating 'justice and fair play'.

The day after, he went further. 'Arrogant Ponting Must Be Fired' was the front-page headline. It became a huge national story. As Australian as Roebuck might have wished to be, he was now judged by many on the premise that he was a 'bloody Pom'. The story quickly became one about the writer and his agenda. More than 50,000 responses appeared by the end of the day the article was published, with around 60% of respondents supporting Roebuck.

Yet many of his colleagues, admirers among them, took the view that it was far from his finest journalistic hour. 'I was very surprised,' says Harsha Bhogle. 'My first instinct was: is it just to arouse attention? Using that to present a completely contrarian point of view?' Agnew was one who applauded Roebuck's bravery: 'I sent him an email. I really admired him for doing that. He might have been wrong, or right, but he had the guts to do it.'

Steve Waugh, who admits to taking notice of Roebuck even when he made for uncomfortable reading, believes it to be a rare error. 'I think the morning after he wrote that he would have realised that he went too far,' says Waugh. 'At the time, he would have been emotional and upset about certain things that happened in the game and knowing Peter he would have said, "Right, that's it! I've had enough of this – it's gone too far." And he would have written it, filed it and then thought, "Hang on, what have I done here?" I think it's the only time I ever saw him apologise or backtrack in subsequent articles.'

Three days later, Roebuck wrote:

> Time to shake the tree. Sacking the captain was the only
> story remotely dramatic enough to bring everything
> out into the open ... Of course the players were angry,
> even shocked. Some of the column was too forceful.
> The comparison with wild dogs was unfair. Just that I
> have six dogs in Africa, likeable canines until they form
> a hunting pack. The reaction was startling, phones
> ringing, offers of money to go on television, threats,
> compliments. But the journalist is not the story.

Perhaps it sounds feeble. Yet some who worked with him over time were familiar with the theme: what he committed to paper, he often said, was his opinion at that moment. It might shift, it might change, but that was what he felt when he wrote the words.

While Ian Chappell could not agree with Roebuck over Ponting, he did feel his point of view was inevitably worthwhile. 'I always found it interesting to go and talk to Peter if there was a subject of controversy or conjecture. Peter so often came at it from a different angle.'

Lalor is critical not just of the original column – 'He didn't express himself very well in that article and there was a lack of conviction about it' – but of Roebuck's handling of the fallout. 'He didn't get out and defend ... He ducked and weaved, which I think was pretty poor. He hid in his bedroom and wouldn't take calls. If you're going to get out on the front foot with that sort of stuff you've got to stand by it. He threw a match and then ran away.'

The episode was a rare questioning of Roebuck's journalistic courage. He was not, though, seen as beyond reproach on some other basics of the trade. The post-stumps media conference, for example – Roebuck spurned them. 'It's fairly consistent with players turned correspondents: they don't do interviews,' says Rob Steen. 'He, out of all of them, went down the psychological road, he wanted to burrow into people's minds, but he wasn't talking to people. Maybe there was a lack of comfort in one-to-one situations – who knows? I don't know how he justified it.'

Roebuck's justification lay in his adherence to the Bill O'Reilly line: he chose to remain at arm's length and not cross paths with the players. 'He didn't go to press conferences and ask questions; he operated from a higher plane in a way,' says Lalor. 'And that was fair enough because he understood the game so well and had good contacts.'

Waugh believes Roebuck saw things, from outside the boundary, that others did not and could not see, and that his refusal to form relationships with players enabled him to write penetratingly about them. 'He would take the mask off players, their personalities, what they were really like,' says Waugh. 'He was almost too good at times, but I respected the fact that he never got too close to players so he didn't have biases. He was that one step away.'

An incident that prompted legitimate peer criticism of Roebuck was the 'dirt in the pocket' affair at Lord's. Mike Atherton, leading England in the field against South Africa, faced allegations he had sought to alter the ball's condition – Roebuck filed his copy early, not taking a major story to anywhere near its fullest extent. 'There was a sense that he was above it,' says Steen. 'He would have done his first piece around tea-time … He should've been doing a second piece after the close of play. He should have at least covered the press conference and done a rewrite of what he'd already written because that is your job.'

Atherton, too, is bemused looking back on it. 'Peter was writing for the *Sunday Telegraph* and I remember years later, because I also wrote for the *Sunday Telegraph*, the boys on the subs desk telling me that he had ducked off home at seven o'clock, leaving somebody else to pick up the pieces. It was quite a story but Peter just wrote on the game and left.'

It was not only in England that Roebuck was inclined to duck away early. 'He hated leaving the SCG at the end of the game because the traffic was so bad,' recalls former Cricinfo writer Peter English, who spent time as a boarder at Roebuck's Bondi house. 'So he left early. Sometimes very early. When I was living with him he always left one-dayers not long after the first innings. One night he arrived home in a flap because in his fifteen-minute commute the wrong team was suddenly on top. He hated refiling; this night he didn't. To his credit, he became more professional later on – and would have no problem changing one or two paragraphs before resending.'

* * *

Herein lies a curious contradiction to the perfectionism Roebuck demanded as a coach of young cricketers. Despite his early resistance to the methods of his father, he would later adopt similarly unbending standards. Geoff Lawson witnessed this on a promotional tour of Sri Lanka in the late 1990s. He and Roebuck were making up the numbers with a group of promising Sydney teenagers in a game against a local team at Kurunegala. Batting at ten and eleven, the two retired cricketers had to rescue the team, coming together with scarcely 50 runs on the board and digging in to take the total to around 120. Things followed a similar pattern in the field. The early bowlers lacked discipline and again it was left to the veterans to provide a contest. In the end the home team scrambled to victory by one wicket. Roebuck's reaction, according to Lawson, was one of bewilderment and concern. He asked Lawson for permission to address the team.

> He spoke to them harshly, but fairly it must be said; he didn't use any bad language, didn't yell, he just spoke sternly, to the point. They did not escape responsibility for what happened in the game. He was really strong on it. But it was all within a framework. It wasn't just a failure of your cricket; it was a failure of your life because cricket reflects life. One under-nineteen, who's a really good kid, ended up getting a tertiary education ... I think he said thanks to Peter at the end of it.

Whatever the relevance of this tale to later events, Roebuck clearly had a strong conviction that discipline and the correction of young people could not be adequately performed in a half-baked way. Five years after the Taunton court cause, there was a sensitive moment on air during the 2006–07 Adelaide Test. 'I was talking about Shane Warne and his pantomime dame–type appealing,' Agnew recalls. 'The umpires had a chat or something and I suggested, figuratively, that Warne would be up in the ref's office and we'd hear the swish of the cane. I didn't think anything about it. Except that he [Roebuck] was sitting on my left and I was aware of the headset going bang on the desk and him storming out. I remember thinking, what was that all about, and I spoke with someone in the box, whether it was Kerry [O'Keeffe] or Jim, and they said "Yeah, he's not happy" so I went and found him.

'And I said to him, "Peter, how long have you known me? You've known me a very long time and you know I didn't mean it like that." And he said, "But Jim has said it before and now you've said it", and I said, "I don't care – you've known me a long time and I've always supported you." He stopped for maybe three or four seconds and said "OK" and we shook hands and that was it. Never mentioned again.'

That he would so misinterpret Agnew revealed Roebuck's ongoing fragility. Yet if it showed in his work, it was usually only in an increased fervour over events that concerned him. Foremost among these was Zimbabwe. In 2010 he wrote:

Of the Zimbabweans under my roof, one was abominably tortured with 20 friends by security forces angry that they had protested food shortages, another saw his friends tortured by the youth militia because

they did not know the words of a Zanu-PF (Zimbabwe
African National Union–Patriotic Front) song, another
escaped from a house burnt down by the militia
after his father dared to stand against a government
candidate, another has recently been threatened after
criticising Mugabe. All of them have suffered family
deaths, sisters forced into prostitution, siblings unable
to obtain medicine, and so forth. All of them yearn to
go home.

He had been campaigning ferociously about Zimbabwe for
a number of years. He had the two most powerful men in that
nation's cricket administration, Peter Chingoka and Ozias Bvute,
in his sights. In his newspaper columns and online he labelled
Chingoka a drunk and a man who had corrupted his soul and
said Bvute was, if anything, worse: 'As thick as thieves with the
crooks running the country.'

Malcolm Speed remembers being shocked by these and other
claims. 'I was amazed at the allegations he was making and if
they weren't true they were clearly defamatory.' The ongoing
stream of invective so roused the Zimbabwean and South African
administrations that they urged the ICC to fund a defamation
action against Roebuck; ultimately, their request was rejected.
Speed points out that no defamation action was ever pursued.
'Peter,' he says, 'had very good sources within Zimbabwe and
South Africa about Chingoka and Bvute.'

This war was waged for what would be the last five years of
Roebuck's life. As Ian Chappell observes, 'Taking someone on in
the sporting field is not that bloody dangerous; you might create a
few enemies but they're not going to be serious enemies. But you

take on Mugabe and you don't know where that might end up.'

Roebuck the cricketer waged war every time he walked to the wicket. Struck on the head by Andy Roberts, he came back for more. He defined personal failure as the failure 'to discipline myself to concentrating every ball every season'. Against Allan Border's triumphant 1989 side, he was one of only two non-Test batsmen (Mark Nicholas was the other) with the stomach for battle to take a century off them. At Somerset in 1986 he waged war off the field and, arguably, suffered for it every day of his life thereafter. 'Under the shameless stewardship of these men the game in Zimbabwe has sunk into a pit of bullying, corruption and despair,' he wrote in late 2006. According to Darshak Mehta, his Sydney friend, Roebuck foreshadowed that these men would come for him one day.

Could that really have been so? Or was this the expression of a mind still tilting at windmills, that knew darkness of another kind, and knew that his day would eventually come anyway?

6

THE MAN WITHIN

'It's personal things that matter –
I really do want to be braver.'

– Roebuck, private correspondence, 1983

The nature of Roebuck's personal life was the elephant permanently in the room. There was about him a difference as manifest as it was indefinable. Some, on first dealings, perceived it as a darkness; for those prepared to befriend him this soon passed, to be replaced by the unpredictability, stimulation and enjoyment of working with someone who was genuinely on another plane.

The exploration that follows is unusual, intrusive. It will be painful for some, yet under the circumstances it is justifiable and necessary. It will add to the understanding of Roebuck and perhaps even elicit sympathy in quarters where sympathy did not previously exist..

Roebuck was a public figure for whom fairness on matters of race held a particular primacy. His death in the aftermath of an allegation of sexual assault upon a relatively disempowered

African male led to journalists on three continents claiming his purportedly philanthropic ventures in Africa were inspired by an ulterior motive – the sexual exploitation of those he took into his care. Many now believe this was so, some enthusiastically because they always suspected the darkness in Roebuck, others because of the circumstances of his death. There is another category, which includes friends – and family – of decades, standing, who seriously question that he could be guilty of such unprincipled behaviour. They argue the man known to them was incapable of acting as his accusers claim. If he jumped from a hotel window, they say, it would have been out of despair at his predicament, not out of shame.

Jim Maxwell was heard to say in bemusement, more than once over the years, 'Roebuck believes he's an open book …' It was a book, all in his working fraternity understood, from which only snatched glimpses were allowed, a book not to be fully opened. He was the most interesting imaginable colleague yet the most elusive on matters personal. There was a sense, without it ever being stated, that his personal space was a zone to be avoided.

Which helps explain the majority view among work colleagues: that Roebuck was a repressed homosexual. Reasons for such repression could be found in his Catholic family upbringing, strong enough for his mother to convert; in the fact that the acceptance of homosexuality remains a universally unresolved issue in men's sport; or in a particular buttoned-up Britishness. Accurate or otherwise, this presumption caused a blockage in communication. Those who would have liked to know him better suspected, even feared, that his personal life was off limits, and so it went undiscussed, danced around, in what felt like polite deference. Roebuck contributed to the stand-off. He consciously cultivated his image of the enigmatic outsider. Rohit

Brijnath, a respected fellow writer and valued friend, might be imagined to have come as close as anyone to gaining Roebuck's confidence. Yet Brijnath remained as bereft as others – and just as sure something was not quite right: 'I got a sense of a man struggling with something. There is no question in my mind.'

The leap from exceptionally private person, to single man with no apparent interest in women, to repressed homosexual was one made readily. 'I had never seen him with a partner of any type; he would come to things alone,' says Agnew. 'We all have our girlfriends or boyfriends but with Peter there didn't seem to be anything.'

Not that this proved a thing. Not that Roebuck fitted any sort of gay stereotype. John Barclay, so fond of his rival county captain, assesses Roebuck as someone who 'couldn't really see the point of women'. Barclay found his friend's likely orientation a puzzle. 'I would have to say Pete didn't really have much of a connection with women that I knew, but the many gay people I know are very comfortable around women and maintain great relationships with them – and Pete was the opposite to that.'

A more definite conclusion was drawn by the journalist Tess Lawrence, who recalled Roebuck's stunning attack on Lara Bingle the previous year. Following his death Lawrence wrote of her reaction to that Roebuck column: 'Here is a man who is afraid of women; who holds them in contempt. Who thinks they are less worthy than men ... I sensed then that this was a man who had probably never lain with a woman, nor was ever likely or wanted to. So. You win some. You lose some. To each their own or none at all. But there was an unpleasant whiff of something else.'

The context and subsequent coverage of Roebuck's death seemed to confirm the idea of a person repressed, tortured. The gay writer and broadcaster Dmetri Kakmi wrote in the weeks afterwards: 'As details about the private conduct of a very private man emerge, family and colleagues realise they did not know Roebuck at all. They say they had access to only a small part of him. That can be said about most of us; there is an inevitable disparity between private and public face. But it is especially true about the closeted homosexual who is forced to operate clandestinely under a cloud of shame and fear of exposure.'

In a tribute to Roebuck, the late Christopher Pearson, then a regular columnist for the *Australian*, reminisced fondly about contributions made to the *Adelaide Review*. Despite the yawning political divide between them, Pearson regularly hosted Roebuck in his Adelaide home during the city's annual Test match. Referring to him as a companionable friend, Pearson recalled discussions they had about Roebuck's work with young men: 'In the course of those conversations he made no attempt to conceal the fact that there was sometimes a heavily sublimated erotic element in his feelings towards his protégés.'

Roebuck, Pearson added, was 'intensely conscious that abusing a position of trust standing *in loco parentis* was a grave betrayal. That was especially the case with the ... house in Pietermaritzburg. The suggestion on some websites that it is an establishment for grooming teenagers with a view to sexual servitude strikes me as highly improbable.'

If Pearson's claim regarding a 'sublimated erotic element' is faithful, it carries with it the tone of an exchange between two men who acknowledged each other's homosexuality.

Yet there are friends outside the cricket circle, of longer standing than most who knew the Roebuck of the pressbox, who insist that not only was their friend not a predator, he wasn't gay.

Toby Jones poses the question: 'Is there anyone at Cambridge who saw Roebuck display or act upon perceived homosexual impulses? Not that I've heard. I reckon the uni environment would have been a perfect one for him to launch an experiment – away from family and cricket team.' Jones knew Roebuck from the late 1970s. He was captain of Cranbrook's rugby team and a member of its cricket team. Later, while Roebuck was still teaching at the school, Jones returned as a house tutor in the 1980s. He strenuously disagrees that his friend had a homosexual orientation.

'If Roebuck was a repressed homosexual I never saw him betray the slightest signs of physical attraction to any member of the "malestrom" over many years and in many contexts,' says Jones. 'Not fellow teachers, cricketers, students or various admirers. And I think it likely if Roebuck was gay at some stage my "gaydar" would have gone off. Surely, a blip at least.'

Fabian Muir concurs: 'I knew him all through boarding school and there were definitely a couple of tutors who batted for the other side; you just knew. But there was never that feeling with Peter. He definitely had an appreciation of female beauty.' These testimonies come from men who, as student boarders, lived, slept and showered in areas under Roebuck's watch, or, as tutors, shared sleeping and showering quarters with him. If Roebuck was one whose gaze was drawn towards teenage and/or young adult male bodies, they swear it didn't show. Roebuck spent six months a year from the late 1970s until the second half of the 1980s living in this environment. There has never been the merest hint of even a sideways glance out of place.

As for Christopher Pearson's imputation regarding a 'sublimated erotic element' to Roebuck's dealings with young men, Jones is dismissive. 'When in a bohemian moment of whimsy

Pearson purrs to Roebuck, "You know, I see in your writing an almost erotic love for young men playing cricket", Roebuck could have conceivably replied, "Yes, there may be something there" … Roebuck was a true Englishman in his ability to deliver "Yes" in that polite "Hmmm" way which really means: "You're talking bollocks but here we are, two gentleman of the intelligentsia exploring refined ideas, so I'll indulge you – briefly."'

Nevertheless, in press and broadcast boxes of both hemispheres, the speculation hummed. 'If you knew Peter,' says Agnew, 'you couldn't help but be aware of this scuttlebutt, this murmuring. If you said you're weren't aware of it, you're lying. You might not have believed it, but you'd be aware of it.'

There were believers, non-believers and abstainers. 'Well, the outside scuttlebutt was always scuttlebutt,' says Geoff Lawson, who ignored it. 'It was always rumour and innuendo. I never heard one story about him being either openly gay or in the closet. Not one. I never heard of him ever taking a woman out, not that side of gossip that you get in professional sport. There was just none.'

Rob Steen is inclined to see Roebuck as gay but trapped by an unyielding and old-fashioned culture, unable to 'come out' because the world of cricket wasn't ready. 'The idea that he was suppressed makes me incredibly sympathetic towards him,' says Steen, 'but I felt he didn't help himself.' Engel takes a nuanced view that Roebuck's sexuality, whatever it was, gave rise to a broader psychological crisis. It struck Engel that he had known many people who identified as gay, or who might have been gay but were repressed, but he did not think he had ever met someone who appeared to be so alone in life. 'I think sexuality was at the heart of this,' he says, 'and the guilt.'

'It seemed,' thinks Baum, 'to be a threshold he couldn't cross to be public about, which meant that a whole part of his life had to be more secret than the already secretive Peter Roebuck.'

No one had evidence of anything, even in whispered form, and none of it particularly mattered anyway other than to those whose minds were made up. It was just that Roebuck was single, he was different, and among his cricket media colleagues he expressed not a scintilla of interest in women. And he did seem to enjoy the company of young men.

Occasionally he would bring one of those he coached to the commentary box. It was never furtive, always upfront, and he showed absolutely no unease at whatever observations such companionship might have prompted. And of course those around couldn't help but notice. It led to curiosity and perhaps a slight wincing discomfort. But as there was no indication of anything improper, it wasn't – and nor could it have been – challenged. Disapproval could be found, though, if one went looking for it.

Jim Maxwell was aware of judgement being cast. 'The perception was that because Roebuck might sit in there [the press box] with a young person, and he wasn't married or didn't give any obvious signs he was interested in women, that he was interested in boys. My view always was that if anything stupid had occurred he'd be absolutely nailed. That's why I thought he was basically asexual, not comfortable with who he was and struggling. Some would say he should've come out of the closet but I don't think it was ever obvious.'

Maxwell was correct; it was all far from obvious. So what lay beneath the surface?

Probably only Mike Coward, among members of the Australian media, ever had a conversation with Roebuck about such personal matters. Brief and long ago as that exchange was, Coward remains clear on the message. 'The only time a conversation drifted towards emotional matters he assured me he identified as heterosexual.'

While many will be surprised by that, there are suggestions of early female connections in England and Greece. Jonathan Griffiths, a Cranbrook friend, speaks of an acquaintance in England 'who was into horses and hounds I think'. Nigel Popplewell attests: 'He was very keen on a friend of mine, Kate Buckley. He dedicated *Slices of Cricket* to about fifteen people and Buckles is mentioned. She was in London but he would enjoy her company when she came down, and my missus Ingrid and she were great mates.'

Roebuck's family have never believed their son and brother was anything other than heterosexual but say they didn't see it as important. Rosalie, his oldest sister, declares whether Peter was gay or not simply wasn't an issue. 'He was chased by a few women but cricket came first,' she says. 'In this day and age, why would he feel the need to repress it? I don't think he was gay, but if he was it wouldn't matter.' Beatrice was aware over time of young men staying at his house but saw nothing untoward in this. Neither does she have cause to believe her brother's sexuality was kept a secret. 'He tended to have young males staying in his house because they were aspiring cricketers,' she says. 'I never thought about it from any other angle: the cricket world is male and Peter's passion was cricket. It never entered my head that there weren't many women around. He was comfortable mixing with anybody.'

Roebuck himself made no secret of his enjoyment of the bonds of male company. 'Women constantly underestimate how much men like spending time together, how much they enjoy the rooms with their secrets and vulgarities and laughter, for there they feel understood and appreciated and their full selves,' he wrote in *It Takes All Sorts*.

* * *

There is, however, much more to the story. Elizabeth Roebuck talks of a young Australian woman. Her son wanted to marry the woman. He confided to his mother that he would love to get married but had seen too many divorces and broken families. He believed it was a choice between a life of cricket or a life of being a husband and father. Given the years of speculation, this is intriguing; such was Roebuck's perceived lack of interest in women, the possibility of a serious relationship remained an almost unimagined possibility to those who knew him in the world of professional cricket. Of course, his conversations with his mother could have been just something a closeted gay man would tell his committed Catholic family, something to keep them believing he was, well, on the straight and narrow ...

But it is not the only indication there had been a woman in Roebuck's life.

After Roebuck's death Fabian Muir wrote a tribute for ESPN Cricinfo. Ever since he was a child at Cranbrook, Muir had maintained an active and robust friendship with Roebuck. Once as a young student he was in Roebuck's care for an extended period. 'One holiday weekend I was the only boy left in the house,' he wrote, 'and Peter was master on duty, giving him the dubious distinction of supervising me for three days. In retrospect I think he used those days to test me.' Those tests, as Muir went on to describe, involved cricket and literature.

The adult Muir came to know his former teacher well enough that personal aspects of life were shared in their many conversations. This put him significantly closer to the man than anyone who worked with Roebuck in the world's pressboxes. In his tribute, Muir sought to answer the question that kept reappearing in the obituaries they wrote: 'Why was he a mystery to many who knew him?'

Muir wondered whether the answer was simply that, 'Experience of how the English media can handle public figures had made him build his walls a little higher, even in Australia.' Muir's experience of being taken inside those walls is one for which he feels grateful. 'There was a gate in those walls, which had only to be lightly pushed. Those who passed through it found themselves in a quite extraordinary garden, which revealed something new with each visit.' Muir wrote of their conversations through the years. More often than not the topic was not cricket. Rather they discussed literature, travel, politics. 'Sometimes,' wrote Muir, 'we talked about relationships and the beauty of Russian girls. I know of at least one woman whom Peter loved and lost.'

In an interview for this book, Muir reiterated that Roebuck was genuinely in love with her: 'He said that explicitly.'

* * *

She is out there. This is her story.

She met Peter Roebuck in Sydney in 1981 at which time she was studying at the University of New South Wales. The point of connection was her younger brother, a student and member of the cricket team at Cranbrook. The coach bonded with his players after games by inviting them to the boarding house. These gatherings were notable for Roebuck's pre-cooked stews and the wide-ranging discussions that took place. The mother of the young Cranbrook cricketer was part of a small army who helped out with catering at school sporting events. She became aware of the young English cricket coach, liked him, knew that her son liked him, so invited him to the family home for dinner.

For some time the daughter did not notice that while her parents were taking a shine to the erudite and independent-thinking young traveller, he had eyes for her. The young teacher and cricket coach – later renowned among media colleagues for a conspicuous lack of interest in women – was, in fact, smitten. He began dropping by the house. Ostensibly he was checking how the brother was faring with his studies and cricket. In reality he was seeking to better get to know the older sibling. At some point he enquired of the brother whether he thought his big sister would go out with him. There was disappointment: she had a boyfriend and the answer was no. But by the following summer she was unattached.

It perhaps says something for Roebuck's lack of confidence in such matters that things didn't exactly proceed apace. Not until the end of March 1983 did he invite the young woman to a dinner that had been organised at a favourite restaurant in Darlinghurst. The dinner was a farewell for him, the night before his return to England for the northern summer. It was in full swing when the young woman arrived and the guest of honour cleared the way for her to sit next to him at a long table. Later, when the restaurateur indicated it was time to go, they returned to her family home to continue the conversation, which entered more intimate terrain.

She explained to Roebuck that the relationship with her former boyfriend was over. 'In this ritual of talking about each other's romantic pasts,' she says, 'I have a vague memory that he talked about an English woman in Greece.' As night gave way to early morning, it came time for him to leave, go home, prepare for his flight to England. They exchanged what she describes as 'a very lovely and lingering kiss, not a sisterly kiss but a passionate kiss'. Roebuck said to her: 'I don't want to go.' But neither in the sense of them spending the rest of the night together, nor of him avoiding going to England, was that possible.

As Roebuck jetted off the next day, the young woman was writing him a letter, saying she had thought about their evening together and was interested in pursuing a relationship. In reply, Roebuck admitted he had delayed reading her letter until his various housekeeping matters were taken care of. This was a compliment. Usually he rushed the reading of letters 'amid the chaos of everyday life'. His reply was tinged with humility and deep feeling:

> It was the most warming letter I've ever received. I left Australia with immense regret – for a range of reasons, the main of which (put bluntly) was that I had for a long time wanted to get to know you better but had assumed that this was impossible. It is not often that someone for whom you have the highest regard returns that affection, and it had not really occurred to me that you might …
> You may realise that I have very little confidence in some things – which is why I have very few close friends, though those friendships will last a very long time.

The letter went on to lament a lifestyle that 'encourages a vague and drifting approach to everything' and can serve as an excuse for not daring to enter into 'warm' relationships. He expressed a feeling that he must settle, reside in the same place for a year or more, and that he felt strongly attached to Australian things, 'rather than Australia', as he put it. He added, 'Naturally the fact that you are in Australia is a major influence – though we all realise that there are no guarantees in anything.'

A full year in Australia, if this was put into effect, would mean Roebuck missing a season of county cricket. He was weighing up the life he knew, doing the one thing that truly challenged him, against the prospect of taking a risk on a relationship. It would in all probability be the most fateful decision of his life.

* * *

Julia Horne is the woman whom Peter Roebuck loved and lost.

More than thirty years later she is an academic and historian, married, with a family. Her parents, both deceased, are the aforementioned Donald Horne, father also of Nick and author of *The Lucky Country*, and his wife Myfanwy, a journalist and editor.

Donald and Myfanwy loved to entertain in their Woollahra home. Dinner parties were frequent events, with lively discussion and riotous laughter as integral to proceedings as good food and wine. The young Roebuck became a sometime attendee, capable of fuelling such cut and thrust in his inimitable way, throwing up an opinion whether he truly believed in it or not then enjoying the reaction. 'Authors, feminists, academics, Catholic priests, star journalists and editors, film critics, diplomats and visiting luminaries – my parents saw these events as vital aspects of a civilised life,' says Julia, 'a time to enjoy intelligent discussion and conviviality with space to debate opposing views. For a while Peter was part of that, and even when I was in England my mother invited him to dinner parties.'

Myfanwy liked Roebuck, seeing him as a natural fit in the Horne household. As for Donald, the idea of his daughter forming a relationship with a young man of Roebuck's intelligence and world view held appeal. Here was a newcomer with whom he could converse on all manner of topics. Julia says,

> I remember a conversation between my father and Peter
> over a family dinner about life as a county cricketer, the
> place of county cricket in the English psyche, and life
> in the West Country. My father had lived in Cornwall
> for a few years and was intrigued by the Englishness of
> county life, the strong sense of place and identity that
> attached to one's county, different from his experience
> of Australian country towns. Peter's natural incisiveness
> meant the conversation flowed easily and enjoyably and
> caught my father's interest.

The parents also enjoyed debating Roebuck's sometimes unpredictable positions. Myfanwy observed in her diary that at one dinner he set off 'a big argument with his statement that he didn't believe in subsidies for writing', with everyone relishing the spirited discussion. Roebuck's politics, while generally small-l liberal/social democrat in their leanings, observed no particular dogma or definition. He was, one suspects, an Australian republican, a cause enthusiastically and publicly advocated by Donald Horne. Yet years later, on the day after the Liberal coalition's 2001 election win, he could be found wandering into various media boxes at the Gabba and announcing with wickedly provocative intent: 'So ... you've got John Howard and the Queen!'

Then there were his views on education. In 1990 he wrote in a letter: 'Our big debate in England is about education – at last the right-wing backlash is beginning. I am awfully right-wing in these matters. Teach the so-and-sos to read, write and behave – that's what I say – and it's coming back into fashion!'

In 1983, as their romance began, Roebuck had just turned twenty-seven and Julia was going on twenty-two. He was obsessed with excelling at cricket, she was finishing her history honours degree and planning a trip to Italy the following year. Like every young couple whose relationship spans oceans, theirs was going to be difficult to maintain. If, indeed, it gained a foothold.

'The next five and a half months were extremely frustrating because we'd just established that we were attracted to one another,' says Horne, 'yet couldn't go any further because we were separated. On the other hand, we did communicate by writing letters to each other, and over the course of that correspondence a deep affection developed. Over those five and a half months he wrote to me every week or so, some thousands of words, and we became close, got to know one another quite well, even before he returned to take up where we'd left off.'

This was the season diarised by Roebuck in *It Never Rains*. The book's dedication reads: 'Julia, Nicholas, Toby, Griffo.' Nicholas is Julia's younger brother, Toby is Toby Jones, and Griffo is Jonathan Griffiths. Clearly, apart from cricket, Roebuck's mind was on Australia and his friends. Over the years he was at Cranbrook he used to rave to Griffiths about Australia: the light, directness, informality, egalitarianism, the multicultural flavours of the people. He cut a swathe among the students there. Amid a multitude of colourful and exotic teachers, Roebuck was a standout, the epitome of a schoolboy's hero: foreign, superbly fit, and a first-class cricketer to boot.

But first and foremost Roebuck was consumed with Julia and what might, or might not, lie ahead. For now things were good and the cricketing diarist was enjoying a solid season. At times, when injury or international duty took others away, he enjoyed the challenge of captaincy. Then in August of that year the darkness descended on him in Manchester, a darkness not triggered, as previously, by poor form. Julia read *It Never Rains* in the 1980s. In the light of more recent events, she has revisited it. After all these years she sees clearly the quandary Roebuck was in.

'He wanted,' she says, 'to take our relationship seriously and knew that would be difficult to do unselfishly as a consequence of his peripatetic, self-contained lifestyle. To stay "in the same place for a year or more" – as he wrote to me – and for that place to be Australia would, of course, have meant giving up his career as a county cricketer. But his letters to me show that in early 1983 he was pondering an alternative life, even contemplating different work choices to either cricket or teaching, considering a career as a journalist. And his diary – especially the account of the Manchester melancholy – hints at this conflict.'

In that tortured section of *It Never Rains*, Roebuck declared:

I decided to abandon my cricket career and start afresh with something less tormenting. I wanted to be able to relax, to be sociable, to be more human – it's in there somewhere but one has to suppress so much of it to win the battle. Then suddenly you realise the battle is not worth winning.

The 'battle' was his against the game. He knew a 'more human' side existed within himself and recognised cricket was stifling it. Yet he could not tear himself away. Not only was a major choice facing him, he now had a degree of responsibility to the woman he had wooed. On one hand, cricket was in the way; on the other, she was beautiful, intelligent, came from a family into which he fitted easily, and she disabled the barriers of shyness and privacy that had proved so inhibiting.

When Roebuck returned to Australia in September, Julia was waiting. The night he arrived the couple had dinner with her parents then she drove him back to Cranbrook. They had waited a long time and the longing was evident. Julia recalls both the intensity and humour of that moment. 'He said, "I want to make love to you and how can I do that in a car?" For some reason I thought of country lads and haystacks – because in England he'd lived in the country – and wondered where I would find a haystack in metropolitan Sydney. Subsequently we found some privacy and shared a passionate sexual encounter. We continued to have an emotional and sexual relationship for the following five months we were in Australia together.'

The pair formed a serious relationship and mutual friends enjoyed seeing a young couple deeply fond of each other. Griffiths remembers thinking, a view shared by others, that Roebuck had captured a prize. 'Julia adored him,' he says. 'And we all loved Julia a bit, in a way. She's a very pretty lady and we thought, "Wow, Peter's very lucky."'

However, his good fortune in the relationship was not without qualification. For as well as being blessed, Roebuck was cursed: by common sexual anxieties that may well have eased with time. The effect on Roebuck, though, was undoubtedly profound. It is no great leap to suppose that ultimately, given the subsequent freeze in his emotional and sexual life, it may have contributed in some way to his death.

Julia has asked that the specific details remain private but she is prepared to acknowledge that a feature of their physical relationship was Roebuck's not infrequent over-eagerness that embarrassingly complicated an otherwise normal sex life, creating some internal tension that grew over time. He naturally came to doubt his performance as a lover, which, coupled with the demands of his cricketing life, quite possibly encouraged him to sublimate his desire into an ascetic and all-consuming commitment to career. 'I bring this to light for no salacious reason,' she adds, 'merely to observe that there were reasons why Peter's sexual life may have been curtailed after our relationship ended which had nothing to do with a preference for men.'

The effect of this problem on a shy and intense 27-year-old, now intertwined with a delightful young woman whose wit and intelligence were a match for his own, can only be imagined. The dilemma of career versus love, where one appears to exclude the other, has never been easy.

That aside, through the antipodean summer of 1983–84, and dealing with a sensitive personal problem as best a young couple could, they were an item. Julia's description of the attraction she felt for Roebuck depicts the joy of the time:

> His sparkling eyes captured my attention, along with his
> pleasant and convivial demeanour and a conversational
> style which ranged confidently across any topic,
> inviting others to join in, rarely judgementally though
> not without debate. His conversations covered many

angles – the serious, the absurd, the relaxed and the political, and of course the personal. I loved his sense of humour, sometimes self-deprecating, recognising life's ironies, but also quick-witted. This enjoyment of conversation, sociability, sense of humour, appreciation of irony – along with the idea that books could be good friends – had long been part of my home life and were familiar, enjoyable, comforting.

It did not last.

Unlike the previous summer, this time it was Julia who left Roebuck behind after five months of close companionship in Sydney. For three years she had been planning a trip to Italy. Nothing was going to interfere with that. He, with somewhat typical male insecurity, predicted she would meet an Italian man 'and that would be that'. She took her holiday anyway, managed to escape the clutches of Italian men, and modified her itinerary to divert to England. There, in the season of 1984, the obsessive need to make a success of his cricket remained Roebuck's driving force. Perhaps it had even taken on a new urgency. Julia discovered a very different Roebuck in Somerset.

Her stay coincided with a break in the team's busy schedule. 'Of course it was nice to see him,' she recalls. 'He was pleased too, but for the first few days he seemed very distracted or preoccupied. I just don't know what was troubling him. He may have been tired after seventeen days on the road, or he may have been grumpy that he had not played well.' Whatever it was, Roebuck had difficulty shedding the bonds of his cricket obsession even for a few brief, keenly anticipated days. He spent considerable time in the nets grooving his backfoot technique.

With hindsight, it's conceivable the decision between cricket and love was in the process of being made or, indeed, had already been made. While Julia's stay in Somerset had been timed to offer maximum opportunity for the couple to be together, from her point of view it was a confusing and anticlimactic visit. 'Peter had been keen that I visit him,' she says, 'to see his English life. But he was preoccupied. After much cajoling, I finally got back the Peter I knew in Sydney only a couple of days before I was to return to Australia.'

Still there was disappointment. Somerset had an away fixture to Warwickshire at Edgbaston and Roebuck wanted his girlfriend to see him play. She was scheduled to fly back to Sydney the following day so needed to return to London that evening. Somerset won the toss and Roebuck opened. At least she could see him bat.

'Peter said to me: "It's all right, I'm sure to get out and be able to take you to the bus station, don't worry." And his scores over the preceding weeks suggested that might well happen. But he had a good innings. I think he scored a century. [102 in fact.] All that training had paid off. With him still batting and my bus about to depart there was no opportunity to say goodbye.

'I arrived back in London; he phoned me to see I'd returned safely and told me of his score. And the next day I departed England.'

It's interesting, if futile, to ponder Roebuck's sudden resurgence with the bat. In the month before Julia's arrival he'd reached 50 once in six games. Now, with her looking on, he took a century off an attack that included Bob Willis, Chris Old, Gladstone Small and Norman Gifford. It did not stop there: he scored centuries in his next three matches, the richest vein of form of his career. A dividend of those hours in the practice nets? The soothing effect of an intimate presence, resisted initially though it may have been? Or an outcome of Roebuck feeling released from a relationship's immediate pressure?

Soon after Julia's departure, he wrote to Toby Jones that 'Julia has gone home. I don't know that I gave her enough. I do like her a lot, and she has a real affection but finds me incredibly shy – I think she enjoyed her stay though. Sometimes I could just dive in – but I value distance and privacy so much.' There is commitment and there is independence. As so often, they can be hard to reconcile.

Upon Julia's arrival home, normality resumed; the letters and phone calls started again, and Roebuck did indeed return to Cranbrook in September. Julia remembered how confused she felt during the English sojourn but was happy to see him again and continue their relationship on the same side of the world. But while there were good times again that summer, something had changed. As is often the case, it was the female who confronted the issue:

He was about to return to England and we had to work out where this relationship was going. The discussion took place in his car outside my parents' house. I raised the question of what we were doing and for the first time in our relationship he was lost for words. I became exasperated. He said he was conflicted, but the implication was that there was no place for me as his partner in this nomadic lifestyle. Two things frustrated me: one was that he wasn't really tackling the question – he was running away from it – and the other was that he'd cut me out of the decision-making. So when I saw

I was making no progress, I slammed the car door and
went off with the impression that we'd be continuing this
conversation another time. But we never did.

They would never speak again. Roebuck had lost the person who
appears to have been the great love of his life.

* * *

Every summer for the next twenty-five years Roebuck returned to
Sydney. But their paths never crossed. The end of the relationship
haunted Julia. 'Yes, I slammed the door,' she says, 'but I think
now, looking back on it, he took that as an opportunity to leave
without saying goodbye, slip out of the country, back to England
and his life as a county cricketer, and escape possible further
uncomfortable confrontations with me. I was very cross that
night. Possibly in his eyes I'd walked away from him. That's not
how I saw it, though; I'd slammed the door out of frustration and
walked away to stop the argument and continue the conversation
later. The fact that we didn't troubled me for a long time.'

Toby Jones believes Roebuck was genuinely attracted to Julia
in body and soul, but suspects he was far more at ease playing the
role of 'lover' than actually being in love or sustaining genuine
physical and emotional intimacy. 'Vulnerability and reciprocity
were not Roebuck's strong points,' says Jones. 'He was reluctant
to give away too much of himself for too long. He never liked
being emotionally unguarded for long.'

Sympathetically viewed, Roebuck's perfectionism meant
contemplating the relationship breakdown as a personal failure –
and failure racks at and contorts a perfectionist's very being.

Whether such a response was complicated by his problem of sexual anxiety, as explained here by Julia, can only be guessed at. From the middle of 1985 he was a single man. And perhaps he committed to staying that way. Few, if any, of those with whom he worked knew of this history. Whereas most heterosexual males give a clue at some stage to those around them of their attraction to women, this man gave nothing. It was a conspicuous part of who he was. Most would say there was absolutely no indication from Roebuck – ever – of women being of interest. Yet Julia maintains, 'My friendship with Peter over four years including my physical experience with him for two of these years left me in no doubt that he was sexually attracted to women. I can only reaffirm that Peter did not indicate a preference for men.'

For some, the tempting interpretation of Roebuck's ultimate baulking at his relationship with Julia will be that a sexually complicated man had recognised this was simply not for him. That he excluded her from any discussion of the decision might suggest someone not wanting to explain his reasons. Yet Julia may well be right in interpreting Roebuck's decision as largely one between her and cricket. For the relationship Roebuck had with cricket was decidedly unusual. He did not wish for the game to be fun. In *It Never Rains* he made reference to reading in the letters of F. Scott Fitzgerald that '... the thing that lies behind all great careers ... [is] the sense that life is essentially a cheat and its conditions are those of defeat and that the redeeming things are not "happiness and pleasure" but the deeper satisfaction that comes out of the struggle'. It appears cricket presented itself to Roebuck as an outlet for aspects of his personality in a way that nothing else, including (maybe especially) the profession of law, did. It was important for him that there be no loosening up, light-heartedness, frivolity or any experience other than a rigid, compulsive, self-imposed discipline. He would apply such rationale to others as well as himself, which might offer a psychological backdrop to what happened at Somerset in 1986 and explain his immense frustration with players who were not – in his eyes – as dedicated to the game as he expected them to be.

Did he consciously shut women out of his life? There are barely any references to females in his autobiography. The notion is conceivable, although the memory of his romance lived on. Fabian Muir says Roebuck never forgot Julia Horne: 'He even mentioned her the very last time I had dinner with him, which was in the same year that he committed suicide. I guess I must have seen him in February or March. He was still talking about her. He never mentioned anyone else.'

Julia could not entirely avoid her old flame either. After she married, Roebuck turned up at the family breakfast table on summer mornings, via the *Sydney Morning Herald*.

She is unable to reconcile the personal controversy that unfolded in later years with the man she knew. 'I was deeply surprised to hear about the English court case and assault conviction for caning,' she says. 'I know later he developed a line on discipline and the appropriate use of the cane. But he never spoke to me about the virtues of caning as a disciplinary tool, and if he had ventured such an opinion I would have told him he was bonkers.' As for the tragic end in Cape Town, she continues to wrestle with the facts of his death, with the claims made, and with the manner in which the story was reported:

Independent evidence suggests that he was distraught and in despair, and so we can only imagine what was going through his mind. We know that the South African police did not take care of a distraught person in their charge – he died in their custody. How could that be? I was utterly shocked to hear of the alleged sexual assault, and without a public inquest we're left to speculate as to what exactly happened. We have one side of the story revealed in newspaper reports, an account that presents Peter as a predatory white man, exploitative and sexually dominating. He was none of these things when I knew him.

Perhaps Roebuck felt he would never love again as he had loved her. Perhaps he lost his nerve in relationships. 'He had a very good love relationship with Julia and it nearly worked,' says Griffiths. 'It didn't but it could have. And that was wonderful.'

Julia sees Roebuck, subsequently, as an emotionally diffident man who'd had an important relationship that failed, and who, while over the years being flattered by the attention of women, also clearly understood that women posed real complications, ones his life would not allow. She believes Roebuck left their relationship 'with a determination to channel desires for intimacy into other, non-sexual aspects of his life; to lead an outwardly productive life through a commitment to work, to a disciplined sporting body and to the realisation of good deeds, his interior life nourished by writing, reading and discussing ideas with close friends'.

Toby Jones describes Roebuck not as a repressed homosexual but a repressed heterosexual. Fabian Muir wonders about being so badly burnt by a relationship's ending that a person closes down, never daring to so expose themselves again. He wonders whether that was Roebuck's experience. If true, it would explain why many who knew him use the word 'asexual' in an attempt to categorise him, for, without question, that is how he appeared to them. Yet he was far from asexual, as his relationship with Julia demonstrates. According to Jones, it was more that his approach to life was such that the commitment and responsibility of relationships simply didn't fit: 'There was too much else going on to be diverted by a love affair of the kind he had road-tested with Julia. It had not worked out and I think afterwards Roebuck was pretty much set on a single life.'

As things were to play out, Roebuck's relationship with Julia Horne unfolded in what would be his middle years. Remarkably, the nature of his personal affairs through the second half of his life remains a complete mystery. Put together gossip, rumour, innuendo, speculation and imagination; even the genuine concern and care of a workplace in which he spent a great deal of the twenty-six years after Julia – still no clear answers emerge. Considering the media's propensity to know what is going on in the world, down to minute detail of people's private lives when the machine puts its mind to it, it says much for the capacity of this man to isolate that side of himself from those with whom he worked and spent so much of his time.

He retained friendships with a number of people from Cranbrook and, clearly, kept them separate from his working life. He spent every Christmas Day with two Sydney families of strong Cranbrook and cricket connection. Mark Patterson is a Sydney stockbroker and former New South Wales selector, whose family entertained their friend through the early part of each Christmas afternoon. Roebuck would then move on to the home of Catherine Remond and her family for the second half, before heading to

Melbourne in readiness for the Boxing Day Test. Catherine's son Dominic is general manager of the Sydney Sixers in Australia's Big Bash League. The Remonds, the Pattersons, Toby Jones, Fabian Muir, Jonathan Griffiths, Julia Horne and many other friends of that time in the 1980s see – still – a very different Roebuck from the man of mystery who so perplexed his work colleagues.

While other possibilities regarding the ongoing nature of his private life cannot be ruled out, there remains an absence of hard evidence. After he died came occasional suggestions of Roebuck dealing with young men in a way that made them feel unsure of his motivation. Sydney broadcaster Gus Worland, coached by Roebuck as a schoolboy in 1985, claimed to have been on the receiving end of such an experience while in England for cricket two years later. He described Roebuck's approach to him at a dinner as 'very inappropriate'. After discussing cricket matters, Roebuck allegedly changed tack and asked him a series of personal questions, including whether or not he had a girlfriend and if he liked anyone in the cricket team. Worland admitted to not being especially astute emotionally at the time – understandable given his youth – and the conversation made him uncomfortable. Despite plans to stay at Roebuck's Taunton home that evening, Worland made his excuses. Recalling the evening on radio in the days after Roebuck's death, Worland felt that he had 'dodged a bullet'. Perhaps; or perhaps Roebuck the mentor was seeking to understand and guide a young man. It was a fact that Roebuck's scything directness could unnerve.

The possibility that with the passing of the years something within him changed can't be ignored. The claims made against him, if true, suggest something distorted, dark and punitive fermented in his complex psyche. The idea, though, that Roebuck was homosexual and felt compelled to repress it flies in the face of considerable evidence.

All who knew him, including those who felt he was repressed and in the closet, would agree he was someone who delighted in being different, to a degree that drew strong dislike from certain of his peers. He took to dressing in a deliberately unfashionable way. His physical presence always had reflected an inner feverishness, his movement quick, and his exits quicker still; when stimulated by a topic he would express himself with an easy but not exaggerated hand gesture; he had the fit body of a sportsman, wiry, a hint of tanned leg occasionally revealing itself as the cuffs off his trousers, worn unfashionably high, rode above the ankle. To the consternation of colleagues, he refused to attend to his infamously prolific nasal hair – another issue no one ever dared address! It flourished beneath a swollen-looking, reddish nose that appeared as though it may once have been struck by a searing delivery. It was hard to tell whether the broad-brimmed straw hats, often worn with the cord pulled tight under his chin, spoke of irredeemable gaucheness or of not giving a damn what anyone thought. And, as Greg Baum observed in his tribute upon Roebuck's death, he wasn't one for 'indulging in such fripperies as deodorant'.

Of all people, he marched to his own drum. It begs the question posed earlier in this chapter by his sister Rosalie: why would such a man, in the years following the social upheaval of the 1960s and gay liberation, feel unable to publicly face homosexuality?

Whatever its exact nature, Roebuck's would not be a conventional single life. He was not cut out to be a swinging bachelor of any sort. Instead it is conceivable he committed to denying sex as a factor. And while for most this would be an unrealistic ambition, Roebuck may have been prepared to attempt as a layman what has proved a challenge too great for many in religious orders. 'We need,' thinks Julia Horne, 'to suspend the popular belief that sex is a central part of modern-day living. For many it is. But for some, it isn't.' She wonders if celibacy as a cultural, rather than religious, practice enabled him to focus on the 'rigours of the disciplined mind and body rather than expose their frailties'; and enabled also 'the privileging of the rational self over the emotional or sentimental'.

Certainly Roebuck appeared to take on a monastic lifestyle. Rosalie acknowledges, 'He was an ascetic, unworldly, he lived his life in his head … He would have been a very good monk.' Herein lies an issue of our time: the relationship between separation and restraint on one hand, and men's psychological health on the other. The experience of clergy in many parts of the world who have appeared unable to maintain a healthy celibate existence may see it subjected to increased consideration in the years ahead. Embedded within scientific studies lie questions, of course, as to the level of mental stability in the first place of those who later become sexual miscreants.

Regardless of that, it's the singularity of Roebuck's life, in a fuller sense, that may have posed the greater threat to his wellbeing. 'The lack of any partner in his life stems from his wish to be above,' says Scyld Berry, 'to have acolytes and unquestioning admirers, not someone who is going to say, "Hey, that's wrong what you just said or what you just wrote."' This view of Roebuck is strongly disputed by Julia. The Roebuck she knew – albeit more than a quarter of a century before he died – did not wish to be above challenge or invite unquestioning acolytes and admirers.

A slightly uncomfortable piece of commentary box history lends some credence to this. One day during a Test at the MCG, the straight-shooting Keith Stackpole confronted a terribly delicate issue: he spoke to Roebuck about personal hygiene. Stackpole explained that while he understood single men weren't always good at ensuring they had a supply of clean shirts, it was important in a confined space like a commentary box that such matters be attended to. Roebuck's reply, he recalled, was a genuine 'Thank you for raising it', and their relationship proceeded, unaffected.

The different perceptions of the man live on. But wherever Roebuck was positioned on the spectrum, it is logical, and a matter of medical fact, that for the good of people's mental health they must subject themselves to challenge. Dr David Horgan, an associate professor of psychiatry at the University of Melbourne, and a specialist in the area of suicide, puts it this way: 'People need people. We're programmed to need feedback. People [who are] alone run the risk of being vulnerable under stress. Emotional resilience is increased by jobs, family, friends, and living with someone else.'

In his life after Julia, Roebuck was perceived to become gradually more alone. By the end, as he grappled with this, there are accounts of many and regular night-time phone calls. His mentoring of young men could never provide the emotional security, texture and challenge of a more complex adult connection. Not that this would normally lead an intelligent and moral man to the sort of decay that has been publicly associated with his death.

But then again, his striking singularity and sense of superiority may well have propelled the justification of risky behaviour to the margins of his psyche. The existence or not of a sexual element, said Horgan, doesn't really matter in this context. He also said: 'If you are highly intelligent, you think you know better than anyone else.'

7

CLOUDS OVER THE SAVANNAH

'In an age of reason, he chased the wildest of
dreams. Accordingly, he can be forgiven an awful
lot, including most of the darknesses that also
exist within his uncontained character.'

- IT TAKES ALL SORTS, 2005

Back in the 1980s, perhaps fired by the educationalist zeal of R.J.O. Meyer, Roebuck proposed to a good friend that they open their own school 'in Polynesia … no, in outback Australia first of all', remembers Jonathan Griffiths. 'He said, "I'll do the cricket and sport stuff and you do music and languages and English." I said, "Come on, I'm quite happy here at Cranbrook." But he did have that idea … way back then.'

He was already turning outwards. His Taunton house was an unimposing bungalow with an attic, one of about a dozen in a row on a quiet street in Monkton Heathfield, north-east of the city centre. Roebuck hosted young cricketers there – two, three or four at a time – for nine successive summers from 1992 onwards. Around that period he also bought an old Federation-style house, in need of some repair, in Bondi, situated on a decent-sized property within easy walking distance of the beach. It had a long, dark hallway and a wire door that was usually flapping in the breeze. The three or four boarders were typically school leavers or on a gap year, perhaps with a Cranbrook connection, or possibly from overseas. When Peter English stayed there in the 2003–04 summer there were three other house guests: a Zimbabwean teenager whose father had recently died, a magazine publisher, and a recently graduated doctor.

'It was a fun house, something was always happening,' says English. 'He literally had an open door policy. It was not a place for secrets. I had a key but don't remember using it. Sometimes the broken front door was closed at night, but usually it was just the screen door flapping about. Roeby wasn't concerned about being broken into or having his private sanctuary exposed. There certainly wasn't much to steal. In his room he slept on three mattresses stacked up, with a curve like a skateboard bowl. He was not a man for luxury or comfort.'

Griffiths occasionally watched him work from Bondi on one of his *Sydney Morning Herald* pieces:

He'd come in, have a shower, put on this bathrobe, do his hair and then, refreshed, he'd be able to speak into the telephone ... He just had a few scribbled notes on a piece of paper, which I found very hard to read. He'd read that, but he'd also improvise it, develop it, from the sparse notes that he had there, and he'd read it and it was almost, like, word-perfect. 'You make yourself a cuppa,' he'd say, 'I'll be there in a minute, we'll listen to some Dylan, no drama.'

With the aid of Darshak Mehta, Mike Coward and others, he established the LBW Trust in Sydney. 'I got a call out of the blue in 2006,' Mehta recalls, 'saying "Come over to my place for a barbecue." I didn't know what to expect or who would be there. There were a couple of solicitors, Coward, me, someone from KPMG. Peter told us he was supporting ten or twenty students in a house, Zimbabweans coming to South Africa to study, and they have nowhere to live, they are very poor. I thought, my god, surely this is not possible, and said "Peter, we should formalise this – we should set up a charity." So the next thing you know four of us had a board meeting and I was conned into being chair.'

The house Roebuck was talking about was Straw Hat Farm, surrounded by bush in the hills outside Pietermaritzburg. He'd designed it himself with a local architect. He considered the winters in KwaZulu-Natal 'glorious'. There are farms nearby, and game reserves. The view of the huge Albert Falls Dam is spectacular. It is a grand, two-storey brick lodge with polished concrete floors and a lookout on the roof, and multiple bedrooms upstairs. The ones facing the dam have balconies. Roebuck's bedroom doubled as his office. 'If you had a problem,' recalls housemate Chris Mandivavarira, 'Peter would call you into his office and talk to you about what was going on in your life and your current situation.' Roebuck employed a maid, Weza, who was devoted to him and the young guys at Straw Hat. She lived in a tiny squatter's camp on the side of the hill, next to Roebuck's property, in a cluster of mud huts.

His coaching took him into the heart of Mugabe's Zimbabwe, rising at dawn to run with boarding-school pupils in Chinhoyi and Bulawayo. He spent time at the academy in Harare and in the 'high density' areas, as the outlying slums are called. In South Africa he coached at Grey College in Bloemfontein, welcomed back year after year. African sojourns became a part of Roebuck's life, for short spells initially and later for extended periods.

And all the while there was India – as his profile widened, so did his appetite for venturing into its backstreets and markets, striking up conversation. 'He was always curious about India, curious to know the political situation, the different cultures, and he would travel by train,' says Bhogle. 'I met him at an airport in India once. I didn't know he was around. He had lost everything on the train. He had wandered out to talk to someone on the platform, came back, and it wasn't there. Peter was like that. I took Peter home and gave him a few dollars to help on his way back. When I was next in Australia I got the money back straight away; I might have forgotten but Peter hadn't.'

Some have suggested he was close to relocating to India. 'All the guys in my office really loved him,' says Brijnath. 'I used to think of Peter as a strange bird that people had never seen. I don't know why, maybe it was the way he walked, and his funny hat. There was always something wrong with how he was dressed; trousers pulled up a little high … It was nice because he wasn't a man conscious of vanity. His vanity lay in his writing.'

Certainly he was finished in England. He had been ever since the 2001 court case in Taunton. 'Never the same person again,' according to Coward. 'Intense with everything' in later years, says Baum. References to 'my enemies' crept into conversations with trusted sources.

Now actively scouring the gloom for the hand of Botham, he was espousing the view that the conviction was all due to the muckraking of his nemesis.

'I distinctly remember Peter seeking me out at the SCG,' says Ian Chappell. 'He's come down from the pressbox or the ABC radio box. He said, "I've got to get writing." I said, "What are you talking about?" And he said, "Everything I'm hearing is that Botham is going to get a knighthood – I've got to put an end to this. There's been a book going around in my mind and I've thought it's not quite the time yet, but I've got to get writing now. This has got to be stopped."'

History tells us Roebuck was not successful, though he did his utmost to spoil the moment. On the eve of the announcement he filed a column that was, perhaps mercifully, published only in the *Natal Witness*. In a destructive, almost vindictive tone, he labelled Botham a bully, drug-taker, liability, liar and hypocrite, and the rest of the piece wasn't overly kind either:

Enough. Botham's knighthood is a fait accompli. It was also an inevitability. With its declining culture and absurd aristocracy, England is welcome to him, deserves him. Swept along by the bonhomie, his chums salute him. Recognising his malice, wary of his populism, his opponents avoid him.

For the harbingers of doubt amongst his English colleagues, the Taunton court case confirmed the scuttlebutt and triggered a note of contemptuous satisfaction for those discomfited by his sense of ambition.

Roebuck's stated belief in corporal punishment was a red rag to a bull for his antagonists. It left him exposed.

'He clearly had a dark and very unattractive side to him, but at the time I knew him well it either didn't exist or, if it did, was much more embryonic,' says Popplewell. 'It may have developed as he got older and got more extreme, wanting to test people and wanting to be in control, manifesting itself in mental or physical abuse. I don't know if that was still balanced by the good sides of his character – the generosity, insight, and he was very funny.'

Geoff Lawson was someone who did spend a great deal of time in later years socialising, travelling, dining and working with Roebuck. 'We spent a lot of hours together and I've never, ever, seen anything untoward, any behaviour, any suspicious words he ever spoke. His behaviour, to me, was totally consistent with a disciplinarian – not just a disciplinarian, but a person who wanted young people to do well. And through discipline, that was the way you did well.'

'He had,' says Maxwell, 'some sort of old-fashioned principle about disciplining people. That's how he coached Ed Cowan – "If you don't turn up at six o'clock, that's it, it won't happen." He was very driven and intolerant and impatient with people who didn't go with his method. There was a kind of rigour to it, which had good results you'd have to say.'

Roebuck was forever talking up the latest news of his Zimbabwean orphans to various friends in Australia. Occasionally he mentioned them on air. Colleagues remember him passing around photographs of students with names like Integrity, Justice, Diamond.

'You never got any hint,' says Baum, 'that it was anything other than a philanthropic, educational passion of his. I'm still certain that's what it was at heart, but maybe it opened him up to temptations that even he didn't quite understand or admit to himself.'

* * *

A fleeting encounter at the Harare Sports Club on 14 October 1999 set Roebuck on his ultimate course. It was day one of the Test between Zimbabwe and Australia. Roebuck's eye was drawn to a group of marimba-playing youths brought in to entertain the crowd during the lunchbreak. Showtime over, one member of the group asked Roebuck to find a telephone and relay a message: 'The captain would like the bus to come now.' The boy was the leader of the band. According to Roebuck's own reporting of events, he was intrigued. One other who was present, Mark Ray, struggles to find the right word for the look that crossed Roebuck's face. 'Bliss,' he suggests, 'best summed it up.'

Some days later Roebuck turned up at the address provided in the message, in the Harare suburb of Belvedere, and was surprised to learn it was an orphanage, St Joseph's. The boy, Psychology Maziwisa, was then a slightly built sixteen-year-old intent on completing his schooling. Sixteen years later he is an entrenched, avowed propagandist for the despotic and corrupt Mugabe regime.

Maziwisa's journey is curious enough, the cat-and-mouse game he and Roebuck played over the next decade curiouser still. As it transpired, one party wanted affection and devotion, the other wanted money. In the end neither had his wish fulfilled.

Through an African-based intermediary the authors sought to establish face-to-face contact with Maziwisa in Harare. The response was an unconditional refusal.

The quotes that follow from Maziwisa were relayed in person to an Australian freelance journalist, Adam Shand, during an interview at a property outside Harare in the wake of Roebuck's death. Shand's piece ran in the *Sydney Morning Herald* on 1 January 2012 and across the globe thereafter. Given the ongoing conjecture about the veracity of the claims against Roebuck, Shand offered to hand over his recording of the interview. Maziwisa's enthusiastic displays on behalf of the murderous henchmen running Zimbabwe into dust mean any utterances of his about Roebuck are understandably compromised. Against that, the nature of what Maziwisa has had to say, in a notoriously homophobic state, has done him no favours, making him the constant subject of vicious attacks from opposition supporters. Shand also supplied the audio of his interview with Petros Tani, who was subsequently interviewed by the authors as well, the crucial intermediary leading up to the incidents in Cape Town.

'He seemed very generous and was quite concerned by my story,' said Maziwisa of that first encounter with Roebuck. 'I told him how I had been raised, difficulties I'd come across, my family and my siblings.' With their mother dead from an HIV-related illness and their father penniless, Maziwisa and his younger brothers Immigration and Integrity were vulnerable. 'So we exchanged contacts and he visited me.'

According to Maziwisa, however, the ensuing visit at the orphanage was uncomfortable. After spending time talking with him and some friends in the bedroom, Roebuck asked the other boys to leave. With the door shut behind them, Roebuck allegedly embraced and kissed Maziwisa.

'I was a little quiet for a few days, especially because as soon as he left people started saying "he must be gay." The matron was the most vocal, saying "I don't want to see this guy back here, I think he might just corrupt our boys." But she never actually confronted him personally … I said to myself, I cannot judge this man based on this incident … The future is a lot brighter, it's just one incident … I think it's wise to keep this to myself. So we stayed in touch. It worked out to my advantage because Peter paid for tuition, my varsity education. As it went along and he made advances and I told him, "Look, I'm not comfortable with this, I'm not that kind of person", he continued to assist me without any grudges. I cannot imagine what my life would be like without Peter. It was an important relationship, it was warm. He would show me love and affection at times and, to be honest, I got my first hug from Peter. In African culture a handshake is enough.'

When Maziwisa faced expulsion from high school in 2001 because the Department of Social Welfare could no longer fund his tuition fees, Roebuck set up a bank account in Harare. Soon after, he also paid for the funeral of the boys' father.

In South Africa, Roebuck invited friends Andrew and Larika Dickason to act as caretakers of Straw Hat Farm. House guests were treated to the sight of loping giraffes on the valley floor, warthogs in the undergrowth, chattering monkeys in the trees.

In early 2004 he arranged for Maziwisa to cross into South Africa on a student visa and study law at the University of KwaZulu-Natal. By now, via constant correspondence and the occasional visit, Roebuck had tapped into the lives of the St Joseph's orphanage boys. He began referring to them as 'my orphans'. Maziwisa believed it was Roebuck's attempt to procure a family, and attributed his allegedly tactile ways to a lonely childhood. 'Peter made reference at some point to his childhood, where he grew up. He said, "I grew up as a lonely guy, I didn't have much love around me." He told me one day, "This is a way of making things right."'

According to Maziwisa, however, Roebuck's idea of making things right involved a relationship with him – after a period of grooming. Maziwisa said a year after he moved to Straw Hat, on a day when the caretakers were absent, Roebuck called him upstairs to his room and began touching him inappropriately while asking about his welfare.

'At that time he had his hand in my pants and he was feeling my buttocks,' said Maziwisa. 'He had done that on previous occasions but this time he went a little bit further. He said, "Look, Captain, I have something to tell you, I hope you're comfortable with it. You know, Psychology, I love you."

'And I said, "Thank you, I appreciate that." My understanding of his love and his sort of thing … were very different. He said "Are you not comfortable with this?" and I said "You've got to tell me what you're talking about."

'He finally said, "I love you, I've been meaning to tell you this," and he was hugging me and pulling me to his chest. I think he was ready that day to have sex with me because Andrew and Larika were going to be away for a while. So I just had to stand up and say, "It's not my thing, I don't do that kind of thing, I'm sorry." He looked devastated and said "Captain, are you sure?" and I said "Yes, I'm positive, I can't do this." And he said "Do you need time to think about it?" and I said "No, I don't think so, I'm not comfortable with it and I'm sorry for letting you down."

He was so devastated, he shed some tears ... I think he felt I let him down, the expectation was that I'd just say OK in return for the favours and everything, despite my straightness.'

Maziwisa said he resolved to tell Andrew Dickason of the advance because the impression people had of Roebuck was wrong. 'But I decided just like 1999 it will die down, just forget about it.' When later allegations were made by young men Maziwisa had invited to Straw Hat, Maziwisa said he would cover things up by telling people Roebuck had a wife and children back in the UK, calculating it was in his best interests to keep a lid on the escalating tensions. He was only part way through his university studies, reliant on Roebuck's generosity, and his brothers Immigration and Integrity were due to arrive in the house. Oddly, Maziwisa did concede that he and Roebuck had shared a room as the house was being finished and no advance was made.

Maziwisa said that after Roebuck's declaration of love, Roebuck treated him with greater respect. As household numbers swelled and a regime of corporal punishment began, he wouldn't beat him. To Maziwisa's way of thinking, it was because Roebuck was uncertain how he would respond. 'If he was going to beat me he wasn't sure how I was going to take that. So the best way to deal with that was to try to make me feel like I was special.'

From then until he moved out in 2007, Maziwisa invited other young Zimbabweans to Straw Hat under the auspices of Roebuck's charity. Down from Harare they came, a trickle at first and considerably more later on, spending a few days or weeks before Maziwisa would consult Roebuck as to their respective merits. As the house filled, Maziwisa claimed he warned Roebuck that 'the whole thing is getting out of hand, but he said, "No, we have an open door policy here – I just find it difficult to turn anyone away." He was genuine, he had this strong sense of helping people, and he constantly told me, "Everyone deserves a chance."'

Costs began to mount: coach fares to and from Zimbabwe, students commuting into Pietermaritzburg (about a thirty-minute journey) twice a day, the maid Weza on the payroll, university fees, food, utilities, large phone bills. As 'captain' of the household, Maziwisa was placed in charge of a debit card to manage expenses when Roebuck was away, a powerful and enviable position for one who had only known poverty. 'I've got to admit I got carried away.' The fox was running the henhouse. Then the jockeying for Roebuck's patronage began. 'People were contesting for power, feeding things to Peter, thinking "if we say all kinds of bad stuff [about Maziwisa] Peter might just put me in charge next time around".'

In 2006, as the Dickasons moved out to start a family, Maziwisa said corporal punishment crept in. He said that Roebuck initially carried out the beatings with a cane and later with a length of rubber hosepipe. 'You can imagine the pain … If you're going to hit someone with a hosepipe on their buttocks and you give them as much as twenty-one strokes … I mean, I thought one day I'm going to take some pictures, it had gone too far.'

According to Maziwisa the system became ritualised, with Roebuck informed which household members had committed infractions – not washing dishes, being lazy, drinking too much, spending too much time on the phone – so he could determine the penalty prior to returning to the house. 'He was getting too much with his hugging, squeezing and making people feel uncomfortable. He was taking liberties, taking advantage of the situation. He didn't know I was painting a completely different picture, telling people he had a wife.'

But with an ever-expanding household and factions developing, other 'sons' had Roebuck's ear. He listened less frequently to Maziwisa's advice and the filtering of new household members became haphazard. Maziwisa suggested this contributed to Roebuck's downfall; the youths coming down from the orphanage would consult with him on all matters but those from elsewhere would not.

Matters came to a head in 2009. Maziwisa's younger brother Immigration composed a letter accusing Roebuck of sexual assault, including an allegation that Roebuck had molested him while he slept. A copy was sent to the *Natal Witness*, one of Roebuck's employers, and Immigration threatened to send further copies to the police and the *Sydney Morning Herald*. Maziwisa was summoned to Straw Hat by a panicked Roebuck. According to Maziwisa, Roebuck told him the claims were exaggerated and irrelevant and he believed the two brothers had dreamed up the allegations to blackmail him. Maziwisa denied this, telling Roebuck if he wanted to incriminate him, he could make such claims by himself.

At that, stated Maziwisa, Roebuck threatened to kill himself if the allegations were made public. It would be a scandal; he would be 'finished' and would go to Albert Falls and 'jump off'. 'He said, "I've made my peace with my god – I can go anytime." He was red in the face and his hair was up.' Maziwisa encouraged Roebuck to make a financial settlement. Roebuck dithered, furious at what he saw as betrayal, patently aware the brothers were colluding. He sought advice from neighbour Adrienne Anderson, a friend who was familiar with many in the house. She believed Maziwisa and his brother were after only one thing – money – telling Roebuck they were conmen. Anderson challenged Maziwisa to take sides if

Immigration went to the police. Maziwisa replied that he would testify against Roebuck but that he had come up with a sensible proposal to bury the allegations: a payout. Roebuck further demurred, called a house meeting, and read the accusatory letter out loud. He was told by all and sundry that Immigration was a crook.

'Almost everyone knew it was all rubbish,' says Chris Mandivavarira, a housemate present at the meeting. 'They just wanted money. Immigration and Ngoni [another housemate], these two guys got together and plotted this ... Peter was very angry and very disappointed.'

But after a spirited debate Roebuck eventually made a substantial payment.

'It was a big plot by Immigration,' says Justice Hakata, another house member who witnessed the whole affair. 'It was a strategy by a group of people planning to extort money – and they knew Peter as a father! It wasn't as though he didn't give them money, but because of greed they wanted more. Immigration was the most corrupt guy; when the trouble started he was running around trying to buy us, get us to say Peter molested us.'

Hakata explains that after graduating the housemates would stay on for a few months while seeking employment. If nothing secure was forthcoming and a wish was expressed to return to Zimbabwe, Roebuck would provide what was known as a 'start-up', paid directly into the beneficiary's bank account. He is adamant that Immigration was no different, receiving both Roebuck's blessing and his start-up. 'You're given something,' says Hakata, 'you have a chance, but you still want more ... when does that come to a stop? But at the end of the day Peter had a big heart, because Immigration came back and stayed at the house.'

A third former housemate, James Gwari, says people used to say to him about Roebuck – 'What does he want in return? He's not married and he's staying in a house full of boys.' Gwari says that's why Roebuck was easily extorted. 'They knew it would make a good story,' he says. 'If people say he did something, it was easy to believe. But that wasn't happening in the house.'

Maziwisa believed Roebuck's friends contributed to his demise by not believing the rumours: 'They didn't warn him of the dangers of his behaviour.' With corporal punishment still a part of Roebuck's agenda, Maziwisa said he left himself exposed. 'We've got his mum saying it wasn't suicide, it's a farce, people are lying ... That kind of assertion can only come from someone who didn't know Peter as well as some of us did.'

Despite such episodes and threats of testifying to the police, Maziwisa went back later to Roebuck for money. Indeed, when pressed about why he switched camps politically midway through 2010, he stated it was because neither Roebuck nor the LBW Trust would furnish him with more funds. It was something of an about-face, given that he had just savaged Mugabe in the *Zimbabwean*, multiple times:

> The right to vote for a government of our choice
> has effectively been negated through ZANU PF's
> manipulation of the political environment by means of
> sustained violence, intimidation, abduction and unlawful
> killings.
>
> I fail to comprehend how as a person and as a
> Zimbabwean you choose to remain indifferent to the
> hungry, desperate and shuttered voices, loud and clear,
> of the very people you purport to lead.

I am literally disgusted by your sort of leadership
especially in the light of your stunning indifference to
a humanitarian crisis occasioned by your own greed
and that of your stalwarts. The mere thought of your
atrocious regime makes me feel like I want to puke.

Unfortunately, you cannot be trusted. It is as simple
as that.

Upon being rebuffed by Roebuck and the LBW Trust, Maziwisa wrote a number of pro-Mugabe articles. 'I thought, I've got a family to look after,' he said, 'I've got to make some money, let me change course here.' It had the desired effect. In November 2010 a Zimbabwean government minister, Saviour Kasukuwere, visited Maziwisa in South Africa and effectively recruited him on the spot. Roebuck expressed disgust at the prospect of Maziwisa changing sides but told him 'go well'.

And so Maziwisa returned to Harare. He was put to work as a spin doctor, sprouting a pro-Mugabe stance on an online blog, and has since risen through the ranks of ruling party Zanu–PF. From being a junior public relations merchant, he gained favour among top officials for his energetic efforts to praise Mugabe and condemn the opposition. In particular, his continuous ridicule of opposition leader Morgan Tsvangirai carried weight with his overseers. In mid-2015 Maziwisa was parachuted in as Zanu candidate for the parliamentary seat of Highlands.

'Psychology,' says James Gwari, 'joined Zanu for money … Right now, I'm not working so if they offered me a well-paid job I would put on a face and do it. That's what I think Psychology did.'

It should be noted that Adam Shand, in writing his story, declared a personal connection with Roebuck: he was coached by him at Cranbrook and they fell out but reconciled, warmly, in later life.

It should also be noted that on the eve of the story's publication, Maziwisa contacted Fairfax Media asking for payment. Denied payment, he withdrew consent to use his quotes. The story ran unchanged.

* * *

Shand remains convinced of Roebuck's wrongdoing. 'You've got someone there who purports to help people, but has a passive sexual agenda underneath. You've got people wanting education, needing money, needing shelter, and prepared to compromise themselves. The whole thing is a bit warped. It's not unusual for this sort of stuff to be hiding in plain sight in Africa and the third world generally. Exploitative behaviour – but it's a mutually beneficial transaction.'

He believes Maziwisa's version of events was factual, although he is not blind to the strategies employed to relieve Roebuck of money, suggesting a significant effort was made to prevent the Maziwisa faction from blackmailing Roebuck because the other students realised they were in danger of losing their meal ticket. That aside, by detailing an older white man's alleged romantic or sexual advances, Maziwisa made himself a target. 'Psychology has copped heaps in Harare about the fact that he was even tolerating such a relationship,' says Shand. 'The opposition media calls him a fag to his face. For mine, his recollections were accurate and genuine; he was willing to disclose his vested interest and even express sorrow that had they not fallen out this would not have happened.'

Three and a half years on, Shand displays a nuanced approach to Roebuck that was not necessarily immediately evident in his story. 'We all manage to maintain some pretty decent double standards in our lives, but I think over time it got worse. I don't think he set out to fool anyone; he wanted to uplift people and he did and we can't lose sight of that. There was this unfair coverage of my story afterwards that he was somehow this aggressive paedophile, which he wasn't. It was sexually motivated, but coming out more in the control and discipline and beating than straight sexual advances.'

Shand believes both parties were vulnerable. Roebuck was utterly reliant on Maziwisa as his guide, translator, adjudicator and point of contact. Then Maziwisa departed and the two severed ties. On this point, his family has stated that Roebuck admitted fear over the last twelve months of his life, in part due to the uncertain qualities of those who now formed part of his household. 'Peter relied so heavily on Psychology,' says Shand. 'I mean, he was surrounding himself with people he didn't know culturally, didn't know their language, didn't know their families. I don't think anyone did take over leadership of the house. That was the problem; he was now isolated.'

As for the students, they were at the behest of their benefactor – invited into South Africa, away from relatives and everything that was familiar, their food, shelter, education fees and living expenses all taken care of by Roebuck, whose renowned hostility towards Zimbabwe's ruling regime and the country's cricket chiefs meant the students were increasingly isolated. It was supposed they were being monitored by Zimbabwe's Central Intelligence Organisation (CIO), leading Shand to describe them as 'exiles' and 'stateless people'.

All of the former members of the Roebuck household interviewed in person for this book soundly repudiated the claims made in the Shand piece and openly questioned the testimony of Maziwisa. The most vocal opponent of Shand was Justice Hakata. Alarmed and disappointed to see his name and photograph in the *Sydney Morning Herald*, he called Shand in Australia to vent his anger.

'When Adam Shand came,' says Hakata, 'he was just standing outside the gate. He said he was from Australia and had known Peter. He said he last saw him at the beach. I didn't know if he was joking or what. But he said, "I'm just here to hear some stories." He came unannounced and said he could buy some beer and some meat and have a braai [barbeque]. We said "cool" – we were young guys and anything for free, you know? He didn't mention that he was writing a story. He came as a person who wanted to know about Peter.

'I could see where he wanted to go. He was trying to get the perversity, so guys would say "Yes, this man raped me" and "Yes, this man molested me". To him it was a disappointment. How could all of these boys be having a proper relationship with this man? It was a blow. So the only way for him to get what he wanted was for him to manipulate whatever people spoke of Peter. For me, I just thought I was a person showing him around. There was no interview.

'From there, he went to Zimbabwe and Psychology told him whatever he told him. Psychology just smiles ... he doesn't refuse anything, so I'm wondering if it's true what he said. I've never had the opportunity to ask him. Nobody used to talk like that and because it involves Adam Shand, it gives me more room to doubt. When the article came out I had people coming up to me saying, "Why did you say these things about Peter?" I said show me and then I saw it with my own eyes. I spoke to him and said, "Adam, I helped you but you're quoting names and putting my name into disrepute here." Those photos are now everywhere on the internet. Everyone was just trying to make as much money as possible and that was a best-selling story.' Adam Shand refutes the allegations, pointing out his notes are clear and that Hakata's version of events are untrue.

Another house member, Petros Tani, is still residing at Sunrise – a more modest house Roebuck bought after Straw Hat – and made an understandable, if uncomfortable, retraction of the commentary he provided to various journalists. He'd initially told Dan McDougall of the *Sunday Times*, for instance:

> By this time there was a hierarchy in the house and those who were believed to be having sex with Peter were relentlessly abused by the others.

Tani, under fierce pressure from the Roebuck family's agents, has now backtracked on such claims: 'The only person I spoke with was Adam Shand who twisted the comments I made in order to spice his distasteful and destructive articles. Such exclamations are false and indicate that we were victims and vulnerable people, no, no, no, no … That was a false accusation and so wrong. Peter never slept with anyone from the house, he was determined to give everyone a chance in life, not these false accusations. There was nothing sexual about him.' In the face of these rebuttals, McDougall, like Shand, offered to make his audio recordings and notes available.

Contrary to the evidence provided by Maziwisa, Roebuck's

housemates who we spoke to could offer only praise for their father figure, a man who sponsored females as well as males, whites as well as blacks, and drilled into his charges the benefits of aspiration and education. 'I was coming from an environment where all of the elders are black, then into a house where the patriarch, the father, is white,' says Hakata. 'There's a change of lifestyle ... All of a sudden food is available, 24/7, and there's a man who is available to listen. Peter was a resourceful man; everything I would ask for, Peter would find. So, at first, I was thinking, "Wow, is this true?" For the first time in my life, I'm starting to have things; I'm starting to have hope.'

'It was heaven,' says Gwari. 'He actually came to pick me up from the bus stop in PMB. He had a car full of dogs. I just thought he was a good guy. He asked me about my whole situation and told me how he could help. Coming from a background of no parents, I was able to tell him everything. I used to cry about my girlfriend, who I left in Jo'burg, and once Peter paid for her to come to PMB. It had never happened in my life, to have a father figure. I loved him.'

'Peter wanted to bring light and hope into people's lives,' says Tani, 'especially with education. But after graduation he'd say, "Fasten your seatbelts, go to war!" He was unique, a one-off.' Another student, Tinashe Rutunhu, told Roebuck he wanted to be a writer. Roebuck paved the way for publishing contacts and paid for Rutunhu to study outside of South Africa. 'To me he was a father figure, kind and good. I loved him and admired him,' Rutunhu said.

'He was the father I never had,' says Mandivavarira. 'I'd grown up in an orphanage and here comes this guy. I probably haven't come across a person like that in my life. A lot of us have asked that question. I can definitely speak for myself: Peter had a big heart. He said he fell in love with Zim and he fell in love with St Joseph's because of the marimba band. Almost every guy who passed through Straw Hat or where we are now did well in school.'

They were keen to address the allegations of physical impropriety, sexual advances and savage discipline meted out to them. To a man – and evidence came in some cases from those no longer on speaking terms, thereby reducing the possibility of collusion – they dismissed all such claims. Some testified they felt awkward about Roebuck's hugging as it was not part of their cultural norms, but soon grew used to it. One said he told Roebuck he would prefer if there was no hugging and Roebuck immediately desisted. The others, however, had no issue with it. Hakata says at times he would be the one to initiate it, particularly if Roebuck had just returned after an absence. Gwari had a similar attitude: 'Peter was our father. He would say, "Come here my son, how was your day?", and he would hug you. He would ask if there were any problems. I would say no and I'd be off. I never felt uncomfortable ... I don't see anything wrong with hugging someone.'

None could recall a single incident where they were propositioned, addressed in an inappropriate manner, looked at while changing or washing, or touched in a fondling or sexual way. Indeed, they viewed such assertions as nonsense. They were also at pains to highlight the nature of Roebuck's disciplinary methods, suggesting a crucial fact was either missed or omitted from the feature stories damning Roebuck. And it is this: house members were offered a choice of punishment, one being a physical reprimand with a stick, and the other being physical labour.

'If you did something wrong or messed up,' says Gwari,

'Peter would say, "How do you want me to punish you?" He didn't initiate corporal punishment on anyone. I would say I want a beating, and go and break the stick myself. It might be six [strokes] and then he'd say, "We're good, we're clear." Or you would choose the garden. But I wanted to get it out of the way because I don't like manual labour. I don't think he enjoyed the beatings because he actually wanted us to work around the house. It would have made life easier for him. We didn't have a problem with corporal punishment because we grew up with it.'

Hakata says at Straw Hat, some distance away from the attractions of Pietermaritzburg, they preferred corporal punishment over a ban from visiting the city. 'You took the punishment rather than not being allowed to go into town and see girls. So you go and find the smallest and weakest stick. And the punishment was never in private, it was always public. We'd be laughing while he was doing it. We found a small stick that made a special sound to trick Peter. We'd cry out "Aaagghh!" and after two [hits] he'd say, "OK, that's enough."'

Tinashe Rutunhu goes further, claiming corporal punishment never happened to him: 'My punishment was verbal. He would tell me I can't have something for a month … but then the next day I'd get it! Or he would ask me to do the garden. Go and water the plants or something. It was never physical.'

Mandivavarira says very few of the students chose the option of performing physical labour around the house. 'There was a time when he left and went to Australia for six months and I abused the house phone. I think I raised a bill for six grand or so [rand]. Overseas calls and stuff like that. When he came back he was very disappointed and I was number one on that list. Some other guys also used the phone. So he gave us that option: corporal punishment or work around the house. I chose corporal punishment, because the yard was huge. If you're gonna work around the house it's not just gonna be for one day – you're probably gonna do that for the whole week. Take the quicker option. It was never against anyone's will.'

Deducing the exact situation in Roebuck's households is a fraught exercise. For any claims of self-serving exaggeration or deflection on Maziwisa's part, he is ensconced in Zimbabwe with nothing to gain – except ridicule – by revealing allegations of an intimate nature with an older, white male and admitting he only turned to Zanu–PF when attempts to procure more money off Roebuck failed. But the strength of the contrasting testimonies from the other former housemates lends a distinct ambiguity to Maziwisa's assertions. Self-interest is a factor; Tani, it could be said, is relying on Roebuck to this day in the form of his estate and, along with some others, has been repeatedly warned not to further damage Roebuck's reputation. The others, however, have moved out and moved on.

Considerable conflict between the former house members has continued and factions are rife. Caught between the damaging allegations, the death of their benefactor, pressures on them to speak well of Roebuck, or to not speak at all, the ongoing struggle of eking out a living in a foreign country ... The ordeal has taken a toll. These young men are walking a difficult path.

* * *

Was Roebuck ever fulfilled by his African experiment? Mike Coward believes so, albeit fleetingly. He once paid a visit to Straw Hat Farm, sharing in the stunning vista across to Albert Falls

Dam and seeing a calmness and tranquillity in his host that was previously unknown. 'I remember before dinner,' says Coward, 'sitting outside overlooking this quintessential African scene. One of his favourite dogs had been buried at this spot and another was sitting at his feet as we enjoyed a glass of wine before dinner. I had never seen him as content as at that moment.'

The moment soon passed. He revealed to Coward that due to his worsening financial situation the house would be sold and the small tribe of Zimbabwean students shipped down the hill into the city of Pietermaritzburg. 'On the evidence over this forty-eight-hour period, Peter had an easy rapport with the students,' says Coward. 'He felt seriously let down by one or two, especially by Psychology who had thrown in his lot with Robert Mugabe's regime. But overwhelmingly he could point to many successes. Peter's generosity was well known and at times he felt some students were taking advantage of him by alerting their friends to his generous nature.'

Other friends of Roebuck's remain somewhere on the path between admiration and scepticism. Agnew remembers just how proud Roebuck was when making the latest announcement on the progress of one of his students. 'He was clearly fired by it, but again, because there was that murmuring, it always felt a bit uneasy asking too many questions. I wanted to believe and I still do believe it was done for the right reasons.'

'At the time we thought this is a bloody strange thing to be doing,' says Vic Marks. 'We didn't necessarily correlate him setting up a house in Pietermaritzburg with it becoming a mini-establishment for young southern Africans. But by that stage we weren't that au fait with what he was doing. I'm sure in many ways it was very valuable, noble ... but I don't think Anna and I quite saw it in purely altruistic terms. We were puzzled by it, but there's that shrug of shoulders and, "That's Pete".'

By the start of 2010 his beloved Straw Hat had been cleaned out and sold. Roebuck was already paying rents in Pietermaritzburg for a number of students and this continued despite the purchase of Sunrise, close to the university, a rambling property with two small bungalows at the rear and an in-ground swimming pool to one side, the house hidden behind high walls, overhanging trees and an imposing steel roller gate. It was a boisterous, crowded environment. As many as twenty students would bed down for the night with Roebuck taking a single bed in the smallest, darkest room. He brought his dogs with him. Compared with the space and breathtaking views of Straw Hat, it was a sad comedown.

He could be forgiven, nonetheless, for breathing a little easier. He had evaded the threats of Immigration and ended his relationship with Maziwisa on a civil note. Some of his students were completing their courses and he was pictured, beaming just as a proud parent would, at their respective graduation ceremonies. But life at Sunrise was increasingly chaotic and the financial concerns ever present. It has been suggested by his family that he was planning to wind up his African venture; his brother Paul says he made more than one reference to selling the house and heading to India. It wouldn't have come as a surprise to his students. During the blackmail crisis Roebuck offered to end the experiment, offload Sunrise and send the young men out into the world with a handsome stipend. They talked him out of it. 'He was fed up,' says Gwari. 'It had nothing to do with being paid to shut up.'

Come 2011 the house was hopelessly divided into various factions, all competing for Roebuck's attention and patronage. It

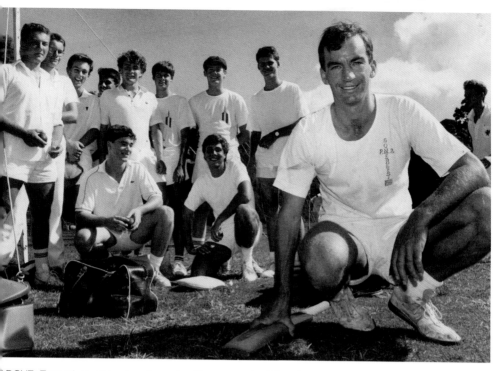

ABOVE: Tanned, energised and popular. Peers remarked that Roebuck was a different man in Australia. Here he is pictured with Cranbrook School cricketers in 1986. (FAIRFAX)

BELOW: Relaxing in trusted company at the Remond family's Christmas gathering in Sydney, 1985. He was welcomed back every year for a quarter of a century.

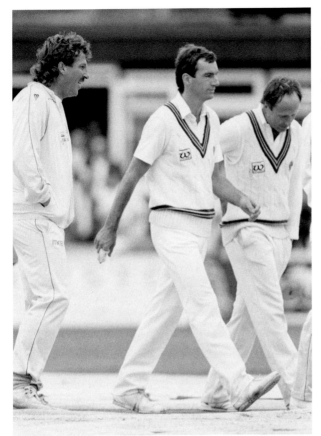

LEFT: Belligerent Botham, rigid Roebuck and the affable Marks during Botham's first appearance back at Taunton after the split. It was tense, uncomfortable and rain-affected, but nonetheless Botham made a gritty ton. (CRICKETPIX)

BELOW: The man apart pictured in 1987. Years later he was to write 'All a man can do is find a niche for himself and then make the best of it.' (FAIRFAX)

ABOVE: Author and columnist amidst the SCG crowd, January 1987. Said Harsha Bhogle: 'He had this incredible ability to use words to make the game of cricket and the players come alive.' (MARK RAY)

RIGHT: Coaching in New Zealand in 1997, complete with his now-familiar tatty straw hat. (CRICKETPIX)

TOP: A golden summer in 1989 brought an unlikely reward: captaincy of an English XI which included Derek Pringle, Alec Stewart and a young Nasser Hussain. (CRICKETPIX)

RIGHT: Another trophy for his adopted Minor County side, Devon, where his idiosyncrasies were humoured and his skills deeply appreciated. These were perhaps his most fulfilling days in cricket. (GETTY IMAGES)

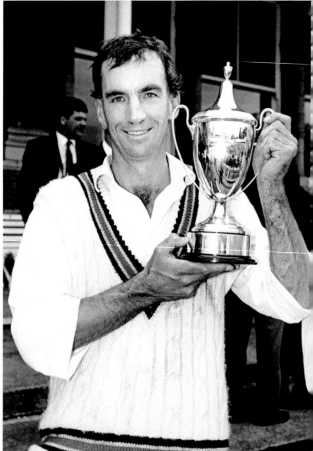

ABOVE: Calling the game like no other. Roebuck focused and in full stride for the ABC in Karachi in 1998 with Tim Lane (middle) and Jim Maxwell (at back). (MARK RAY)

BELOW: Outside Taunton Crown Court in October, 2001. The conviction for assault was a savage blow. 'We had to pretend consent was absent,' he later wrote. His close friends urged him to desist from using corporal punishment. Their pleas fell on deaf ears. (PA via AAP/BARRY BATCHELOR)

Cricketer caned teenage players 'for gratification'

By Simon de Bruxelles

THE former Somerset cricket captain Peter Roebuck was given a suspended prison sentence yesterday after admitting that he had caned three teenage players in his care.

Roebuck, a 45-year-old Cambridge law graduate, beat the young South Africans "for his own gratification", using the excuse that they had failed fitness training, Taunton Crown Court was told. After the canings he had made the players show him the marks on their buttocks.

Judge Graham Hume Jones spared Roebuck a prison term after he pleaded guilty to three counts of common assault, instead sentencing him to four months suspended for two years on each offence, to run concurrently.

Judge Hume Jones said: "These were talented young men far from home, far from their families and they were keen to come under the tutelage of a person like you. Not only were they in your care but you had power and influence over them. That power and influence was abused by you."

The offences were committed between April and May 1999 at Roebuck's bungalow in Taunton, where the teenagers lodged while training.

Ian Fenny, for the prosecution, said that Roebuck warned the players he would cane them if they were unfit.

Describing the assault on Hendrick Lindeque, then 19, Mr Fenny added: "They were forceful. They distressed the young man."

One of the victims, Keith Whiting, aged 19 at the time, later told police: "I was scared and lonely and very vulnerable. It was the first time I had been away from home."

The assaults came to light when he told Richard Lines, coach of the nearby Bishop's Lydeard club. Mr Lines confronted Roebuck.

Paul Mendelle, for Roebuck, said that he was a complex man, adding: "He has never made a secret of the fact that his is a tough regime. It does not suit everyone."

Roebuck said: "I believe I have a great deal to offer to young cricketers and the community at large and I intend to do that."

Roebuck "abused his power and influence"

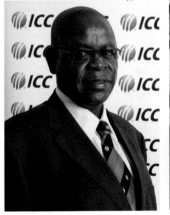

ABOVE: St Joseph's orphanage in Harare, where most of the students Roebuck sponsored spent their formative years.

MIDDLE LEFT: One such student was Psychology Maziwisa. Once the subject of Roebuck's affection, he then took up propaganda for ZANU-PF, Zimbabwe's ruling party.

BOTTOM LEFT: Zimbabwe Cricket power-brokers Peter Chingoka (left) and Ozias Bvute. Roebuck's condemnation of the pair was so fierce that colleagues worried about his safety. Bvute later questioned Roebuck's sanity. (GETTY IMAGES)

BELOW: The view of Albert Falls Dam from the rooftop of Straw Hat Farm, Roebuck's first and grandest African hideaway. Pictured here, one of his former 'sons', Justice Hakata, remains a staunch defender of Roebuck's efforts to educate and uplift impoverished young men from southern Africa.

ABOVE: Roebuck's 'Blue House' in Pietermaritzburg, KwaZulu-Natal, a far cry from the splendours of Straw Hat Farm and now in a state of neglect.

1. My findings are:

   a) Identity of deceased:

   ~~Q~~ PETER ROEBUCK
   ~~(± 50 YR OLD MALE)~~

   b) Date of death: DOB 704719801)
   12/11/2011

   c) Cause of death:
   MULTIPLE INJURIES

   d) Whether the death was brought about by an act
   or omission *prima facie* involving or amounting to
   an offence on the part of any person:
   NO

TOP LEFT: The stark finding of the original inquest into Roebuck's death. No witnesses were called, no forensic evidence was presented.

TOP RIGHT: Police photograph of Roebuck's room at the Southern Sun Hotel in Newlands, Cape Town. 'A' denotes the bed, 'B' the chair where he was sitting before the incident, 'C' the window Roebuck allegedly opened and 'D' the position of the policeman supposed to be standing guard.

BELOW: Falling from the sixth floor, Roebuck landed on the hotel's concrete awning. Unable to see the body at first, given its position on the awning, police initially suspected Roebuck had 'got up and run away'.

was always about money. Jealousy erupted when one particular camp appeared to gain more favour than another. The students devised ways to get Roebuck's assistance. 'There were many people in the house putting pressure on him,' says Hakata. 'They always waited until he was about to go back to Australia because they knew he had a visa, he's travelling, and couldn't change the date. They needed Peter to be around to make the big transfers of money. They knew it was the time to pressure him.'

Leadership changes – with the god-given privilege of controlling the debit card – were campaigned for and fought over. House members clamoured to make further recommendations of people – brothers, cousins, friends – who were desperate to flee Zimbabwe and come under the patronage of this famous benefactor. With Roebuck back in South Africa in November of that year, spot fires broke out at Sunrise. In desperation, he finally laid down the law, instructing the students to make no further invitations to others to join the house. The pressure was building. 'That last week was a stressful week because there was a change in the leadership order,' adds Hakata. 'He wanted to place me as leader but the rest of the crew never liked me. There were many fights in the house … I've never seen it in such political turmoil.'

It seemed to be getting away from him. Roebuck promised Gwari a trip to Cape Town – where he would be covering the Test between South Africa and Australia – but backed away at the last moment, stating he simply couldn't afford it. He wrote an impassioned reminder to his students of just how hard he needed to work in order to pay for their needs and expenses. In a critical misjudgement, however, a moment of weakness, generosity or otherwise, Roebuck buckled under repeated requests from Tani to change his mind about offering help. Tani kept mentioning someone in Cape Town, a young man who needed Roebuck's attention. Roebuck acquiesced. He made contact via Facebook then flew across the country to prepare for his media commitments.

In the afternoon of 7 November 2011, a Monday, Roebuck checked into room 623 at the Southern Sun Hotel. A meeting with the young man had been arranged for that evening. He had time up his sleeve as the cricket didn't start until Wednesday. He responded to some emails – almost as soon as they were received, according to friends and colleagues – and waited for the appointed hour.

At 7 p.m. there was a knock on his door. Roebuck had five days left to live.

8

INTO THE ABYSS

'Alas, the dismayed will continue to take their
lives for it is all more fragile than it appears.'
– SOMETIMES I FORGOT TO LAUGH, 2004

It is inevitable, isn't it? The tendency we have to wish upon our
heroes, even unlikely ones like Roebuck, attributes, morals and
ideals we believe we ourselves do not possess.

Here is a man who criss-crosses the globe, throwing missives
at dictators in one breath and national cricket icons in the next.
A fearless generator of comment. A writer read by millions. A
broadcaster, an author, a philanthropist, a contrarian, an intellect,
a captain, an eccentric and, above all, a composer of character
assessments and judgements considered so distinct, so piercing.
He is not one of us.

So we impart expectations of behaviour. Curiously, celebrity
brings its own pact between the exalted and the exalters. Even the
unlikely hero Roebuck was during his cricket career became adept

at looking over the heads of fans who clamoured to meet his eye. By no means a superstar, he still warranted attention – he was a first-class cricketer and a writer – and to acknowledge them, to meet their gaze, would have meant engagement. His siblings recall that look, because he walked right by them at times when they had come to see him play.

In print he liked to disavow this assumption. 'The notion that famous sportsmen inhabit a world separate from the rest of mankind is dishonest. Like the rest of us, they are made of flesh and blood,' he wrote in 2005.

And if this appears as a contradiction, Roebuck might have countered with a Whitmanesque flourish: 'Very well, then I contradict myself, I am large, I contain multitudes'. Yet perhaps it wasn't a contradiction at all. One of the multitudinous elements within Roebuck's labyrinthine personality was extreme shyness, a significant factor in why he was so difficult for so many to understand. Put simply, he would not reveal himself and the majority with whom he engaged did likewise in reciprocation. Inevitably, this could only lead to some degree of isolation. Here was a man so separate that he forsook the fundamental, almost universal, instinct for human closeness. But he was not devoid of yearning. An independent man, yes, yet more than capable of forming an intimate relationship and tasting its fruits. If we believe Psychology Maziwisa, he lacked affection as a child and develops tactile and ritualised behaviours that intensify behind the walls of his 'family' compound in South Africa. It is wrapped in hopelessly misplaced affection, but affection all the same. Who are these 'ungrateful African bastards', as Maziwisa puts it, to refuse the endearment expressed by their patron?

In our hearts, it is not difficult to concede that even Roebuck needed contact, despite the constant reminders of a man alone, a man willing to upend social graces in order to spend more time by himself.

Yet if we are to accept the deposition made by another young Zimbabwean, one who called for Roebuck's help in Cape Town, it is difficult to find either sympathy or understanding, even on the basis of a clumsy attempt at human contact.

* * *

Roebuck's colleagues weren't at the Southern Sun when his guest arrived that Monday evening. They checked in a few hours later and didn't see Roebuck until the following day. By then the alleged act had taken place, leading its instigator to desperately summon help from Sunrise. Roebuck kept the incident to himself, betraying nothing during that three-day Test at Newlands, Cape Town. 'Sometimes you'd notice that Pete would get into depressions,' says Peter Lalor. 'He'd come into the box looking like he hadn't slept. He was always dishevelled and agitated. I really can't remember anything outstanding about Peter in Cape Town.'

Yet behind the scenes, communiqués were being sent back to Sunrise – a last gasp, one final effort to contort and conceal? A bizarre three-way amalgam of communications crisscrossed the country when the pair at the heart of the matter were separated by a couple of suburbs. A concerted attempt was made on Roebuck's behalf to smooth things over, as had been done before by Maziwisa, but the injured party this time around was in no mood for conciliation. He had been honest about his age when outlining his situation to Roebuck – despite being encouraged to do otherwise by his intermediary, Petros Tani – and was not about to buckle afterwards. The intervention failed. Five days after the incident, on Saturday, 12 November, the young man went to the police.

About the same time as he was walking into the central Cape Town SAPS police station, Roebuck walked into the Southern Sun's breakfast room. The Test was over and a free day in Cape Town beckoned. 'We all finished our breakfast and off we went,' recalls Drew Morphett. 'I was using the time to go up the cable car, up the top of the mountain. Jimmy [Maxwell] and Henry [Lawson] were going to play golf. Roeby was being picked up by a fella at about nine o'clock in the morning.'

Contrary to some other observers, Maxwell remembers Roebuck as being on edge that morning. 'That day was quite extraordinary,' he says. 'Peter was there with a young lady, Zimbabwean I think, who was engaged to one of the boys. He was wound up, very excited and carrying on. So I sense when I think back that something had already happened and he was aware, maybe, that whatever happened in terms of an arrest was around. I said to him, "I need to get ten minutes with you on this game", and he said, "That's fine, that's fine, that's fine", and he was wound up. And that was the last interview he would've done. It never went to air.'

Roebuck left the hotel and headed first to Basil D'Oliveira Oval in Elfindale and later to the Old Mutual Sports Club in Pinelands. By that time his accuser had filed a formal complaint of sexual assault and returned home. The two may have passed each other along the way; the complainant lived ten blocks from the sports club where Roebuck spent part of the afternoon. But Roebuck was oblivious. Prompted by a telephone call, his friend from the University of Western Cape, Nic Kock, a man also involved in charity work, drove to Pinelands to meet him.

Just before four o'clock he and Roebuck left by car and headed to another cricket venue, the UWC's oval in Bellville, where the university's first team was playing.

It may be comforting to his family and friends to know that Roebuck's final afternoon was spent watching cricket in the company of cricket people. He and Kock stayed at the university until well after the day's battle had ended, mixing and chatting freely with players in the clubrooms. Roebuck even shared a Castle Lager with them. The young cricketers were thrilled to have him in their midst and as the shadows lengthened they invited him and Kock to dine with them. Roebuck demurred and asked Kock for a lift back to the hotel. It had been a pleasant afternoon and evening by all accounts. 'Peter was in a very good mood throughout the day,' says Kock. 'We spoke about plans for the future. We chatted cricket. We talked about the future. There was no sense of stress.'

He was dropped at the entrance of the Southern Sun at 8.50 p.m. and bid farewell to his friend. As Kock drove off, at least two policemen – and it would appear a number of others – were preparing to depart from different stations to rendezvous at the hotel and arrest him or be present when it went down. After the event, Lalor spoke to Kock and confirmed there was nothing in Roebuck's demeanour during the day to suggest he had something on his mind. 'The Peter I knew, under that strain ... you would've seen it,' says Lalor.

So what exactly happened in room 623 five days earlier? What was it that so traumatised a young man to file a complaint of sexual assault? And what led a detective from the Cape Town police to effect an immediate arrest on the alleged perpetrator?

For upon learning of the accusation the police responded in a manner that struck some observers as unusually expeditious in a city weighed down by violent crime. It was a black-on-white accusation, made by a foreigner against a foreigner, and related to an offence that was days old. It was also a male-on-male affair, not the stuff of headlines in a country that suffers from a staggering incidence of sexual assaults against women – in Cape Town alone it is reported that six women every day are victims of sex crimes, with the real figure estimated at upwards of nine times that number.

Here was an overtaxed police force, on a weekend, patrolling an urban area with a homicide rate fifteen times that of London. Yet within a matter of hours of receiving the brief, the commanding officer had visited the hotel (twice), met with and interviewed the complainant, organised back-up, and moved in to arrest the alleged perpetrator. Witnesses also recall seeing 'many' uniformed officers in and around the hotel before the arrest. The commanding officer deflected this in his official statement, putting it down to mere coincidence. However, the station commander of nearby Claremont SAPS had also called for an update during the operation, before the arrest occurred; it would appear the detention of a prominent figure had aroused a sense of excitement among local police.

Later the Roebuck family was informed by a source at the *Sydney Morning Herald* that one of the Murdoch tabloids in the UK, the *Sun*, also had a presence on the ground before the event. It was implied an exposé featuring the complainant was due to run, irrespective of the police's actions. Ultimately, those actions triggered a far more significant and infinitely more awful story. But all that was to come.

The incident in Roebuck's hotel room the previous Monday evening remains a subject of conjecture. We have the alleged victim's statement and speculation from the police, Roebuck's colleagues and his former students. In the days that followed, the victim went to ground, speaking only to his then girlfriend and turning up at his workplace. He wrote a lengthy message to Roebuck via social media then cut him off, and exchanged a number of text messages with Petros Tani back at Sunrise, a flurry of communications that ended badly and prompted him to make a formal complaint to police. That Saturday morning he was greeted by uniformed officers. Once the gravity of the alleged offence was outlined, they asked if he would make an official statement and appear in court if necessary. He told them he would. He was led to a meeting room and interviewed at length.

Under oath, this is what he said:

I am an adult male, a Zimbabwean refugee, 26 years of age, a student. On the 2011-11-07 between 19:00 and 21:30 I arrived at Southern Sun Newlands Hotel. Mr Peter Roebuck allowed me into his room 623. He said I must have a seat on the couch next to his bed. He asked me to tell me more about myself after what we had discussed on Facebook. I told him a little bit about myself. After I finished he told me about the student he has been sponsoring.

I told him about my expectations, goals and ambitions and he told me about his. He said I must work hard, he likes discipline, he disciplines hard, he used a cane to discipline if you step out of line. He asked me about my talent. I told him I can fix computers.

He told me that he currently stays with 17 boys at his house in Pietermaritzburg. He then said that he currently sponsors students that are studying at the University of KwaZulu-Natal and he wants to move them to UNISA due to the costs. He said if he takes me he will also move me to UNISA.

He then said he expects me to be tough and though I was a little bit of a push [over] cause I fix computers for free, discipline was not installed right on our generation. He then said I must take off my jacket because it was hot. I took my jacket off. Mr Pete then said I look thin. I responded that is my metabolism that is like that. He emphasised on male bonding, he then said women won't understand; we as males must bond to be successful. I must be comfortable with him in order to have a father-son relationship.

He then said I must take off my t-shirt, pants and remain in my underwear. When he noticed that I was uncomfortable, he's said there's nothing sexual about it. It is about openness, that is what he and the other boys are doing. He started hugging me, assuring me that there was nothing wrong, it's all about a son and father bonding. When we create bonds we create bonds that last forever.

He took his pants off and pinned me down from behind. He held me down with his left hand and holding his penis with his right hand, he put his whole body weight on top of me. He forcibly tried to kiss me, instead he was biting me on my right cheek. I tried to push him over to stop. I was in shock. While pushing off he grabbed my genital parts, that's when I realised he ejaculated all over my stomach. That's when my phone rang. It was my driver that had to pick me up for work. Then he stopped.

Mr Peter started apologising, went to the bathroom to fetch a towel, saying 'I'm sorry, I've never done this before.' I was so traumatised. I just wiped myself and got dressed and left. While I was leaving he said I must come see him the next day.

The day after the incident he tried to contact me via Facebook twice, I didn't respond. I only responded on 2011-11-11, telling him he must never contact me.

Cape Town SAPS
28 Buitenkant Street
2011-11-12, 08:00 hours

Detective Warrant Officer Aubrey McDonald of the Family Violence, Child Protection and Sexual Offences Unit (FCS Cape Town) received a brief containing the above statement at 3.50 p.m. Twenty-five minutes later he was in the foyer of the Southern Sun interviewing the desk manager. After some to and fro, the desk manager told the detective the guest name and dates of occupancy for room 623. McDonald established Roebuck was due to check out two days later. He left, announcing his intention to return.

By five o'clock he was at the local police complex, Claremont SAPS, where he rang the complainant and arranged to meet. At seven o'clock McDonald was in the complainant's home in Pinelands, about ten minutes away by car. Another interview was carried out and Facebook communication that had purportedly occurred between the complainant and Roebuck was given to McDonald. Satisfied with the bona fides of the allegation and the urgency of the task at hand, McDonald returned to his own office and made a series of calls, arranging back-up. By 9.15 p.m. he was back at the Southern Sun, where he met a Lieutenant Jacobs from Claremont SAPS in the foyer. He briefed his colleague on the case, reaffirmed the need for assistance, and then approached the hotel's front desk.

After being informed that the hotel could not state whether Roebuck was in his room or not, McDonald requested the presence of the hotel's security official. Together they took the lift to the sixth floor.

* * *

It had been a fraught time at Sunrise. Just back from covering Australia's tour of Sri Lanka (from where he had emailed Peter English: 'No idea about babies except don't read books and just respond as a human – no one is perfect!'), Roebuck was deeply concerned about the viability of his South African venture. Somehow he had managed to keep the house going and keep a lid on the rumblings that could have brought him down. It was quite a balancing act. When he emailed his family in the UK, letting them know he missed them and would be visiting in 2013, they detected a rueful, almost sentimental tone.

All the while, like clockwork and with a surgeon's precision, he hammered out his columns, dashing off sublime copy and poking his nose where angels feared to tread. His targets were match-fixers, the bullies of the Board of Control for Cricket in India, player behaviour, prejudiced views of bowling actions, decaying Britain, media standards and the game's governance. 'The world is a battleground between the corrupt and the common man. Everyone has to choose his side,' he wrote in one of his final columns for ESPN Cricinfo. But one issue above all defined his reputation as a brave and controversial agent of protest: Zimbabwe.

For years he had railed against Mugabe and those he considered to be the lickspittle cronies of a despicable regime. He decried the ruination of a nation and the degradation of its cricket. No term was too strong, no opportunity lost on air or in print, to castigate Zimbabwe's cricket chiefs, Chingoka and Bvute, for what was unfolding in their backyard:

> Under the shameless stewardship of these men, the game in Zimbabwe has sunk into a pit of bullying, corruption and despair ... Chingoka's deterioration has been painful to behold. Money has been his undoing. He has always enjoyed flash cars, malt whiskey, tailored suits, elegant houses. Alas, he sold his name to obtain them ... If anything, Bvute is even worse. He who does not bother to hide his ignorance about cricket, his contempt for the players or his greed.
>
> *Sydney Morning Herald*, October 2006

> Obviously Zimbabwe is the issue that has forced everyone involved in the game to examine their hearts and heads and stomachs. Specifically the manner in which Peter Chingoka, Ozias Bvute and their loathsome henchmen have run the game in that wonderful country.
>
> *ESPN Cricinfo*, April 2008

> As someone assisting 36 impoverished Zimbabwean students, I have long been aware of the collapse of

hospitals, justice, free speech, schooling and hope. Bright girls have been forced into prostitution, brilliant students sweep streets to avoid starvation, critics are killed and all the while the corpulent cats widen their girth.

Sydney Morning Herald, **January 2009**

Zanu and ZC have fed greedily upon the carcass of the country and game they are supposed to care about ... ZC tries to scare off critics by spreading little stories about their foibles, even publishing them in tame little newspapers that omit to mention torture camps, rape, corruption, and the hundreds of millions of dollars and diamonds stolen under the noses of people desperate for food and medicine. Can there be normal sport in an abnormal society?

Sydney Morning Herald, **February 2010**

'Could he have been putting himself in harm's way?' asks Malcolm Speed. 'It didn't cross my mind at the time but it's fair to say they were angry about these allegations.'

At one point, South African writer and broadcaster Neil Manthorp asked for Roebuck's advice. Manthorp had hosted Roebuck in his Cape Town home and their association went back many years. He'd had an offer from Zimbabwe Cricket to serve as media liaison officer and he told Roebuck he wanted to see the issues first-hand. He went one step further and suggested Roebuck do the same. Roebuck wished him well, only to later criticise his decision in print and lump Manthorp as an apologist for a corrupt body. Not surprisingly, Manthorp considered this a duplicitous act. Only in the final week of Roebuck's life did they speak again on a civil basis.

And in the months before Roebuck died, one of the 'shameless stewards' – Ozias Bvute – confronted him in Pietermaritzburg. It was a surprising move, given the enmity between the two men and Bvute's standing in cricket circles. He was cordially received and shown around Sunrise, where he met some of Roebuck's students. Bvute remembers thinking it odd there were only young men in the house but was convinced that Roebuck passionately believed in the merits of his guardianship.

According to Bvute, he was not there to change Roebuck's views but to outline both sides of the story. He told Roebuck he was free to come to Zimbabwe at his invitation and witness changes he said were taking place there. Bvute explained he was motivated to spread the game of cricket through all communities in Zimbabwe, not just leave it in the hands of a privileged few (i.e. the whites): 'Sometimes, by virtue of the historical circumstances, it was very difficult because people were marginalised. But, you see, I think he really wanted to associate me and Peter [Chingoka] with everything that was wrong about Zimbabwe, and we were politicians according to him.'

Bvute says that in talking with Roebuck he attempted to understand what lay at the heart of his anger towards him and Chingoka. Perhaps inevitably, given Roebuck's conviction in the UK and the rumours dogging him, Bvute easily deflected Roebuck's denunciations by raising doubts over his sexuality. 'The articles were defamatory,' says Bvute. 'What Peter was writing did not matter to me, but nevertheless in his spirit I felt there was something much greater than what he was writing about. He seemed to have an affinity for Zimbabwe and he felt he could no longer travel there based on accusations that he was having improper relations with young men. Given the stance of the Zimbabwean government on sexuality he probably felt trapped.

'My conclusion thereafter was that he thought he was being denied entry to Zimbabwe and that Zimbabwe was a playground of his that he thoroughly enjoyed. He could not vent directly at the government so Peter and I were soft targets. Obviously, he had an alternative lifestyle and it is widely publicised that in Zimbabwe the law is not very tolerant to alternative lifestyles. He felt denied. Let me put it like this: he certainly had relations with those young men that were not proper. I'm not sure if it was easier to pick them up [in Zimbabwe] and when that was no longer possible it drove him to insanity. When I visited his house that was the opinion I formed, just as he had formed opinions of me.'

Soon after Bvute's visit, and completely unrelated, came Roebuck's edict to halt the introductions of new students. Sunrise was full and Roebuck's finances were stretched. It mattered not. Tani continued to press Roebuck to meet a fellow called Itai Gondo, another Zimbabwean student in need of assistance. Gondo was living in Cape Town and had fallen behind in his tuition fees. His girlfriend was studying at the University of KwaZulu-Natal, on the other side of the country, and knew some of the Roebuck housemates. She was friendly with Tani and had mentioned her boyfriend's plight.

This introduction has remained a sore point inside and outside Sunrise, and the intermediary between Roebuck and Gondo was keen to play down his role. 'His girlfriend was here [in Pietermaritzburg],' said Tani. 'I met him here. About a year later she said, "Remember my boyfriend Itai? He's in Cape Town now and needs help."' Tani said he took the information to Roebuck and that it was nothing more than an offhand approach. 'We exchanged a couple of emails and I put him in contact with Peter.'

The other students disagree. They say Tani was insistent and they still don't know why. 'Peter wouldn't ever say no,' says James Gwari, 'but later he would come back to us guys and say, "Please don't introduce me to other people at the moment – we have a full house – so let's get the old crew out of the house and then we can start looking for new blood." But Petros went through with Itai.'

'At some stage,' says Hakata, 'Itai was here in Pietermaritzburg because his girlfriend was here, at the university. Peter had never met or spoken with him but Petros pushed it. Peter had this thing in him ... he never ignored anyone who came to him for help.'

* * *

A Facebook message sent by Gondo to Roebuck on 3 November started the exchange. He had been coached by Tani as to how to broker an approach.

'I briefed him on how the family worked,' said Tani. 'Peter Roebuck was the father, and we were his sons.' Tani suggested that Gondo's real age (he was twenty-six) might count against him gaining Roebuck's patronage. He told Gondo to consider lying about it, as Roebuck typically supported younger students. 'Tell him that you are twenty-one and you are doing your first year ... If you tell him you are older than that you are out. Communicate with him as your father,' wrote Tani on Facebook. 'Your focus needs not to be on financial support but neediness as of a father and a family. The rest will then come.'

Gondo refused to partake in the subterfuge, stating should a father-son relationship be forged, it would be along honest lines. His introductory message was warmly received and he wrote again to Roebuck a day later, this time in greater detail:

> Sir, with regards to my age I'm 26 and I admit that is a matured age and most paternal adoptions encompass ages ten years younger than that, but even though that appears disadvantageous, I believe even when older one still looks towards the wisdom of a father figure to guide one through this life ... I want us to get to know each other better, that even if college assistance or not aside, I know I always have someone to turn to for advice ... Seeing you're coming to Cape Town, I don't mind having a meeting and we can have a heart to heart conversation.
> Kind regards, Itai

He mentioned he was studying at university but had to withdraw due to financial constraints. He also raised the notion of shifting to Pietermaritzburg in order to study at the University of KwaZulu-Natal, where many of Roebuck's students were based. Roebuck, in turn, replied also in greater detail:

> I have a better picture now ... I think money can go a lot further elsewhere, plus accommodation costs come into it ... Anyhow these are things to be discuses [sic] and explored further this way or when we meet ... In terms of adoption u r right of course, younger is normally the way as then character is still forming and lessons can

be taught with words and punishments ... But u missed a father and so might benefit from a father figure if not to direct and discipline as least to offer counsel and comfort.

Stay in touch my boy,

Cheers, PR

Between them, arrangements were made to meet at the Southern Sun.

After the incident in the hotel room, Gondo said he was left reeling. Over the next four days Tani attempted to placate Gondo after the latter had been prompted by his employer to take the matter to police. 'I said this was not the way to proceed,' said Tani. 'I wanted us to talk about this first but events went too fast for us.'

He was right about events moving too fast. He and an increasingly anxious Roebuck exchanged a series of Facebook messages as the week wore on, against the backdrop of that incredible match at Newlands:

Tani

Finally I spoke with Itai ... he said he is no longer interested in your assistance and that's why he removed himself on Facebook.

Roebuck

Oh well, not too sure what he said. He was a bit strange but he needs a lot of help. He needs to call me or other way round. Sometimes things go wrong the first time but you have got to fight back. He's basically a good person.

Tani

Dad, do you have any idea why he does not need your help anymore?

Roebuck

Not really, it was a strange meeting but am only here one more full day and he has many skills e.g. repairing laptops

Tani

Anyway Dad my advice would be to forget about him. We cannot force him because he doesn't need anything to do with you or us. Worse off he doesn't need any contact with anyone.

Roebuck

Oh he's depressed. Isn't that dangerous? Think he needs to uplift his life. Sometimes I go a bit far in first meetings. I suppose outsiders not used to it but his life is important whereas our relationship is not. It's his future.

Gondo then sent his final message to Roebuck:

It's funny how you ask me how I am doing as if what you did to me you find that justifiable? So that was your intention all along? To lure me and pretend you were interested in forming some father-like relationship, yet your intention was to do the sick, pervert disgusting thing you did to me? Well Mr Roebuck, you can stuff whatever form of support you blatantly faked to be interested in. You have greatly humiliated me and I feel very violated, disgusted with myself, your acts were of the purest, sickest kind. It makes sense why you pretend to help out orphans, whilst you prey on their financial difficulty for your perverted satisfaction. I shudder to even think what sick sex-related things you're doing to those 17 boys staying with you! I don't need your assistance, I don't shake hands with the devil, don't bother replying for I will block you after this message. One day the long arm of the law will catch up with your evil misdeeds, rest assured, then all the money in the world won't save you. Goodbye, Mr Molester and good riddance!

Roebuck must have felt his world closing in. Yet only Maxwell sensed something awry. Roebuck got back in touch with Tani and wrote: 'Itai has sent me a nasty message and am sick about it. I will try to call him but not sure it's any use. I'm upset, don't tell anyone or they will worry.'

He was upset and he did a remarkable job hiding it.

* * *

McDonald, Jacobs and the security official approached room 623 uncertain whether Roebuck was inside. It was now approximately 9.25 p.m.

Jacobs was dressed in his full SAPS uniform and McDonald was in civilian clothes. The security man knocked on the door and it was promptly opened. A warrant was produced and permission to enter requested. Roebuck stepped aside, let the three men in, and then sat on his bed. McDonald explained the purpose of their presence. He said Roebuck would be charged with sexual assault. Allegedly, Roebuck responded that he knew 'this is about Itai, who visited on Monday'. He was then placed under arrest and read his rights.

The security official was excused from the room and Roebuck became agitated. He said he was well known in the media and the cricket world and his arrest would be front-page news. He raised the subject of his students in Pietermaritzburg and asked McDonald what was going to happen next. McDonald told him he would be taken to the Claremont police station and detained in the cells. A formal charge would follow on Sunday and he would appear in court on Monday. The news distressed him. He was permitted to make a call and immediately rang Jim Maxwell, who was staying on the same floor. 'He rang me in my room,' says Maxwell, 'saying, "You've got to come down … Something terrible has happened." He was just wound up.'

As Maxwell reached the door of room 623 McDonald met him and briefed him in the corridor. McDonald said that Roebuck was under arrest for a sexual assault and would be charged to appear at Wynberg Court. Maxwell was then allowed into the room. There, in a chair by the window with his pants lowered, was a dishevelled Roebuck.

'He was totally apoplectic,' says Maxwell. 'He was off his face completely, so distraught, going on about me ringing up his boys to tell them he wouldn't be able to catch a plane the next day – he was going back the next day to catch up with them. "Have you got a number?" I asked. "No, I haven't got a number! You'll have to go on Facebook." He was just blithering about it all. I imagine they had taken his computer. He was beside himself, in an awful emotional state. They only let me in the room for a minute or two. I guess he [McDonald] was worried about something going on between us that would compromise their investigation.'

Embarrassed by his state, Roebuck stood and pulled his pants up. He pleaded with Maxwell to find a lawyer, a difficult task given the day and hour. 'He was getting what clothing he had organised, as they were taking items of clothing, the sheets on the bed, everything; they were going to be evidence quite obviously. He was in a dither, on the other side of the bed as I recall and behind him was a chair and a sliding window. He was in a very agitated state. I said, "Can I ring Fairfax and get them to intercede in some way?", and he said, "They'll know soon enough!" Whatever that meant. There wasn't much more to it than that. McDonald was speaking mainly in Afrikaans to the other guy. He escorted me out of the room and then went back in.'

Events to this point can be corroborated. Maxwell left the scene, stunned, and went straight back along the corridor. Before he entered his room Drew Morphett – who was right next door – stuck his head out of his room and asked what was going on. 'So we stood one step inside my room and had this conversation,' Morphett recalls. 'We were out of sight of the corridor. And he said: "I've just come from Roeby's room and he's being investigated by two coppers on some sexual charges. They're fuckin' going through all his gear. They're looking at his underpants for signs of semen. When I last saw him he had his pants down around his ankles."'

What happened next is open to speculation and interpretation.

According to the official SAPS version, McDonald told Jacobs he wanted to call the police photographer and would leave the room to do so. Jacobs replied by saying he would also make a call in order to arrange for others to assist McDonald as he had other duties to perform. The policemen's respective statements are identical in this respect. McDonald went so far as to write: 'Lt. Jacobs had his cellular phone in his hand to make a call.' The testimony from Jacobs reads: 'I was about to phone one of the patrol vehicles since my duties don't allow me to stay any further and had to attend to inspections.' They both testified that Roebuck was sitting in the chair.

Given Jacobs, to begin with, had been requested to assist McDonald, and together they had been on the hotel premises barely twenty minutes, it could be viewed as incongruous that Jacobs was already making arrangements to leave. That aside, Jacobs then attempted to explain what unfolded. Under oath, he stated that he was standing diagonally opposite where Roebuck was sitting as he went to use his cellphone. 'When I lift [sic] my head up, I saw Peter Roebuck standing in the window. I screamed at him but he jumped without looking back.' In stark contrast to Maxwell's testimony, Jacobs said that at the time of the incident – approximately two minutes after Maxwell left the room – Roebuck 'appeared very calm and in control of himself'.

For his part, McDonald testified he had been outside in the corridor for only a few seconds when he heard Jacobs shout '*Hey wat maak jy?*' ('Hey what are you doing?') Seconds after that: 'I heard a sound which I now know was Peter Roebuck falling on the first-floor balcony.' He further testified that Jacobs then opened the door and reported, '*Die man het net gespring.*' ('The man jumped.') McDonald said he re-entered the room and saw that the window was wide open and Roebuck was gone. He noted in his statement that the window was closed when he and Jacobs initially entered the room to confront Roebuck.

At exactly the same time, Maxwell was delivering the news of the police's actions to Morphett. 'Drew was next to me,' says Maxwell. 'I said, "Mate, things are bad – they've arrested Roeby." I was talking to him and then I heard McDonald coming down, on his phone. We're just in Drew's room so I can hear him but he can't see us. We could hear him saying, "There's been an incident", and then he broke off into Afrikaans.'

'This is a hell of a bombshell,' says Morphett. 'The last time I saw the bloke was ten hours before and he was on top of the world. We're talking, a step inside my room, and he's [Maxwell's] filling me in and we hear a voice. It's one of the coppers and he's come out into the corridor, ten metres down. We couldn't see him. We didn't poke our heads out to see. And we can hear this bloke on a mobile phone saying: "There's been a complication – he's gone out the window." Jimmy and I looked at each other. "Fuck! Who's gone out the window?" Reasonable guess was: has Roeby gone out the window?'

Down on the third floor was Geoff Lawson. He heard the sound that McDonald claimed to hear. 'I remember sitting by the window with my laptop,' says Lawson, 'writing a story of the Test match, and life was pretty good. And I did hear a noise outside. "Fuck, what's that?" It was a very strange noise 'cos the car park's right outside.'

Jacobs raced downstairs. McDonald stayed briefly in the corridor and rang Colonel Naidoo, the Claremont station commander. He also called another detective to ask for assistance, before going down to the ground floor. Upon reaching the foyer and heading outside he could find no trace of Roebuck or Jacobs. He looked left and right. 'For a moment I thought Roebuck got up and ran away.' While searching the ground at the hotel's entrance he was informed by 'other SAPS members that I must go to the first floor'. What those other police were doing at the time of the incident has never been explained.

McDonald went back inside the hotel and up to the first floor. He found Jacobs and yet another SAPS officer at the scene. He saw Roebuck's body on the portico but did not venture any closer. It was immediately clear his suspect was dead. Calls were made to commanding officers, paramedics and forensics specialists. McDonald returned to the sixth floor and was joined by three other officers.

The Australian media corps was shell-shocked. They gathered together downstairs, scarcely believing the unfolding drama. 'Cops came running in,' says Morphett. 'There was activity everywhere. There was a woman – a psychologist or something. She came over and said, "Are you connected with so and so?" She was just asking questions. Not taking notes. It didn't take long for sirens and lights, tape to go up, cordoned off the area. He'd gone out the window, which was right on top of a portico, which was the roof over where cabs and cars pull up. It was just a flat concrete roof.'

Maxwell rang Lawson and told him 'something really bad has happened' and he better make his way downstairs. Once there, he was confronted with the sight of anguished senior colleagues and men and women in uniform rushing by. 'He was as panicky as you'd ever see Jim,' says Lawson. 'Told me the story and if someone's writing that for a Saturday-night thriller you'd go: "Nah – got to make it a bit more believable." The ER people rushed in. We didn't know he was actually dead then. They rush in, rush upstairs. "What's going on? What the fuck's going on?" Jim said to us, "Roeby's jumped out the window. We think he's jumped out the window."'

The hotel staff responded as best they could. The hour was growing late and guests were returning from a night out. They offered the media men drinks as the police went about their business. A discreet word had the SAPS officers take a more subtle approach. The car park was kept relatively clear with activity confined to the portico and Roebuck's room on the sixth floor.

'Our group waited to hear what the situation actually was,' says Maxwell. 'We were being comforted by the hotel staff and a very nice counsellor from the South African police. About an hour later, I can't remember precisely, someone said, "Will someone please come up?" – one of the paramedics. The first thing he said, and this is when you know your worst fears are confirmed, "I'm sorry for your loss." That was pretty shaking, to find out that – bang – he was dead.'

Lalor and Baum were dining at a restaurant near the Cape Town waterfront that evening and oblivious to the situation at the Southern Sun. They were in a mood to make merry; logistically and for other reasons it was proving to be a difficult tour to cover, and the wine was flowing. When Lalor's phone rang any such concerns paled into insignificance. It was Maxwell and he asked for Baum.

'I just handed the phone across to Greg,' says Lalor, 'and I was watching him and there was something really odd about this conversation. His chest was moving ... I could see he was upset. I heard him say "how high?" and I heard him say "hospital" and "ambulance" and I somehow knew they were talking about Roebuck. Then he hung up and said, "Roebers has jumped out the window." He was in shock. I said "Is he dead?" and he said "No, no, the ambulance is there."'

The pair sat astonished in the restaurant. Lalor was the first to suggest they finish up and get over to the hotel. The phone rang again. It was Maxwell, this time confirming Roebuck was dead. Lalor relayed the news. Baum, who was much closer to Roebuck, was visibly shaken. Lalor roused his friend to settle up and organised a taxi. By the time they reached the Southern Sun the car park was dark and devoid of police presence. Lalor at first thought they had gone to the wrong hotel. But once inside they were met by Maxwell and the others and told the body was lying above them on the portico. Lalor did a lap of the hotel before realising all the external lights had been turned off in order to keep guests calm. Once back inside, his thoughts turned to Roebuck's family.

'Jim was just rattled,' says Lalor. 'Henry just sat there and stared into space. Drew was talking … I suppose that was his way of dealing with it. So I said, "We have to work out what we do here." At one point I said, "Guys, are we sure there's no family in the UK? Are we sure there's no mother?" And Jim said no and Henry said no. So I said let's ring Mike Coward and check. I rang Mike and said, "This is bothering me – is his mother alive?" I knew the news was about to get out. And he said, "No, there's no mother." That's one of the things that really bothers me about it; we got that wrong.'

McDonald and his fellow officers were meanwhile carrying out a search of Roebuck's room. They dusted for prints and took photographs. Numerous items were packaged up and removed for forensic testing. Later that evening, a representative from the Independent Complaints Directorate – the body charged with responsibility for investigating all deaths in custody – attended the scene. The ICD's representative, senior investigator Lamla Tyhalisisu, decided not to pursue the matter for reasons that have not been explained.

Over the course of the evening and into the early hours of Sunday morning, the Cape Town police carried out their grim work. Exhibits relating to the case, including Roebuck's laptop computer and mobile phone, were seized and booked in at the Claremont station. The one officer left in the hotel room when Roebuck went out the window, Lieutenant Jacobs, was later seen transporting exhibits through the foyer. Although he provided an official statement as per SAPS (and general worldwide) policing protocol, Jacobs was never formally questioned, for reasons that have not been explained.

In the next five days, articles of clothing, bedsheets and blood and hair samples from both Roebuck and his alleged victim were taken and then booked in for forensic examination. Despite the thorough work of McDonald to collect, document and transport the various samples to the police laboratory, the forensic testing was not carried out and made available for the subsequent inquest, for reasons that have not been explained.

Baum believes it might have been an hour or more after the event by the time he and Lalor made it to the hotel. He praises the conduct of the police, particularly the liaison officer who provided some comfort. 'We probably sat there till about two o'clock in the morning,' he says. 'It was quite odd really, we were already reminiscing. I think someone bought a couple of whiskeys. There weren't a lot of people around. I do remember feeling this surreal feeling: we were talking about this bloke in the past tense already.'

After the body was removed, Lalor put his hand up to make the formal identification at the morgue, to spare the others.

* * *

As Roebuck grimly predicted, the incident and the reason why police had moved to arrest him was flashed around the cricket world within hours. Lalor's nagging fear also came to pass – albeit without the need for blame to be apportioned. After all, for so many years Roebuck had insisted he had no family to speak of. People were horrified to discover that he did in fact have siblings and a mother in the UK who, awfully, learned of his death in fits and starts. Of all people and of all places, it was Roebuck's brother Paul, living in Colombia, who discovered the news via an email from a friend offering condolences. He then tried to call Beatrice, in Bristol, who thought at first it was a prank caller. She estimates it was about three o'clock in the morning.

'Eventually I stagger downstairs and it's Paul phoning in complete and utter distress,' she says. 'It was jaw-dropping shock. We turned on the radio and the computer; Peter's dead. We discussed how to let Mum know. I decided the only way to find out at that hour was to call the police. They told me I needed to phone the Foreign and Commonwealth Office. They didn't know anything about it. I'm hearing on the radio that Peter Roebuck has died. Half an hour later it was a fall from a hotel, half an hour later suicide. That's how quick it was, and we're still trying to verify it with the FCO. Officially, we still haven't heard from the South African authorities that he's dead yet. We, as a family, have never had any direct communication of any kind from the South Africans. Peter was a dual passport holder, but we've had nothing from Australia either.

'So here we are, dead brother, dead son, and nothing from anybody. We've been ignored, basically. We obviously wanted to try to find out what had happened. But the biggest thing is that he's gone. He's not coming home. Then we have prior warning about a story in the *Sun* about Itai Gondo and we have to make a decision within a couple of days of the death about whether we want to try to stop that. We didn't attempt to stop it. I was told very early on by the *Sydney Morning Herald*, "You do know, don't you, that it's impossible to slander or libel a dead person." So we were being warned to prepare ourselves.'

Beatrice did manage to track down Maxwell and Lalor to convey her appreciation for their efforts and share in their sense of loss. She feels the family has been rendered voiceless in the clamour to condemn her brother.

The story was breaking. The broadsheets led with respected writer and broadcaster dies, the tabloids went with sex scandal. Numerous former teammates and colleagues were compelled to pay tribute without knowing what exactly happened, while those in Cape Town were faced with the prospect of dealing with the shocking event and moving on with cricket's caravan to the next date and destination, in this case, the second Test in Johannesburg.

Amongst themselves, the various theories were canvassed. 'At first Jimmy and Drew said – "The police must have thrown him out" – because you can't believe he'd jump out,' says Lawson. 'Then you start thinking: a young junior policeman placed on guard in a room ... The police were very good. I thought they were really professional and caring. They obviously had some doubts about the guy's [Gondo's] story. It was a story that needed to be proved. So I found the police very professional. And if you look at those rooms you understand how easy it is. It would be much harder to be thrown out than to jump out. There's a sign on the window and if you're in that frame of mind it *prompts* you to jump out. It says: "These windows are openable. This is dangerous. Do not open these without due care." If you're sitting it's at eye level, right there.'

'Pretty much as soon as Jimmy left that room,' says Morphett, 'Roeby went out the window. Now, how he went out the window is anyone's guess. It was down the corridor and opposite. Probably unlikely, but if there was screaming, let's say they grabbed him, one on each side and head first out the window, you could imagine he'd have screamed. We might have heard it, I suppose, if it was a hell of a hullabaloo but we didn't hear anything.'

'My theory is he didn't actually commit suicide, he just had to get out,' says Lawson. 'His brain was elsewhere. "I've got to get out of here. Ah, that window opens." That's just my take on a guy who's obviously incredibly intelligent and pretty rational. The human mind is a very strange thing. He's gone, "I've just got to get out of here …"'

A media pack descended. A SAPS spokesman, Captain Frederick van Wyk, took the initiative within hours of the incident, stating: 'A cricket commentator committed suicide by jumping from the sixth floor of his Claremont hotel on Saturday night. He died on impact.' Colonel Naidoo from the Claremont police station was somewhat more circumspect with his language but he, too, made an immediate judgement on the circumstances. 'There is no crime suspected as far as Mr Roebuck's death is concerned,' Naidoo told reporters.

Key witnesses were pressed for comment despite their confusion and grief. Maxwell did his utmost to remain composed, saying Roebuck was a very caring human being and 'given his state of mind, he just had a brain snap'. He summed up Roebuck's frame of mind in those last few minutes as 'utter despair'. Nic Kock described his friend as a compassionate man who never hesitated to help. By way of countering news of the alleged assault, Kock told the press Roebuck was spending A$100,000 every year to care for his students and 'his behaviour around them was impeccable'.

Maxwell had to give a formal statement at Claremont station. He took Lawson along in case of irregular behaviour from the SAPS officers. 'The first question the police asked me,' says Maxwell, 'was: "So, did you know Mr Roebuck was a homosexual?" Obviously in their mind he was guilty and they'd made their call. Like they did about his suicide. There was no inquest before they told the world he'd committed suicide.'

Just after lunchtime on Sunday, Lalor was collected by police in uniform and taken to the Salt River morgue. He had called Maxwell in case there was a last-minute wish to say farewell but Maxwell wasn't up to it. The police escorted Lalor into the morgue. They admitted they knew little about the case.

'It could have been a boarding kennel, quite frankly,' says Lalor. 'It was a really low-rent joint in Cape Town. They had the wrestling on really loud in the reception area. The cops didn't have the right paperwork and I was going to have to come back the next day, so I helped the cops get some phone numbers so we could get the right paperwork. You realised the difference in the value of life in South Africa. Some guy led me down and I had to fill out some forms. There was a sterile room and I asked, "What's it going to be like?" And the guy said, "I dunno – you'll find out." There was a box of tissues; one bit of sympathy I suppose. Then they made me sign a document saying I was the legal guardian of the body. I said, "I'm not sure about this", and they told me too bad and gave me seventy-two hours to move the body. It was a difficult time.'

The focus shifted to Pietermaritzburg. Money and other inducements were thrown around as newshounds and photographers tried to get a foot in the door. Roebuck's students were rounded up and urged to spill the beans on their deceased benefactor. None would do so. The most recent house leader, Dennis Chadya, was floored by the death and circumstances. 'We cannot comment on the allegations as we have not heard anything official,' he said. 'But he was a father to me and I don't think any son would take that lightly. He was not only supporting us financially, he was helping us with all accommodation and living expenses. All that he was doing here was giving. He was one of a kind.'

As for Itai Gondo, the knives were out. 'Are you happy now?' read one text message sent to him from Sunrise. The students were as bewildered as they were furious. To some, Gondo had killed the goose that laid the golden egg. To others, he was responsible for the downfall of the only father figure they had ever known. Accusations and speculation swirled about the possibilities of Gondo's involvement: it was a honey trap, he was a rent boy, it was another blackmail attempt – this time with unforeseen and deadly consequences. Another theory doing the rounds had him doing the dirty work of Mugabe.

Gondo's response was low-key. He refused all media requests bar one, refused any payment to tell his story and – in a notoriously homophobic culture – admitted he was subjected to a homosexual advance. 'For an African to say "this guy tried to rape me" is a big step … For a man in Africa, you're almost instantly feminised,' says Adam Shand.

Not accepting payment seemed unusual. A struggling Zimbabwean student in South Africa must have realised there was money to be made from such a scandal. It is easy to suppose that the temptation to cash in might have held some allure. As it turned out, ironically, it was an alleged attempt to buy his silence that ultimately led him to press the complaint to police.

The only journalist Gondo spoke to was Mike Behr, a Cape Town freelancer, who acquired Gondo's address from a sympathetic police officer. (It says much about contrasting jurisdictions that contact details for the complainant in a sexual assault case were passed on to a journalist by police.) Behr warned that the world's press was about to lay siege. Gondo agreed to be interviewed on the basis that Behr shepherded him from any other media attention and vowed never to disclose his whereabouts. He told Behr that Roebuck tricked him into stripping and forced himself on top of him and that he felt like a coward for not fighting back. He then revealed to Behr the entirety of their Facebook exchange, including the final message he sent Roebuck before he went to the police and the earlier details of the agreed meeting. On Facebook Gondo had confirmed:

> 7pm tonight is superb Dad, I'll come on route to work, so
> it will be most convenient. Have a great day!

Roebuck's reply, which went far beyond any preceding context, read:

> ok my boy, bring stick in case I need to beat you!

It was ruinous, unseemly material. The tragedy that had befallen a revered figure morphed into a full-blown sex scandal. It may not have been rape but it was aggravated sexual assault. Sympathy for Roebuck's fate turned in many corners to damnation. 'I regret meeting this man,' Gondo said during the interview. 'All I wanted to do was get the hell out of that place and go to work and forget about it. He has ruined my life. Now I don't know what my future holds. I wish I had never met him. As far as I am concerned he took his own life because he didn't want to face the law; he didn't want to face up to what he did.'

Four days after Roebuck's death, police escorted Gondo to Victoria Hospital in Cape Town where DNA and blood samples were obtained. A second, formal statement was then recorded.

From Harare, Psychology Maziwisa composed a generous tribute (although it included a discreet reference to Roebuck not being a 'saint') that was published three days after Roebuck's death. He wrote that he had a lost a mentor, a parent and a friend, and that Roebuck had left the world a better place. It didn't convince some. Rumours spread that Maziwisa may have conspired with CIO agents to stage the arrest and then murder him. Contacted for comment, he dismissed such claims as 'nonsense' before throwing the spotlight on Gondo.

'It could have been an extortion attempt,' Maziwisa said. 'This could have been about money.'

In Cape Town, Gondo went into hiding.

* * *

There was palpable confusion in the days that followed. Conflicting accounts emerged, as did rumours. Some could not resist the opportunity to sink the boot, for he was nothing if not an easy target for those who may have received more than an ounce of Roebuck's withering tongue. 'Facts rarely featured in his work,' wrote sports journalist Paul Newman in the *Daily Mail* a mere twenty-four hours after the news broke. More typical were the tributes and obituaries attempting to convey a sense of loss of a noteworthy figure, and to unravel the enigma. For his friends and those who knew him well, the news was a shock, but not a total surprise.

'I received,' says Agnew, 'a text message from Jim saying "Peter Roebuck has died" and I texted back to him "Suicide?" It seemed highly possible, without knowing any of the circumstances. You did feel that there was this thing bubbling away inside that could perhaps lead him to do that.'

Vic Marks recalls: 'We came back from a party and there was a message with the fact that Pete had died in South Africa, having been interviewed by the police. We looked at one another and surmised at exactly the same time, "I bet he's finished it." I was stunned; he had been a big part of our lives. We wondered, after that experience in 2001, whether Pete had made a note to himself – "I'm not going through this again". That was our reaction. Anna was angry that he hadn't acknowledged that there would have been a lot of people out there, more than he could ever imagine, who would love to have tried to help him. But he didn't let you in easily.'

Baum puts forward a succinct and credible theory. 'I reckon he was a smart enough bloke and an intense enough bloke to understand everything that would ensue from being exposed in this way, and in a mad but sane moment thought: "I can't deal with that. I can't go through it. I can't live with what's going to come now." It was almost a rational decision to do an insane thing.'

His family was grieving, his students in Pietermaritzburg aghast. Revelation followed revelation. An inquest would be held, said Colonel Naidoo, but reiterated there was no crime suspected in Roebuck's death.

So many questions remained.

9

AFTERMATH

'A man only has his reputation.'

– IT TAKES ALL SORTS, **2005**

The testimonials and obituaries kept flowing in, yet none could quite grasp what lay beneath the cloak. Most told of a hovering foreboding, while acknowledging that they themselves had not been in a position to express concern, or hadn't felt compelled to, or any attempt to do so had been rebuffed. The puzzle remained to the end. 'I've known one or two people in cricket where I've felt they may not see life out to its ultimate long-lived conclusion and I felt a bit like that with Peter,' says Michael Atherton.

A common thread was a disquieted soul and his bleak, numbered, dark, angst-ridden days. 'And I thought about this when he died,' says Marks, 'the way he had been painted by many well-meaning writers, but that's not particularly my memory – he was obviously different and incredibly bright, in his own world in many ways, but it wasn't as though he wasn't gregarious ... He would bare his soul on anything to do with cricket, or politics, fearlessly, with wit and brutal honesty and often at great length. About himself he would reveal practically nothing.'

In the end, he embraced Australia, South Africa and the subcontinent and openly shunned England. 'I would say that he was brush-stroking part of his life away,' says his old captain Brian Rose. 'If you don't confront it, you're going to spend the rest of your life dealing with it.' In the wake of his death, when the tabloid exposés broke, less sympathy or praise was afforded in the country of his birth than elsewhere. There was a quiet acknowledgement of his capabilities, a chance to retell the Somerset feud, and then a note of inevitability over how it all played out. When Matthew Engel announced the news to Scyld Berry, editor of *Wisden* at the time, and told him he would be writing the obituary, Berry asked him to be generous. 'All of his faults were far outweighed by what he contributed,' says Berry.

'He polarised people; sometimes he didn't see the other side of the argument, or saw it but didn't want to acknowledge it,' says Steve Waugh. But Waugh found him, in his dealings with him, 'a good person. And it was such a loss for cricket. Cricket needed him, needed his writing and opinions. There is a massive gap now that he's not there.'

* * *

South Africa is a country burdened by shocking rates of serious crime, racial tensions and glaring deficiencies in policing and judicial processes. Inquiries made for this book about anomalies in the Roebuck case were met with polite but weary indifference. As things stand, the courts are choked, the police underpaid and saddled with a culture of rampant corruption. Graft, assaults, political machinations, murder and attempted murder are rife. For the financial year of 2011–12 a staggering 932 deaths were recorded in police custody. In the UK at the same time there were fifteen. Internal sources point to upwards of an eight-year backlog in forensic testing. Detective McDonald could perhaps be forgiven in his investigation for going through the motions.

'Typically, the first responding officers are not on the level that you find internationally,' says Professor Rudolph Zinn, a world-renowned forensic and crime investigation expert based at the University of South Africa in Pretoria. 'There is a lack of skill, a lack of judgement. Unfortunately the processing of crime scenes in South Africa seems to be our biggest problem. It seems that the police are overwhelmed with the volume of cases they have to deal with, especially when it gets to the forensics. But there are other ways to ensure a person appears in court. So the question here is why did they think it was necessary to arrest him and not just warn him?'

The fundamental issues for those uncertain about the police's version of events concern the legitimacy of the sexual assault allegation made against Roebuck, and his ability to jump out of a hotel window while under police guard. According to the police, Roebuck was able to escape attention long enough to open the window and clamber onto the frame without being noticed. This occurred while Lieutenant Jacobs, as he testified, was looking down at his mobile phone.

'From the sketch, what is strange to me,' says Professor Zinn, 'is that the police officer is positioned furthest away from the window and where Mr Roebuck was. To me, that already raises a question: is the police officer deliberately putting him at a distance? The second thing is I would have expected with the

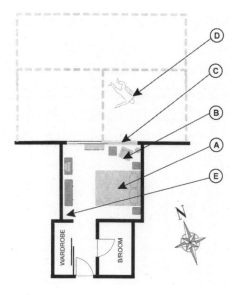

The police sketch of the scene at the Southern Sun hotel in Cape Town:
A: The hotel bed
B: The chair where Roebuck was sitting
C: The sliding window
D: Roebuck's body on the portico roof
E: The position of the policeman on guard

opening of the curtains, the pulling away of the drapes, the person should have seen movement. Then the opening of the window would have definitely caused a sound and you would have heard the traffic noise from outside and the wind blowing. The police officer's attention should have definitely been drawn to the fact that he's opening the window.'

'It is expected,' adds Zinn, 'that a person will be traumatised by the accusation. You will have a person who is emotionally upset and you will have to act in such a way as to prevent an attempt at suicide or potential harm to themselves.'

The initial post-mortem examination found severe injuries to the head, chest, pelvis, legs and feet. There were punctured lungs and multiple fractures to the skull. It appeared Roebuck tumbled but landed feet first, shattering both tibias, then struck his head on the raised ledge of the concrete portico. Paramedics declared him dead half an hour after the incident but in all probability the fall killed him instantly.

As for the sexual assault, it was a case of one man's word. The police were sufficiently concerned to act promptly on the accusation and it is folly to hypothesise whether their actions had more to do with landing a prominent name, protecting the citizens of Cape Town, or simply doing their jobs. Without the forensic results or an adequate inquest – the one conducted in early 2013 was astonishingly bereft of detail and cogent inquiry – it is impossible to know. Roebuck's laptop was scanned and nothing incriminating was found; the alleged Facebook messages between him and Itai Gondo did not appear. The contents of his cellphone have not been released, nor has the phone been returned to the family or to UK police, despite multiple requests. As for the alleged victim, he not unreasonably shunned further attention and for all intents and purposes disappeared.

'The scene described in the hotel room by the police is totally at odds with the Peter Roebuck I knew,' says Lalor. 'I cannot imagine him forcing himself like that ... sexually assaulting someone. Pete was so asexual I can't imagine him in any sexual situation. But the Peter I knew didn't have a mother. He only presented a very small part of himself to us.'

Under scrutiny, the Cape Town police closed ranks. Colonel Naidoo appeared to backtrack: 'I've never once said that it was suicide. I said we are investigating an inquest to determine the cause and circumstances of his death. I said there was no evidence to expect foul play.'

Little further comment was forthcoming, other than that an inquest would be held at some stage in the future.

Without questioning of the officer present at Roebuck's death, or completion of the forensics, or a known determination by a magistrate at an inquest, or an investigation conducted by the ICD into the police's actions, or the interviewing of Roebuck's students by police, or an examination of the hotel's CCTV footage, or the interviewing of other witnesses, or the results of the post-mortem revealed to police, Naidoo's initial comment – 'There is no crime suspected' – appears somewhat premature. Despite repeated requests from the authors, he has refused to say why he immediately publicised this conclusion.

But the general consensus arrived at is incompetence rather than anything sinister.

'I don't see a conspiracy here,' says Professor Zinn. 'They brought in someone from outside – Jim Maxwell – who was allowed to speak to Mr Roebuck shortly after the arrest. What I'm seeing is police work not at a level and standard that I would have expected. They are confronting him with a serious allegation; they thought there was a prima facie case which justified arrest. He was then, legally, placed in their care. It is possible that the police officers were not protecting the person who has been arrested and are now covering up for themselves. It's possible that the police officer who was in the room wasn't paying attention and there's some negligence involved.'

Roebuck's family in the UK do not accept this line of thinking. 'There are two hypotheses: that it was a complete botch-up by the Cape Town police, or that the policeman had been part of some system and had been paid to kill him. I do not countenance the scenario that he took his own life,' says Elizabeth Roebuck.

Roebuck's brother James says, more measured, 'The thing that worries me is that whatever our beliefs are as to what happened in that room, had it happened in this country and there was a police officer who had lost a … a suspect, whatever you want to call him … in that fashion, there would have been the most humungous fuss about it. Inquiries and procedures and that don't appear to have happened. That in itself is suspicious. But from our point of view speculation is fruitless.'

The family insisted on a second post-mortem and appointed legal counsel to assist in the process. London-based barrister David Hood, a product of Millfield who has attracted mixed estimations, was engaged to carry out an investigation. He travelled to Cape Town three weeks after the death and made straight for the Southern Sun. Hood was allowed access to room 623 and tested the window, asserting that it was cumbersome and required some effort to slide open. He also briefed lawyers at the legal firm ENSafrica, who were instructed to uncover the facts around Roebuck's death as best they could and to wind up his estate. Another post-mortem examination was undertaken. Roebuck's body spent Christmas in the Salt River morgue.

'We were reeling – different time zones, not a lot of sleep,' his sister Beatrice, who was appointed de facto spokesperson for the family, recalls. 'That then led to the practicalities of finding lawyers here, in Australia, in South Africa, trying to find a lawyer or a bank, or something or somebody who has got Peter's will so that we can know if he had a particular view about how he wished to be buried. Nic Kock kindly became our immediate contact for repatriation. But there were post-mortems done, so we had to wait for the body to be released. So he spent a very cold Christmas somewhere in Cape Town before we were able to arrange with a funeral home to repatriate. And then he came home and we all felt a lot better.'

From there on, to the dismay of the family, there appeared to be a complete breakdown in communication and cooperation between the South African authorities – police, court and diplomatic – and their UK counterparts. However, as a UK citizen (Roebuck was a dual national) an inquest was required on home soil. On 19 January 2012 it was reported:

> The Coroner for Cheshire, Nicholas Rheinberg, formally opened the inquest at Warrington Coroner's Court on Wednesday and then adjourned the case for a date yet to be fixed. The inquest heard that Mr Roebuck's family ordered a second post-mortem examination to take place in South Africa and that Mr Rheinberg then ordered a third post-mortem examination, which took place last Monday at Liverpool Royal Hospital. Detective Inspector Dougie Shaw said the initial findings of the UK post-mortem examination found injuries of 'severe blunt force trauma consistent with a fall from height'. Shaw said the circumstances surrounding the death were still 'unclear' and that police were still trying to gather information from the South African authorities.

The gathering of information proved impossible. British police endeavours to seek material from South African police fell on deaf ears; the UK coroner's office received not a single piece of evidence despite repeated requests. It was another body blow to the family after Adam Shand's devastating feature article appeared three weeks earlier.

The family was further stunned to learn in early 2013 that the South African authorities had held an informal inquest without notifying the family's lawyers. Lacking notice, no family members were present, despite having retained their legal counsel in the eventuality of the inquest going ahead. They had also set aside funds to travel to Cape Town as soon as an inquest date was announced. Instead a footnote in the South African press revealed that court documents stated that the ruling was death by 'multiple injuries' and reached with 'no additional evidence'.

'This is a mystery,' says Professor Zinn. 'I would have expected that the magistrate would have said that because this was an internationally known person there would be a formal inquest. They should have done it differently, in my opinion, exactly to avoid what is happening now: a lot of speculation and uncertainty. Looking at this objectively, I would have expected a much better police investigation, a formal inquest in an open court, and the family notified.'

Zinn explains further: 'If there is a chance there is a suspect or two involved and it will turn into a criminal investigation, it will be held in an open court. If it's an informal inquest, it means that from the information in the inquest docket [case file] it would appear that nobody will be held liable and the magistrate is able to hold an informal inquest in their office ... but the norm is to notify all of the interested parties.'

The informal inquest did indeed go ahead but the 'interested parties' were none the wiser. On 22 February 2013 magistrate June Snayer, from the Wynberg Court in Cape Town, reviewed affidavits from police and other witnesses, including Itai Gondo, and found no evidence that Roebuck's death involved a crime. The inquest statement amounted to only four pages, containing the signature of the magistrate, the date of the deceased person's death, the cause of death, and the witnesses present and further evidence tendered. On the last two counts the magistrate noted 'no family members present' and 'no additional evidence by parties' was placed before the court.

An explanation was sought from the court. Its senior magistrate, Clive Erasmus, was matter-of-fact: 'The Inquest Magistrate found the evidence placed before her to be sufficient in order to make a finding. I agree with that finding.'

When pressed as to the nature, circumstances and type of inquest that was originally held, specifically, the reason(s) for a closed inquest, the reason(s) why family members or the family's South African lawyers were not informed, and also why the results of DNA samples were not included, Erasmus responded with:

Although the Inquest has been finalised, it can be reopened to include the latest gathered information. The inquest was never a closed one. All inquest [sic] are open to public participation. An Informal Inquest is where the decision is made base [sic] on the documentary evidence alone. The reasons for arriving at the said decision is done in open court and the family or their representative is invited to attend. When the Magistrate is given the case docket he or she study the contents and if the Magistrate is not satisfied with some of the statements they can direct that an [sic] Formal Inquest be held. The state can also request in terms of the law that an Formal Inquest be held.

I [sic] the matter of Mr Roebuck, the state did not make such a request nor did the Magistrate deemed [sic] it necessary. You should note that it is not compulsory for the family to attend. They do not get summons to the proceedings. The family is merely informed of when the inquest will be done. In the matter of Mr Roebuck the family via the British Embassy enquired about the progress made in this matter. As such the Magistrate felt that it would be sufficient if the family is informed using the same canal [sic] of communication. To this end than [sic], the notice informing the family of the date of the Inquest was served on Mr Peter Lalor, at the British Embassy. I do not know if Mr Lalor forward [sic] this message to the family.

I can merely state that neither the State or the Magistrate deemed it necessary for the complainants DNA results to be included in the Inquest. Lastly, it is a very simple procedure to re-open the Inquest and to introduce new evidence.

The justifications put forward by Erasmus were difficult to fathom, namely that: the officiating magistrate saw no need to question the police as to how Roebuck leapt to his death while under arrest; saw no reason to question the officer present; saw no reason to question why an immediate verdict of suicide was reached; saw no reason to call for witnesses; saw no reason to pursue the results of the forensic tests; and saw no reason to inquire as to why there was no legal representation from the deceased's family. On this point, the reference to contacting the family via Peter Lalor 'at the British Embassy' subsequently surprised and bemused the Sydney-based journalist.

As Professor Zinn has noted, such gaps in policing and judicial processes lead only to doubts. 'They had forensics,' says Jim Maxwell. 'If he had opened the window his fingerprints would be all over it, you'd assume. That would be reinforcing evidence to clear the man who was in the room, if there was any allegation that he tossed him out.'

Further complicating matters, no will was found for Roebuck's considerable estate. The lawyer who looked after his interests in Sydney, Peter Strain, attempted to work with Hood but backed off due to irreconcilable differences. After a lengthy and costly delay, Roebuck's mother was appointed sole beneficiary.

Remarkably, more than three years after Roebuck's death, a number of tenants in his former Bondi home refused to vacate. At Sunrise six of Roebuck's former students maintain a tenuous existence. Some claim they were harangued early on by Nic Kock, who became a kind of de facto landlord, for talking to the press. Later, after cooperating with the authors of this book, and despite having uniformly painted an impressive picture of their deceased benefactor, they were threatened with eviction.

* * *

The business of attending to Roebuck's remains and his legacy was fraught. Against a backdrop of accusations, aspersions and attempts to cast his name into ignominy, scores of colleagues, cricketers, journalists and politicians gathered for memorial services in Sydney and Melbourne. The service in Sydney was held, appropriately, at Roebuck's beloved SCG, on 22 December 2011. Mike Coward spoke with passion and gravitas. 'All of us are here because we want to remember the Peter we knew, to thank him for his time among us and for a remarkable body of work,' he said. But he added there were 'too many unanswered questions – how can you explain the inexplicable?'

The funeral was conducted in a small village in Cheshire, England, five weeks later. In the absence of Vic Marks, who was in Australia to cover an Ashes series, Nigel Popplewell delivered one of the eulogies. Others who spoke were Devon cricket identity Roger Moylan-Jones and Jesuit luminary Father Nicholas King, who had helped inspire Roebuck's move to South Africa.

'It was phenomenally depressing,' Popplewell recalls. 'His body was shipped back and one of his sisters rang me to say the funeral is next Tuesday and could I say a few words? Had there been a free hand Vic would have done it. I told some stories about living with him, as a cricketer, what a great time we'd had when he was captain, and about his driving. It was a wet Tuesday and there were very few people there. Brian Rose came, I remember. But the day itself was terribly depressing.'

Even the location of his final resting place was controversial. Four days after he died it was reported that his family had requested the body be returned to England for burial. All those years ago there was a palpable turning away from his homeland, but in death he would lie within its borders. 'I know he wanted to be buried on that hill outside Pietermaritzburg and that he has been buried in England is terribly sad,' says Coward.

By this time one investigative feature story had appeared, followed by another, generating fresh rounds of speculation, defence and condemnation. The pieces portrayed Roebuck as a relentless predator and lecherous oppressor. Dan McDougall's piece, which ran in the *Sunday Times* and the *Australian*, injected into what was otherwise a commendable research exercise the sort of descriptions unlikely to be applied to one still living and, therefore, capable of a legal riposte:

At a memorial service at Sydney Cricket Ground he was described as a humanist, crusader for social justice, cricketer and polemicist. Yet in Pietermaritzburg, South Africa, and in Harare, Zimbabwe, he had a different reputation: to some he was a sexual deviant, sadistic bully and master manipulator. For the past two months, as we have unravelled Roebuck's troubled past, his victims have slowly come forward. They have talked about systematic sexual molestation. His supporters and friends have also spoken out, making robust attempts to defend his reputation. But most voluble is the testimony of those who say they were abused.

Like Shand's piece, McDougall's piece raised eyebrows. The lascivious language did not altogether match the material presented, aside from the claims of unrequited affection as told by Psychology Maziwisa (much like in Shand's piece) and Petros Tani, which Tani later assertively repudiated. The testimonies were confused, contradictory and too easily subject to imputations they had been motivated by less than noble causes, especially in light of the previous efforts at blackmail. To observers, Roebuck's students gave wildly conflicting statements. Much of it seemed to depend on who was asking the questions.

Darshak Mehta was one who took particular umbrage. In the McDougall story a connection was made between Roebuck's resignation from the LBW Trust board and the receipt of anonymous allegations. Those allegations, which were in fact part of the Maziwisa camp's energetic campaign to extort funds from Roebuck in 2008, skewed the article dramatically:

In 2008, Roebuck suddenly resigned from the board of
the sporting charity LBW (Learning for a Better World)
Trust, of which he was a founding director. Little scrutiny
has been given to the episode, but his resignation was
prompted by an anonymous letter detailing abuse.
The LBW Trust admitted to me that it had received
correspondence from at least two young men claiming
Roebuck had molested them.

Mehta insists this was not the case, and that multiple reasons
were detailed, in writing, as to why Roebuck resigned. According
to Mehta the complaints against Roebuck, which were followed
up to no avail, amounted to the last and most inconsequential of
the factors leading to his departure from the trust.

'It was just two lines of slander,' says Mehta. 'Peter said
"this is absolute nonsense, it's rubbish" and that we should ask
this guy [the complainant]. The board decided to instruct our
secretary to write to the complainant and ask for more details.
We never received a reply. There was a second complaint about
a year or so after. I don't even know if that complainant was
aware that Roebuck was no longer involved. Our response to
the complainant was the same: have you informed the police, do
you need legal help, can we help you get a solicitor? There was
no response.'

Mehta says he can only speculate on what made Roebuck
resign. He had been missing at least half the board meetings due
to his work and lifestyle. He felt 'ridiculously shy', according to
Mehta, unable to press the flesh and ask for donations for the
charity. In addition, he was haunted by the breakdown of key
relationships and what bearing that might have on the trust.

'It had got to the point where he couldn't even attend an annual dinner here because we had Botham speaking,' says Mehta, 'so he thought it was best that he stay away. It was a complicated thing all around and we were treading on eggshells. What angered me was indiscriminate talk about the trust. Roebuck had not been a director for almost three years ...'

That the coverage damning Roebuck contained few balancing voices was a further bone of contention; apparently, the oddity of his domestic situation and the sensational charge of sexual assault trumped all other considerations. For all Roebuck's eccentricities and disorder traits, here was a man loved and admired by many of the students he assisted. 'He taught me how to be a man and put my foot down in this world,' says Chris Mandivavarira. 'I'd have never known the things I do know now if it wasn't for him. I've managed to go to a college and finish school.'

'The priceless thing about him,' says Justice Hakata, 'is that the last thing he said, to Jim Maxwell, was "Please call my guys in Pietermaritzburg." It was his only intention, in my opinion, to help. For us, he was our father and a cricket writer and he made sure that life was warm and there was care. Whenever the guys graduated you have never seen him so happy and proud.'

'The family should get on a plane and come here,' says James Gwari. 'Sit down with us and get a better understanding, rather than think and assume things that are in the media.'

'We thought,' Hakata says, 'that Peter's family would come and see us, even just one of them, so they would get a better feeling and understanding of his life here. The Blue House' – as the housemates call Sunrise – 'is the last part of Africa that has his energy and spirit. We have a common denominator: we have both lost a loved one. Let's put everything aside and mourn. We grieved, but nobody came for us. Instead there were fingers being pointed. We were not even told about the funeral arrangements.'

* * *

And then, to our surprise, Itai Gondo surfaced.

The man who vanished from public view three and a half years ago made contact. He expressed a wish to talk, to restore a reputation rocked by those who have attacked his intentions, and to address the ongoing speculation. This would not prove an easy task. Gondo had changed his first name, was no longer in South Africa, and was constantly on the move. In the time this book's authors were liaising with him and an intermediary he hopped across three different continents. But the outcome was positive. Gondo answered questions by email, then sat through an extended interview on Skype.

He reckons it took him two years to stop typing his name into the Google search engine to check what was being written about him. He read it all – every intimation of wrongdoing, every piece of salacious innuendo. Now it is different. He made a point of the need to move on, to get beyond the circumstances that brought him overnight notoriety. An ambitious Christian man with an impressive network of supporters, he has not previously been tempted to break his silence. Without revealing the specifics of his life post-Roebuck, it is something approaching the chimerical. Gondo is much travelled, determinedly independent. At the time of writing he is approaching thirty-one years of age. Asked to confirm his identity, he flashes up his passport, without hesitation, and begins his explanation of how Roebuck came into his orbit.

'I was working for a luxury hotel in Cape Town as part of their food and beverage team for over two years,' says Gondo, 'and had been working in restaurants before that. I had been in South Africa for five years. I made enough money to make ends meet but not to meet my academic ambitions. I had been enrolled once at university as a mathematics scholar, but pulled out halfway after failing to meet the ever-increasing costs. Most times I would work night shifts during college days and early morning head straight to full-day classes. It was really taxing.

'My then girlfriend was aware that I was experiencing financial problems to continue with college – she was the one who suggested I try talking to Roebuck. She told me how he was a businessman, who travelled a lot to India, but had never had children of his own, so was adopting boys from Zimbabwe, sponsoring them to study at UKZN. So she offered to get me in touch with Petros, who was at that time deemed the closest to Roebuck.'

He turns to discussing the meeting in the hotel room. Questioned for the best part of an hour, his manner is matter-of-fact and unhurried. When checked against police and witness statements, his account tallied in every respect. He provided several telling details of the encounter with Roebuck and one detail in particular, at the end, carried significant historical resonance.

Gondo says there was wine on Roebuck's breath. He says he expected an older man, having misinterpreted Roebuck's regular visits to places like India and Australia as the travels of a wealthy businessman. The pair talked about his studies, goals, and financial situation. Roebuck spoke of the students he was sponsoring. Roebuck then said it was warm and that the younger man should take off his jacket. At this point, Gondo says, the mood in the room changed.

In his sworn police statement of 11 November 2011, Gondo stated Roebuck 'emphasised on male bonding', adding that 'women won't understand'. The statement further reads: 'He then said I must take off my t-shirt, pants, and remain in my underwear. When he noticed that I was uncomfortable, he said no there's nothing sexual about it. It is about openess [sic], that is what he and the other boys are doing.' Gondo says Roebuck then removed his own pants and pinned him down from behind: 'At the time I weighed only about 51 kg. Roebuck was quite big, tall, taller than I expected.' By this time, he says, he feared for his life. Having lived in South Africa for five years, he says, he was familiar with the danger a situation like this might present. 'I thought I was going to die,' he says. 'I just wanted to get out alive.'

Reiterating what he had told police, Gondo recalls that Roebuck tried to kiss him, biting him in the process, and that amid the flurry of two wrestling bodies the older man ejaculated on his stomach. Gondo expresses surprise at how quickly this had occurred, wondering aloud if it was due to his assailant's age.

Simultaneously a pre-arranged driver who was waiting outside the Southern Sun started calling Gondo's mobile phone. It was his lift to night-shift duties at his place of work, a hotel downtown. The driver urged him to get downstairs or he would leave without him. Roebuck got off him and went to the bathroom. Gondo was thinking: 'I just had to get out of there.' Roebuck told him that he 'had never done this sort of thing before'. Gondo made his excuses. He says he felt 'disgusting' and wanted to keep washing himself 'like I had OCD or something'. Luckily, he says, he reached a bathroom on the ground floor, near reception.

Dazed by the episode, Gondo says he stumbled through his work duties that night but later revealed the incident – without the explicit details – to his girlfriend. 'Because of my cultural upbringing,' he says, 'I was too ashamed to divulge the details of what had transpired. To be molested by a male is culturally embarrassing. I just told her I was not interested in Roebuck's offer anymore and that he was a sick, perverted person. She tried to find out, but I was adamant about not talking about it; I was angry and just wanted to forget completely that it had happened.'

He says, repeatedly, that had he known more about Roebuck's history the meeting at the Southern Sun would not have gone ahead. 'I was prepared to deal with my own shame and let the matter rest.' He claims he had no intention of making a complaint but, angered by what he perceived as the offer of a bribe and a lack of remorse from Roebuck, changed his mind.

'I don't know if Roebuck told Petros what happened,' says Gondo, 'but I didn't want to speak to him anymore, so texted him to leave me alone. I had not reported the issue because I just wanted to completely forget it had happened. Pressure from Roebuck and Petros to try and bribe me changed my mind. I was never ever going to be violated and then paid off like some prostitute. They had crossed a moral line. I warned Petros first that I would go to the police, and he said I must consider the "big picture" – the situation of the other sons. I would have considered [them] had they not offered to buy my silence, but that was the deal breaker.

'Roebuck told me he was sorry on Facebook! How insulting is that? If he had been remorseful he would have tried to call me, which he did not. He could have easily found my number and called me. Then he had Petros try to entice me by the prospect of being paid off as gesture of an apology, as if I was some rent boy … Petros would tell my then girlfriend how one of the boys at the house had also been abused and was paid off to silence him, insinuating that I could benefit from the experience. That just got me mad; it was an insult to violate me and think that they could throw money at such a serious issue. I decided then I would report him to the police.'

Roebuck's fall and death saddened him. 'I'm not a callous man.' But he felt robbed of his day in court. 'PR was a coward, who knew things looked grim for him legally,' says Gondo. 'He took the easy way out and left me with a media nightmare that brought me unwanted infamy. His sons callously defended him to hide their inherent problems and used me as a scapegoat.'

Embittered by the experience and the chatter surrounding his name, and desperate to avoid further exposure, Gondo says he moved residences around Cape Town. He underwent trauma counselling, lost his girlfriend, and remained the subject of scandal and denunciation. After six months, he applied to an agency recruiting workers to be posted in hospitality roles overseas and left South Africa altogether. For a churchgoing boy from Highfield High School in Harare who once dreamed of studying in the United States, it is a peculiar tale.

Later he drew some comfort from Shand's investigative piece, believing it validated his claim of sexual assault against Roebuck. He even considered making contact with Shand. He says he started to turn his life around with the support of a professor at his former college who doubled as a counsellor in sexual violence matters. 'She was sympathetic and counselled me for free and even tried to find ways to get me back into college. I just wanted to move on with my life.'

But the rumours were maddening, he says – that he was a gold-digger; that it was all a set-up; that he was on the Mugabe payroll. 'Realistically, why would the government of Zimbabwe fret over a small critic in an ocean with bigger critics? PR's own prized son even went to work for them, what more could have been damaging than that? It was just typical stereotypical thinking from narrow-minded individuals who think everything about Zimbabwe revolves around politics.'

He says he feels like he is on the right track. His faith remains important. 'God came through for me because I was faithful.' But he knows that doubters will continue to doubt. After all, it is his word against a dead man's silence.

* * *

'Assuming he did in fact commit suicide,' says Matthew Engel, 'it would be the only case I know of someone committing suicide who everybody thought would commit suicide. So many people over the years said "Roebuck will kill himself." But the circumstances were beyond shocking. I've known people who have committed suicide in an extraordinarily calculated way, but to do so in the heat of the moment requires a certain amount of physical courage. Not moral courage, quite clearly, but extreme physical courage and extreme moral cowardice.'

'Knowing the moody, reclusive person he was,' says Harsha Bhogle, 'and because he looked at life completely differently – geniuses always have a certain side to them – it wouldn't surprise me, in an intensely moody situation he might have just done it. If he had nothing to hide, why did he jump?'

Questions were always going to be asked as to his true motives in housing scores of young black men. Even some formerly close associates in the UK are unable to state with certainty they had full confidence in his charitable intentions. Speculation and hearsay dogged Roebuck for the bulk of his adult life. Most of it was proclaimed as reaction to his eccentricities; a lot of it, in truth, had his sexuality at its core.

Griffiths was mortified by the turn of events. He speaks for many when he says that it just didn't make sense. 'I can't reconcile the person that I knew then with that alleged person now. At Cranbrook the whole community has a pretty sensitive nose for that kind of thing. And I never saw any indication of that kind of predatory behaviour at all.'

Yet the most uncomfortable take on it all was, justifiably, posited. 'You don't want to think of this bloke who put money into these kids' lives,' says Rob Steen, 'who made things possible for them, coming from exactly the direction you want our sporting heroes to come from, and yet he's taken advantage of them?'

'I remember being in Kolkata when I heard about it,' says Rahul Dravid. 'Darshak sent the message. You know, I have not tried to get the truth behind it. There are people whose job it is to find out the truth and to investigate it and we'll wait for that to happen. It may come out, it may never come out. It's very hard; on one side you have those who respected and admired what he'd done and then you hear these other things. It's hard to reconcile that.'

As he bustled and broadcast around the world there was a careful operation of familiarity with comrades he perceived as on his side of the trench and sidestepping – with the occasional swipe at – those he believed were not. It wasn't unusual for certain parties to be unsure from one year to the next where cordiality ended and hostilities commenced.

'You wouldn't have an easy conversation with Peter,' says Mike Atherton. 'He was always rubbing away [at something] and would not take a backward step. I wouldn't say he was deliberately provocative but he put you on your guard and that's fine. If life was more like that it might be more interesting.'

He was scintillating company for some; his baffling, impenetrable conduct puzzled, or infuriated, others.

'He was an intelligent man but a strange man,' says David Frith. 'Am I surprised at the way it all ended? The horrible way it ended? Of course I am, for whatever his sexual proclivities may have been, much of it was circumstantial: a bloke of his age not married, not ever seen with women, so what's going on? Well, you judge him on what he writes and says, but it was very disturbing to read some of the things that circulated shortly after his death. It throws everything that went on before into some sort of perspective. You always felt slightly uncomfortable in his presence and you always wondered what he was really made of. And now we're closer to knowing. It really is one of the oddest stories I've known first-hand in my long life in cricket.'

And, without prompting, without pause, there was immeasurable sadness. Brijnath, one of the dozens to whom *Sometimes I Forgot to Laugh* was dedicated, heard the news from Australian journalist Chloe Saltau and was stricken with grief. 'I will never forget that day,' he says. 'The image of Peter flying out the window does not leave my head. It is an extraordinary, terrible image. I don't know what right or wrong he did, but I just wish sometimes that I could have done something so that this image is erased from my head. Could I have helped my friend so that he didn't have to fly out of that window? It troubles me … it troubles me. I know he was a different type of man and an eccentric man. But I miss him.'

* * *

Naturally, while there is the merest hint of doubt, the believers will retain hope. They are considerable in number and their loyalty runs deep. For the believers, the circumstances and revelations are too fantastic to accept. Lifelong associations remain shrouded, difficult to contextualise, or compromised. That numerous unlikely-seeming conspiracy theories attached themselves to Roebuck's demise was not surprising.

The idea that he was thrown out the window gained some traction in the aftermath, fed oxygen by the demonstrable failure of the Cape Town police to protect their prisoner and the subsequent judicial processes that bordered on farcical. This theory casts Robert Mugabe's Zimbabwe as villain, ridding itself of a journalist who ritually excoriated the rogue African nation. It was a possibility considered by Bhogle even before Roebuck's death, and given weight by Darshak Mehta's recall of Roebuck's words: that one day these men would come for him.

Then there are the accounts of Maxwell and Morphett. They could not be certain whether one officer or two witnessed, or indeed participated in, Roebuck's fall. Yet such uncertainty, even in a nation troubled by a shocking incidence of deaths in custody, does not amount to state-sanctioned murder. The more likely scenario, as Professor Zinn hypothesises, is that two officers covered up for all-too-regular negligence. At any rate, the prospect of the government of a neighbouring country arranging for two Cape Town policemen to do their dirty work is difficult to reconcile. 'Ninety-nine-point-nine per cent he just opened the window and went out,' says Maxwell. 'In those old hotels they have sliding glass windows and he could have been out before they even knew. I'm pretty sure that's what happened.'

Another theory contended Roebuck was murdered because he knew too much about match-fixing. More plausible than murder is the possibility of a set-up that produced an unintended consequence. Is it possible any one of Roebuck's particular enemies would have set out to humiliate him? This would involve a variation on the honey-trap scenario: a young African man creates the circumstances for a hotel-room meeting then makes a complaint. It becomes one man's word contesting another's, with history running against the target; after all, that was the vulnerability so successfully exploited by the Maziwisa faction to extort funds from Roebuck.

Again the evidence falls short. The young African man at the heart of the complaint, Itai Gondo, made himself available to the authors and presented credibly. His back-story checks out and his description of the meeting with Roebuck, almost four years on, was detailed and convincing. It even contained a particular graphic element, at the end, with a certain historical resonance, which was perhaps coincidence or may well be much more significant.

Supporting the conspiracy theory, Gondo's personal circumstances – which we are bound not to reveal – have since improved immeasurably.

And, yet, he refused payment for his story at the time and refused as well the offer of payment that came from Roebuck's 'sons' to keep quiet. Moreover, the temptation to view the testimony of a struggling young African student through the lens of a dubious, white, western perspective remains enticing. In this light, Gondo's position as a victim is rendered mute and irrelevant. But he sought neither justification nor sympathy for his actions and much like Henk Lindeque, the young cricketer on the receiving end of Roebuck's discipline in Taunton all those years ago, he refused to play the victim card.

One former colleague asks: why did Roebuck take these risks? But he was essentially a humanitarian, counters a friend.

'Maybe,' concludes Engel, 'there is something we don't know that is even more extraordinary than what we half know.'

EPILOGUE

by TIM LANE

'Good luck on an almost impossible task.'

So wrote Vic Marks when we contacted him about our intention to write about his long-ago best man and teammate. Given Marks was seen by some as the one who knew him best, it was a telling statement of our subject's elusiveness. After Roebuck's death it had been Marks who summed things up pithily: 'It was a terrible shock … but not a complete shock.'

All the same, and as we learn on occasions in life, there are moments when the shock of bad news can for a moment be too much to grasp. I once met a legendary old footballer at Melbourne airport late on a Friday afternoon. He was bound for a dinner in one state capital and I was heading to a football game in another city the same night. Arriving back in Melbourne early the next morning I bought the local paper and read of his death.

Occasionally things seem somehow impossible until we realise how distinctly possible they are.

It was like that with Roebuck. I'd been listening to him broadcast on the Friday night of that Cape Town test match and thought I heard a sound of particular wellbeing. Early Sunday morning there was a voice message from Malcolm Conn, the long-time News Limited cricket writer. Although this was unusual, as I was no longer part of the cricket media, the grim possibility didn't occur to me. Conn's voice had resignation in it: 'There's terrible news from South Africa. Peter Roebuck has committed suicide.'

The suggestion this might be the manner of Roebuck's end had been around years earlier. I'd heard it floated more than twenty years before. Yet to some it was totally unpredictable. One such person was Luc Remond, whose family in Sydney hosted Roebuck annually for part of Christmas Day. Upon hearing the news from Cape Town, Luc told his mother, Catherine, that Roebuck could not have died in this way. He remembered something Roebuck had once said to him, in the wake of a tragedy at Cranbrook many years earlier. 'Nobody should get to a state of committing suicide.'

My own experience of working with Roebuck and getting to know him, insofar as that was possible, revealed a character of rare strength and insight. It occurred to me that if there had been demons in his past to prompt so gloomy an outlook, perhaps they'd been conquered. The circumstances of his death, though, suggest he may have been heading in the opposite direction.

We had hoped, one way or the other, to find certainty about what happened and why. When we met members of the Roebuck family in October 2014 we expressed this to them and said we could but promise an attempt at the truth. Perhaps it was naive but we believed it was a mission worth undertaking. If nothing else, we feel gratified at having placed on the record the story of a rare cricketer, teacher and media figure, thus painting a fuller picture of the character Engel describes as the most unusual he had ever met.

In death Roebuck continues to baffle, perhaps even more than in life. Seeking to understand him, it is as though he had two different lives interpreted in very different ways by the two largely discrete groups who witnessed them. The matter of whether the difference was real or whether it existed in the perceptions of the two coteries is part of the mystery. And yet within each group there is near unanimity.

One Roebuck life was that defined by his coaching, teaching and mentoring; the other by his work as a writer and broadcaster. Then there was his life as a cricketer, which overlapped both. Those from the educator and coach's landscape saw – still see – him as a gifted and generous person, at times amusingly odd, though they ascribe that to a certain English awkwardness and eccentricity. Very close connections were formed, involving open exchanges and confirmations – by written and spoken word – of genuine friendship. Some particularly close to Roebuck in this part of his life explain him by saying that he consciously and deliberately presented himself as an enigmatic figure to keep people guessing. 'I can see no point in trying to widen my circle here – really the range does not exist. Better to be an enigmatic hero...' he once wrote to Toby Jones from England. He appears to have been happiest when dealing in a nurturing way with young men and this became his life's true mission.

The degree to which such a course seems to have excluded women remains curious. Who knows the reason? Is it possible that after his relationship with Julia Horne he surrounded himself within walls? That he presented in two quite distinct ways according to the gender of whomever he was dealing with is a point noted by Catherine Remond. Although she places herself among those who admit to knowing she didn't really know Roebuck, she was fond of her regular Christmas guest. A mother of four boys and two girls, Remond observes that while her guest gravitated easily to her three sons 'there was an awkwardness with girls – I wonder if it was because no cricket connection existed.'

Roebuck said of himself near the end that he hoped the good outweighed the bad, and certainly there was more that was good and constructive about him than most people would achieve in two lifetimes. Expressions like 'life changing' are not unusual from those educated, coached or mentored by him.

A Sydney cricket administrator and player manager, Peter Lovitt, studied HSC English literature under Roebuck at Cranbrook and uses the word 'brilliant' to describe his teaching. The novels his class studied that year were David Malouf's *Johnno* and A.B. Facey's *A Fortunate Life*. Lovitt says the itinerant Englishman's ability to explore the themes of these Australian books and open them up to his students went beyond any of their expectations. Russel McCool, who – like his father Colin – played cricket at Somerset, became a tenant at Roebuck's house in the northern summer of 1982. He calls the man who was his landlord 'an extraordinary person'.

Roebuck's time as a writer and broadcaster was a less harmonious existence. Here he was dealing with a group generally older than those he taught or coached, perhaps more set in their attitudes and levels of acceptance. While many of these people admired him greatly, some liked him at first but grew not to, some didn't like him, and some fell out with him acrimoniously. His cultivated enigmatic persona was not everyone's cup of tea. It would seem he was less at home in this milieu, although this was scarcely an issue in Australia. The tensions were due in part to competitiveness, especially in his relationships with English media figures, but appear also to have been generated by aspects of Roebuck's nature.

Then there was his overlapping life as cricketer. Such was Roebuck's need for fulfilment as a cricketer that it exposed the brittle side of his make-up to a greater extent than any other field of endeavour. Few of the relationships forged in his playing days endured.

So different were the types of relationships formed in these phases of his existence that there is a fierce clash of opinions about the man and what became of him. Those who knew him as teacher and mentor loved him for what he gave. They feel strongly, virtually to a man and woman, that his integrity was unimpeachable. It seems he opened himself to them in a way that left them in no doubt that they knew him.

For those in the media it was different. There is not one among them who would claim to have really known him. Few of them would claim to have experienced his generous side. So the dynamic was not the same and Roebuck wasn't cut as much slack in this domain. And, journalists being journalists, he was viewed with a cynical eye.

Many of his working colleagues were inclined to the view he was a repressed homosexual. When his life played out the way it ultimately did, this supposed repression and the prospect it had driven him to a dark place seemed real. It's possible that those of this view were all wrong and those in the circle of Roebuck-the-educator were right. Many people from his Cranbrook days knew of Roebuck's relationship with Julia Horne and therefore have an unambiguous picture of him as nothing but an eccentric, English, heterosexual male who gave up on romance.

The heavy collision of opinions makes an already mysterious man just as enigmatic as he apparently set out to be.

Of course, there's a third possibility: that both groups are right and Roebuck changed as he grew older, becoming more isolated, more prone to aberrant behaviour. Not that those who knew the educator even agree that he did become more isolated.

* * *

The case of Roebuck continues to undergo consideration, some of it at lofty levels of learning. The August 2015 edition of *Australasian Psychiatry*, the Journal of the Royal Australian and New Zealand College of Psychiatrists, included a paper on what it refers to as 'Predicament Suicide'. The authors cite three cases, including that of Roebuck. Their conclusion in his case: 'There is no report of any history of mental disorder. The evidence suggests sexual sadism disorder ... [Roebuck's suicide] appears to have been triggered by potential disgrace.'

It should be pointed out that reports from London's *Daily Mail* and the *Mail Online*, both published in the immediate aftermath of Roebuck's death, are the authors' only references. Our own enquiry into the possibility of a medical background to this case offers an alternative view.

When the opportunity arose to build a relationship with a beautiful and intelligent young woman, Roebuck initially clutched at it. Then he encountered physical difficulty, the emotional effect of which can only be guessed at. But what neither he nor the woman knew was that beyond a specific and inconvenient condition, he may have suffered from something less apparent but more debilitating.

In considering Roebuck's life, we consulted a psychoanalyst. He insisted he would not place a diagnostic label on someone he'd never met, let alone professionally consulted. But he did offer an interpretation that might help lead us to a better understanding of Roebuck. Upon consideration of anecdotal material and written words, the psychoanalyst suggested Roebuck displayed aspects of schizoid personality disorder (SPD), pointing to the apparent absence of a normal level of engagement and normal levels of emotional ebb and flow. The World Health Organisation classifies SPD as being characterised by at least four of the following criteria:

1. Emotional coldness, detachment or reduced affect
2. Limited capacity to express either positive or negative emotions towards others
3. Consistent preference for solitary activities
4. Very few, if any, close friends or relationships, and a lack of desire for such
5. Indifference to either praise or criticism
6. Little interest in having sexual experiences with another person
7. Taking pleasure in few, if any, activities
8. Indifference to social norms and conventions
9. Preoccupation with fantasy and introspection

The applicability or otherwise of these criteria to Roebuck will be disputed. Herein lies the man's irreconcilable paradox: he was a different person to different groups of people.

It's a fair guess those who knew the later Roebuck will find many points of identification within the WHO's nine criteria.

Schizoid personality disorder, it's important to clarify, is quite distinct from schizophrenia and the potential for confusion causes concern in some medical quarters. Whatever the accuracy of the assessment, it raises a possibility that might help explain the trajectory taken by Roebuck's life. For as well as being blessed with undoubted talents, he may have been afflicted by something that he not only couldn't quell but of which he was unaware. The broad condition of schizoid personality disorder is the least commonly diagnosed of the personality disorders and those so affected rarely seek medical assistance. Perhaps, then, there was a medical backdrop to much of what was unusual about Roebuck, not that it can be automatically attributed to the kind of conduct with which he has been associated.

Whether it offers insight into his having ultimately baulked at his once-in-a-lifetime chance of a mature, loving relationship with Julia Horne, one can only guess. She, it must be said, doesn't accept this possibility, believing he simply made a choice between a relationship and his cricket career. What is unarguable is that he pulled back. And maybe that was as it had to be. For those who knew the later Roebuck would agree it was impossible to imagine him living in a conventional relationship.

Maybe Roebuck didn't dare pursue love. Ronald Fairbairn, a Scottish psychiatrist who specialised in the study of SPD, formulated the pivotal issue for schizoid people as 'an unconscious fear that their love is destructive'. It is imaginable that somewhere deep in his soul Roebuck sensed this of himself. Perhaps it caused him to shy away not only from romantic possibility, but also from interpersonal connection with those of his own age group.

Self-disclosing human discourse seems to have been something he either studiously avoided or could not maintain. If there is an exception to this general pattern of Roebuck's, it seems to be that he was more able to sustain relationships with those he had known, and taught, as young adults.

Yet for two joyful Australian summers, as a young man in the mid-1980s, he hovered on the threshold of romantic attachment. But no, the game of cricket would be his excuse, his crutch, and largely his life. He opted for it, and for something else he knew well: the education and development of young men. Alas, his nature was such that he also opted for a particular solitariness. He appeared to shun intimacy of any sort, thus taking himself to a potentially vulnerable place. One close to him has commented upon the many, apparently lonely, night-time phone calls in later years.

When Mike Coward addressed the memorial service held for Roebuck at the SCG he spoke of craving 'a more complete picture'. And that is what has been sought in this book. Delivering certainty, though, has not been possible. Indeed, barring the unlikely outcome of a reopened inquest finding evidence Roebuck was murdered, it's almost certain that certainty can never be achieved. To do so would require the evidence of Itai Gondo and Psychology Maziwisa to be subjected to courtroom cross-examination. Bearing in mind that they had no physical involvement in Roebuck falling to his death, it is virtually impossible to see how that could happen. The reality that neither currently lives in South Africa only adds to that impossibility.

While the claims of Gondo and Maziwisa have again been given voice here, the confidence that could be brought only by an exhaustive legal process and cross-examination under oath is inevitably lacking. Gondo repeated to us the sworn allegation he made to Cape Town police in November 2011. His evidence relating to what happened within his alleged physical exchange with Roebuck contains one specific detail that lends particular credibility to his claim. Perhaps the most interesting few seconds of our interview with him occurred when this aspect was pursued. On being asked whether he found it odd that his alleged assailant ejaculated as quickly as Gondo says, his otherwise emotionless face became momentarily animated. Whether this was an honest expression of his bemusement at what had happened, or whether it reflected a moment of anxiety at the need to sustain the veracity of his account, we cannot say.

As for Maziwisa we did not see his face – our access was via a sound recording of an interview with journalist Adam Shand. To us he was a disembodied voice, at times difficult to understand with total clarity, sometimes descending in volume to not much above a whisper. This is not to impute the honesty of his claims, merely to underline the compromised nature of their evidential quality. It must be stated, too, that the interview was not a cross-examination and did not involve strenuous questioning.

The case against Roebuck is also built on one established fact: his earlier conviction on a charge of common assault. It's almost impossible not to be surprised and disturbed by an intelligent man, in this day and age, practising corporal punishment in his training and teaching of young men. He was doing it outside the boundaries imposed by a school. A close male associate of Roebuck's, with a lifetime's high-level legal experience, shrugged his shoulders in exasperation at the degree to which Roebuck left himself exposed by doing this. When this aspect is sketched into an identikit picture of one already seen to be unusual, emotionally distant, and apparently secretive, the leap to negative judgement becomes more able to be taken.

Other voices have been heard that, if not absolutely condemning Roebuck, have articulated greater concern off the record than has been expressed on it. Not that they delivered more than opinion. In some other instances a refusal to speak has been difficult to interpret as anything other than an admission of concern at where the realities of the case might lie.

Yet some who knew Roebuck well would say he truly believed in the worth of corporal punishment. He had taught at Bloemfontein's Grey College and was impressed by the Spartan toughness of South African boys' schools, particularly compared to what he regarded as the politically correct English educational system.

Arguments have been offered in defence of Roebuck that range from the possible to the highly improbable. The most plausible is that he was set up and his suicide was an unintended consequence. Like the prosecution's case, it links the caning episode in Taunton to what happened in Cape Town, but by suggesting that the damage the caning did to his reputation was used for vindictive purposes by various aggrieved parties pursuing him. This is a scenario in line with the old joke: just because you're paranoid doesn't mean people aren't out to get you.

Roebuck's defenders argue more needs to be known about the lives of Maziwisa and Gondo. Maziwisa's transition from beneficiary of Roebuck in South Africa to servant of the Mugabe administration in Zimbabwe clearly invites questions. Gondo, too, has enjoyed better circumstances since late 2011; on his account he changed jobs and saved enough money to leave South Africa in mid-2012.

The defence is also founded on Roebuck's commitment as a mentor of young men and his impeccable record over eight years at Sydney's Cranbrook School. There he not only guided and cared for young men but did so in such a way that in dormitories and shower blocks there was never the slightest suggestion of 'interest', let alone impropriety. Witnesses to this stage of his life insist Roebuck was a cleanskin. One of these witnesses was Toby Jones, who offered his view shortly before deadline:

> Some people have sought to demonise Roebuck as a lonely crackpot with a dark side. Alien, odd, often out of step with his family, community, institutions and/or surrounds. Hard to pin down but somehow sinister, indeed deviant. 'Stranger Danger' in a straw hat.
>
> His presence, bearing and manner sought to proclaim that he was distinctly different – sharper than the rest, briskly challenging to the status quo, a force to be reckoned with. In Roebuck's worldview, life was never a bowl of cherries. It was a contest and a struggle. All life happened in a political context or, more precisely, in a political theatre. It paid to keep your rivals and other factions guessing. In the end life might be futile, but it was worth caring about. As were those on the wrong end of power. It was a serious business alright, but when you stopped for a breather, and looked at the characters on stage around you, you could still chuckle at the farce of it all.

Jones also acknowledged some less desirable qualities:

The Roebuck I knew had some narcissistic tendencies,
was capable of crossing some lines and of driving
himself and others fiercely to commit their utmost. He
was a complicated, caring human being who did much
good in the world, but who left himself vulnerable –
much to his cost.

Suicide in a situation such as Roebuck's should not be automatically interpreted as a guilty plea. This is a point made strongly by Dr David Horgan, who says people commit suicide as a means of ending emotional pain that they perceive will be permanent. A famous twentieth-century example is the London osteopath Dr Stephen Ward, a central figure in the Profumo Affair of the 1960s. Scapegoated by the establishment, Ward faced charges but was found guilty of little. According to Geoffrey Robertson QC, who has written a book on the subject, the high-society doctor was in fact guilty of nothing. But that didn't save him. Subjected to humiliation and isolation, Ward took a fatal overdose of sleeping pills as his court case was nearing its end. There are many stories of innocent people committing suicide in the face of damaging accusations.

Various conspiracy theories have flourished in relation to this case. One is founded on the improbable reality that Roebuck's was the third bizarre death of an international cricket figure inside ten years. Hansie Cronje died in a plane crash in South Africa in 2002 and Bob Woolmer was found dead in his Jamaican hotel room during the 2007 World Cup. Apart from the suddenness of their deaths, the point of connection is all three had some link to match-fixing: Cronje as a practitioner, Woolmer as a coach of cricket nations that had been implicated, and Roebuck as a journalist consistently ferocious in his denunciation of the malpractice.

A former South African cricketer, the late Clive Rice, linked the deaths of Cronje and Woolmer to match-fixing and Ian Chappell says he is in no doubt Woolmer was murdered: 'I've got his supposed last email, just the contents, and I showed it to my wife Barb, who worked for World Series Cricket and knew Bob. And she said "what's this?" and I said "supposedly Bob Woolmer's last email" and she said "no way". Then I showed it to Greigy [Tony Greig] and he said "no way in the wide world it's his". The reason I showed it to them is that there's no way it was written by someone whose first language is English. Then I showed it to Peter and he said the same thing.'

The suggestion of murder is dismissed by Malcolm Speed, who was the International Cricket Council's CEO at the time of Woolmer's death: 'When you think about it, he's collapsed, he's lodged between the toilet bowl and the door, it's very hard to get into the room, it's hard to get out of the room if he's there.' Speed says the investigation was botched but he's sure there was no foul play.

Speed is also confident there was no criminal intervention in Cronje's case: 'Yes, I would rule it out ... Hansie's decision to get on that plane was something of a spur-of-the-moment decision so you'd have to be right on his tail to do anything about that. And it's quite difficult to get an aeroplane to fly into a mountain.'

The other conspiracy theory in relation to Roebuck is that his frequent, vituperative commentary on Zimbabwe and its cricket administration may have prompted either an attempt to embarrass him or an actual assassination. Given that the latter required the involvement of the police force of another country, the former seems the less unlikely. The fact that there is only one living witness to Roebuck's meeting with Itai Gondo, though, and the likelihood that whatever occurred between them on that Monday night will never be investigated, leaves us with nothing beyond Gondo's testimony.

* * *

One day at the MCG, as Roebuck and I awaited our next stint at the microphone, the conversation turned fleetingly to the mysteries of the universe. Considering the haziness of my view that the concepts of faith and hope bear a relationship to optimism, I was a little surprised to hear him reply that he didn't rule anything out. It was surprising because Roebuck wasn't widely perceived as an optimist, and he certainly wasn't identified as one whose life was guided by commitment to any religious doctrine.

There have been moments, during the writing of this book, when some sort of entreaty to the great beyond has seemed in order. And occasional haunting coincidences have made one wonder. The first came right at the beginning: the friend who floated the idea of this book to me once fell from a roof himself and talks of having had time to face his mortality on the way down. Fortunately he contacted a protruding section of the building, which changed his configuration, and he landed on his feet. He survived, albeit with bad injuries and a permanent hobble. Then, in David Frith's extraordinary cricket library, the first book I picked up and opened contained a clipping of a column I'd written for the *Age* in Melbourne. Frith cuts out newspaper reports relevant to his books and tucks them inside the front cover. Somewhat apologetically, he informed me the one I'd happened to locate was the only contribution of mine within his collection of thousands of books. A few months later, as we dined with Julia Horne one evening following an extended interview, we suddenly realised it was 6 March – Roebuck's birthday. All coincidences no doubt, but somehow vaguely reassuring.

Another time, again at the MCG, I mentioned to Roebuck my reasons for finishing up at the ABC, saying I'd formed a relationship with a woman and needed to alter my too-passionate relationship with my job if we were to stand a chance. Roebuck responded to the effect that getting the personal side of one's life right was ultimately the most important thing.

The expression of Graham Greene's that so amused Roebuck again comes to mind: 'The world is not black and white. More like black and grey.' Uncertainty enshrouded in murkiness. It resonates more strongly than ever. Many of those closest to Roebuck in later years have long feared the worst amid the uncertainty, and without the emergence of something unexpected that is where the case must reside; at least for now.

Some will forever feel the grief and pain. Others will simply be bothered by the permanent lack of resolution. The Roebuck family is left to wonder what happened and why. No doubt they will continue hoping for some form of salvation for their son and brother, and for themselves. How they must wonder about that young boy in the photo, described so perceptively by Howard Jacobson: 'Look at photographs of the young Roebuck and you see a shy boy uncomfortable in his skin.'

Was he born that way? Is there some early experience that caused him to be who he was? Did he wake up one day on a treadmill with only one ultimate destination in store? Or could different decisions at crucial times have led to happier outcomes?

Such questions are applicable to all manner of people whose lives take bad turns and they don't excuse bad life choices. At best they are explanations. Nevertheless, they are also part of the mystery of individual fate within the human collective.

Regardless of the circumstances that precipitated his death, could this man have been helped? Many have asked themselves if there is something they could have done. Vic Marks embodied the complexities and frustrations felt by one close to an apparent suicide: 'I wasn't aware of how complex everything had become. If I'd been a better friend perhaps I would have sat down and had a harder try. I was angry and infuriated, in a way, that he had allowed everything to unfold as it did.'

Yet Roebuck was a man who had to have known people were there for him. He had rare perception. He was regarded fondly by many. But you can only take a horse to water. And so it was for so many friends in their relationship with this mule-stubborn human; this man of mystery who saw himself as an open book; this singular citizen of the world who craved his own community; this brilliant man of words who at a crucial moment, as a woman sought to give herself to him, was rendered speechless; this man who detested a lack of serious commitment yet who gave his life to a stupid, bloody game; this man who demanded life not be wasted yet who threw his own away; this man who said of such a prospect 'it will not be so'.

And yet ...

SELECT BIBLIOGRAPHY

Books

Akhtar, Salman, *Comprehensive Dictionary of Psychoanalysis*, Karnac Books, 2009

Bloch, B. & Singh, B., *Foundations of Clinical Psychiatry 2nd Edition*, MUP, 2001

Border, Allan, *Cricket As I See It*, Allen & Unwin, 2014

Botham, Ian, *Head On: Botham The Autobiography*, Random House, 2008

Botham, Ian, *My Autobiography*, Collins Willow, 1994

Frith, David, *By His Own Hand*, Hutchinson, 1991

Frith, David, *Frith's Encounters*, Von Krumm, 2014

Garner, Joel, *'Big Bird': Flying High: The Autobiography of Joel Garner*, Arthur Barker, 1988

Haigh, Gideon, *Game for Anything: Writings on Cricket*, Black Inc., 2004

Haigh, Gideon, *Sphere of Influence: Writings on Cricket and Its Discontents*, Simon & Schuster, 2011

Hair, Darrell, *Decision Maker: An Umpire's Story*, Random House, 1998

Hobson, Barry, *History of Millfield 1935–1970*

Marks, Vic, *Somerset County Cricket Scrapbook*, Souvenir Press, 1984

Marqusee, Mike, *War Minus the Shooting*, William Heinemann, 1997

Martin-Jenkins, Christopher (ed.), *Seasons Past*, Guild Publishing, 1986

Oborne, Peter, *Basil D'Oliveira: Cricket and Conspiracy*, Little, Brown, 2004

Radford, Brian, *Caught Out*, John Blake, 2012

Richards, Viv, *Sir Vivian: The Definitive Autobiography*, Penguin, 2002

Richards, Viv (with David Foot), *Viv Richards*, Star, 1982

Robertson, Geoffrey, *Stephen Ward Was Innocent, OK?*, Biteback, 2013

Roebuck, Peter, *From Sammy to Jimmy*, Partridge Press, 1991

Roebuck, Peter, *In It to Win It*, Allen & Unwin, 2006

Roebuck, Peter, *It Never Rains: A Cricketer's Lot*, Unwin, 1984

Roebuck, Peter, *It Sort of Clicks*, Willow Books, 1987

Roebuck, Peter, *It Takes All Sorts*, Allen & Unwin, 2005

Roebuck, Peter, *Slices of Cricket*, Unwin, 1982

Roebuck, Peter, *Sometimes I Forgot to Laugh*, Allen & Unwin, 2004

Romanos, Joseph, *Martin Crowe: Tortured Genius*, Hodder Moa Beckett, 1995

Speed, Malcolm, *Sticky Wicket*, Harper Sports, 2011

Tossell, David, *Sex & Drugs & Rebel Tours: The England Cricket Team in the 1980s*, Pitch Publishing, 2015

Waugh, Steve, *Out of My Comfort Zone*, Penguin Viking, 2005

Whimpress, Bernard, *Chuckers: A History of Throwing in Australian Cricket*, Elvis Press, 2004

Magazines
Australasian Psychiatry
Cricketer International
Eureka Street
Outlook India
The Spectator
Sportstar
The Week UK
Time Out
Wisden Cricket Monthly

Annuals
Benson & Hedges Cricket Year
John Player Cricket Yearbook
Playfair Cricket Annual
Wisden Cricketers' Almanack

Newspapers
The Age, The Australian, Bristol Post, Canberra Times, Cape Argus, Cape Times, Courier Mail, Daily Mail, Daily Telegraph, Financial Times, The Guardian, Herald Express, Herald Sun, The Hindu, Hindustan Times, The Independent, Mail & Guardian, The Observer, Saturday Star, Somerset County Gazette, Straits Times, Sunday Mirror, Sunday Times, Sydney Morning Herald, The Telegraph UK, Times Of India, Western Daily Press, Western Morning News, The Witness

Online resources

BBC News Online, Cricket Archive, Crikey, DNA India, ESPN CricInfo, Fox Sports, Nehanda Radio, news.com.au, Rediff.com, SABC News Online, Sportal Australia, Talk Sport, World Cricket Watch

ACKNOWLEDGEMENTS

My old mate, AJ Lillas, is not especially interested in sport but has always been interested in life's events and people. It was he who suggested this undertaking over a lunch, and when he raised it again the next time we convened it began to be taken seriously. Soon after, I saw Sandy Grant across a sea of heads at the market one morning and mentioned it to him. By the time I checked my emails a couple of hours later he had sent an enthusiastic exhortation.

So many interviewees gave generously of time, memory, perception, and encouragement: commodities all greatly appreciated. Special and sincere appreciation, though, is extended to Julia Horne. Such honest telling of her story speaks not only of the Peter Roebuck she knew, but of Julia's own courage and loyalty.

Then there are the surviving members of the Roebuck family. Elizabeth, Rosalie, James and Beatrice all spoke to us at length and with unwavering belief in, and love for, the family member lost to them. Their uncertainty, both then and later, about a pair of authors wanting to write their late brother's story, is understood. May they find peace and resolution.

The list of those whose witness guided us along the way is too long to chronicle here, but we are especially grateful to Vic and Anna Marks, Matthew Engel, Jim Maxwell, David Frith and Toby Jones. We also thank Neil Manthorp and Peter Lalor for their help on either side of the Indian Ocean, and Roy Kerslake and Peter Robinson for making us welcome at Somerset County Cricket Club. To all those others who contributed, our heartfelt thanks.

Friends and family who offered support are appreciated in a way that, too frequently, words don't express. Maree, in particular, endured much. Sam and Andrew were also great listeners.

I am also deeply grateful to the two people with whom I tackled this book. Without Elliot's optimism, belief, experience, and relentless attention to detail it would never have happened. And without the ability of our editor, Christian Ryan, to synthesise the thoughts and expression of two writers into one final product, the book wouldn't be what it is.

A final word is in order on the subject of this work. For apart from his good qualities, and whatever his flaws may have been, Roebuck was living proof of the diversity and complexity of humanity. Perhaps that is the ultimate message of the preceding pages.

Tim Lane

This book has been a complicated and demanding undertaking. That it has come to fruition speaks volumes for the generous assistance we have received along the way. Those who gave so willingly of their time and views, on occasion in difficult circumstances, are hereby acknowledged.

Terrific guidance and advice was provided by the likes of Ginny Stein at the ABC, Andre Odendaal, Craig Marais and John Young in Cape Town, Mike Tarr and Millfield School in Somerset, Darshak Mehta and Fabian Muir in Sydney and Adam Shand and Gideon Haigh in Melbourne. Sincere appreciation is also extended to other parties in South Africa and Zimbabwe who opened doors and provided information and who prefer to remain anonymous. A special note of thanks should also be expressed to our publisher, Pam Brewster at Hardie Grant, for her unqualified support.

On a more personal note, my thanks to the Cawdron family in London, the Smiths in Sussex and the Marshalls in Melbourne for their respective, and always splendid, hospitality. Due to the contentious nature of our subject's life and death, not to mention the complexities of the project, the counsel I received from family and friends has been invaluable.

And thank you to my co-author, Tim Lane, who made the original suggestion to research and write about Roebuck. It has been a remarkable journey.

EJ Cartledge

Claims made by Justice Hakata about the journalist, Adam Shand, have been withdrawn. The authors and publishers of *Chasing Shadows: The Life & Death of Peter Roebuck* apologise for any imputation Shand acted unethically when compiling stories on the death of the cricket writer in 2011.

INDEX